Doping in Sport – Global Ethical Issues

Doping in Sport considers ethical arguments about performance enhancing drugs in sport in a global context. It examines:

- The forces that are bringing about the debate of ethical issues in performance enhancing drugs in sport
- The sources of ethical debates in different continents and countries
- The variation of ethical arguments in different cultural, political, ideological and sports systems.

It provides a thorough review and analysis of the ethical literature on performance enhancing drugs in sport in the global society; as although there has been a significant body of work that has looked at the importance of ethical issues in performance enhancing drugs in sport, little has been written on the various ethical concepts in different countries and cultures involving sport. This book makes a major contribution to the international anti-doping campaign in sport.

This volume was previously published as a special issue of the journal *Sport In Global Society*.

Fan Hong is Director of the Irish Institute of Chinese Studies at University College Cork, Ireland.

Angela J. Schneider is an Associate Professor and former Assistant Dean, Ethics and Equity, in the Faculty of Health Sciences at the University of Western Ontario, Canada.

Sport in the Global Society
General Editors: J.A. Mangan and Boria Majumdar

Doping in Sport
Global Ethical Issues

Sport in the global society

General Editors: J.A. Mangan and Boria Majumdar

The interest in sports studies around the world is growing and will continue to do so. This unique series combines aspects of the expanding study of *sport in the global society*, providing comprehensiveness and comparison under one editorial umbrella. It is particularly timely, with studies in the aesthetic elements of sport proliferating in institutions of higher education.

Eric Hobsbawm once called sport one of the most significant practices of the late nineteenth century. Its significance was even more marked in the late twentieth century and will continue to grow in importance into the new millennium as the world develops into a 'global village' sharing the English language, technology and sport.

Other Titles in the Series

Doping in Sport

Global Ethical Issues

Edited by
Angela J. Schneider and Fan Hong

Routledge
Taylor & Francis Group

LONDON AND NEW YORK

First published 2007 by Routledge
2 Park Square, Milton Park, Abingdon, Oxon OX14 4RN

Simultaniously published in the USA and Canada by Routledge
270 Madison Ave, New York, NY 10016

Routledge is an imprint of the Taylor & Francis Group, an informa business

© 2007 Fan Hong & Angela Schneider

Reprinted 2007 (twice)

Typeset in Minion 10.5/13pt by the Alden Group, OxfordShire
Printed and bound in Great Britain by MPG Books Ltd, Bodmin, Cornwall

British Library Cataloguing in Publication Data
A catalogue record for this book is available from the British Library

ISBN 10: 0-415-34832-3 (hbk)
ISBN 10: 0-415-35223-1 (pbk)

ISBN 13: 978-0-415-34832-4 (hbk)
ISBN 13: 978-0-415-35223-9 (pbk)

CONTENTS

Notes on Contributors

Nellie Arvaniti is the Consultant of Physical Education of the Greek Ministry of Education. She is a member of several national and international science committees that design, educate and evaluate educational programs, an evaluator-critic of the Greek Ministry of Education for Physical Education didactic material, and a former member of the World Anti-Doping Agency's Ethics and Education Committee. She has authored several articles and books on Olympic Education.

Gunnar Breivik is a Professor of Social Sciences at the Norwegian University of Sports and Physical Education in Oslo, Norway. His research interests include philosophy of sports, psychology of stress and risk taking, and sociology of values. He has published numerous books and articles in these areas.

Runar Gilberg is a graduate student at the Norwegian School of Sport Sciences in Oslo, Norway. He currently works as a journalist for the Norwegian running magazine Kondis.

Vassil Girginov is Reader in Sport Management/Development in School of Sport and Education at Brunel University in UK. He lectured at the University of Luton, England until 2005. Prior to 1995 he lectured in Sport Management at the National Sports Academy in Sofia, Bulgaria and collaborated with the Bulgarian Sports Union and the National Olympic Committee. His research interests and publications (including four books) are in the field of the Olympic movement, sport management and policy analysis, and Eastern European sport.

Fan Hong is Professor and Director of the Irish Institute of Chinese Studies at University College Cork in Ireland. She has authored and edited several books and articles on gender and sport, doping and sport in the global society with particular reference to China. She is an editor of the International Journal for the History of Sport and member of several editorial boards. She was the Chair of the Research Sub-Committee of the Ethics and Education Committee of the World Anti-Doping Agency (WADA).

Yoshitaka Kondo is Professor of Comprehensive Human Sciences at the University of Tsukuba, Japan. His main research interest is sport ethics. He is the author of *Inquiry of Sport Ethics* (Taisyukan Shoten, 2004) and co-editor of *Questions of Sport Ethics* (Taisyukan Shorten, 2000) with H. Tomozoe. He has also published several articles in both Japanese and English.

Sigmund Loland is the Rector of the Norwegian School of Sport Sciences in Oslo, Norway and a Professor of Sport Philosophy. His research interests include the areas of sport ethics, epistemological aspects of human movement, and sport and the history of ideas.

William J. Morgan PhD is a professor in sport humanities and Director of the Center for Sport, Citizenship, and Society in the John Glenn Institute of Public Policy, Ohio State University. He has a forthcoming book in press entitled *Why Sports Morally Matter*, which will be published by Routledge, and is the editor of the forthcoming *Ethics in Sport*, which is an anthology of readings that will be published by Human Kinetics.

Dr Jim Parry is Senior Lecturer and former Head of the School of Philosophy at the University of Leeds, England, working in applied ethics and social and political philosophy as well as philosophy of sport. He is former chair of the British Universities PE Association, Founding Director of the British Olympic Academy, and a collaborator of the International Olympic Academy for 20 years. He is series editor, with Mike McNamee, for the Routledge series *Ethics and Sport*.

Angela J. Schneider is an Associate Professor in Kinesiology at the University of Western Ontario in London, Ontario. She has numerous publications in the areas of applied philosophy and ethics in sport, including: drug use, gender equity, fair play, definitions of sport, and Olympic Studies. She was the Director of Ethics and Education at the World Anti-doping Agency (WADA).

Claudio M. Tamburrini is a Research Fellow and teacher at the Stockholm Bioethics Centre, in the Department of Philosophy, University of Stockholm, Sweden. He is the author of *Crime and Punishment?* and of several international articles on issues of penal philosophy. In the area of the philosophy of sports, together with numerous articles on sports and ethics, Tamburrini has published *The 'Hand of God'? – Essays in the Philosophy of Sports*. Both in Sweden and in Argentina, Tamburrini has accomplished pioneering work in introducing the philosophy of sports as an academic discipline.

Sarah J. Teetzel is a doctoral student in the School of Kinesiology, Faculty of Health Sciences, at the University of Western Ontario, Canada. Her research interests include sport ethics and medical ethics. She is planning to write her dissertation on the ethics of enhancement in sport.

Series Editors' Foreword

SPORT IN THE GLOBAL SOCIETY was launched in the late nineties. It now has over one hundred volumes. Until recently an odd myopia characterised academia with regard to sport. The global *groves of academe* remained essentially Cartesian in inclination. They favoured a mind/body dichotomy: thus the study of ideas was acceptable; the study of sport was not. All that has now changed. Sport is now incorporated, intelligently, within debate about *inter alia* ideologies, power, stratification, mobility and inequality. The reason is simple. In the modern world sport is everywhere: it is as ubiquitous as war. E.J. Hobsbawm, the Marxist historian, once called it the one of the most significant of the new manifestations of late nineteenth century Europe. Today it is one of the most significant manifestations of the twenty-fist century world. Such is its power, politically, culturally, economically, spiritually and aesthetically, that sport beckons the academic more persuasively than ever- to borrow, and refocus, an expression of the radical historian Peter Gay- 'to explore its familiar terrain and to wrest new interpretations from its inexhaustible materials'. As a subject for inquiry, it is replete, as he remarked of history, with profound 'questions unanswered and for that matter questions unasked'.

Sport seduces the teeming 'global village'; it is the new opiate of the masses; it is one of the great modern experiences; its attraction astonishes only the recluse; its appeal spans the globe. Without exaggeration, sport is a mirror in which nations, communities, men and women now see themselves. That reflection is sometimes bright, sometimes dark, sometimes distorted, sometimes magnified. This metaphorical mirror is a source of mass exhilaration and depression, security and insecurity, pride and humiliation, bonding and alienation. Sport, for many, has replaced religion as a source of emotional catharsis and spiritual passion, and for many, since it is among the earliest of memorable childhood experiences, it infiltrates memory, shapes enthusiasms, serves fantasies. To co-opt Gay again: it blends memory and desire.

Sport, in addition, can be a lens through which to scrutinise major themes in the political and social sciences: democracy and despotism and the great associated movements of socialism, fascism, communism and capitalism as well as political cohesion and confrontation, social reform and social stability.

The story of modern sport is the story of the modern world-in microcosm; a modern global tapestry permanently being woven. Furthermore, nationalist and imperialist, philosopher and politician, radical and conservative have all sought in sport a manifestation of national identity, status and superiority.

Finally, for countless millions sport is the personal pursuit of ambition, assertion, well-being and enjoyment.

For all the above reasons, sport demands the attention of the academic. *Sport in the Global Society* is a response.

J.A. Mangan
Boria Majumdar

Series Editors
Sport in the Global Society

Introduction
Angela Schneider and Fan Hong

This book focuses on doping, sport and ethics in a global context. The perspectives covered range from athletes to administrators, from specific countries to the international community and from skepticism to optimism. The specific countries are China, Japan, Argentina, the United States, the United Kingdom, Greece, France, Norway and Bulgaria. On the international policy perspective, the question of why the World Anti-Doping Agency (WADA) has been asked to deal with issues surrounding transgendered athletes' competition in elite sport is analysed. At the international level, questions of fairness and anti-doping policies and their application in different countries are raised. The goal of this book is to give the reader an understanding of some of the breadth, depth and complexity of the problem of doping in sport and its relationship to different cultures and society.

The first chapter, entitled 'Fair is Fair, Or Is It? A Moral Consideration of the Doping Wars in American Sport', written by William J. Morgan, asked the question whether or not the newfound will in the United States and the international community to catch athletes doping in sport constitutes any real moral progress? Although Morgan believes that the greater number of positive test results reflect improvements in the drug tests themselves, and perhaps most of all a greater resolve on the part of the United States Olympic Committee and the International Olympic Committee (IOC) to catch violators, he is not inclined to think there is any real moral progress. His skepticism is based on his criticism of the approach used to expose and punish violators as having little to do with moral efforts to level the playing field, and almost everything to do with morally questionable efforts to get athletes to tow the company line. He further argues that the system used constitutes a breach of fairness that is as morally egregious as the unfair use of performance-enhancing drugs by the athletes it was supposed to stop.

Morgan's argument for his controversial claim begins by examining the notion of fair play not just as a moral feature that is widely thought pivotal to the conduct of sport, but to the conduct of American life in all its various forms. He discusses two important aspects: fair play as a reciprocal regard for the interests of individual participants in sport; and fair play as 'respect for the game'. Morgan tries to show how the current anti-doping strategy undermines these two moral principles. He concludes by arguing that to deal with doping, we need a moral solution to a deep moral malaise, rather than a technical solution for what is wrongly perceived to be essentially a technical problem. Taking a hard moral look at the great emphasis we place on winning in sport, as evidenced by the outsized economic rewards we attach to it, is one of the places we should start. Although we are well within our moral rights to oppose doping in sport and to take appropriate steps to deter its use, Morgan argues, we have good reason to worry not just about the fate of any proposed moral reform of sport, but whether any such reform is even in the offing.

The second chapter is written by Claudio Tamburrini and is entitled 'Are Doping Sanctions Justified? A Moral Relativistic View'. It reviews literature on doping and responses to Morgan's views. Tamburrini claims that, although some authors have criticised doping controls for being invasive and violating athletes' privacy, and that Morgan attacks the lowering of legal guarantees that the new liability standard for doping offences implies, few sport scientists and philosophers have overtly defended the right of athletes. He states that even fewer have discussed the ongoing standardisation of doping regulations and sanctions attached to doping offences.

Tamburrini argues that doping is not only compatible with, but also incarnates, the true spirit of modern competitive elite sports. He is not suggesting that athletes should violate current bans on doping, but rather that the current bans be lifted. His position is that if the doping ban is kept, fairness demands current policies consider the social and sport-ethical particularities of the different communities, rather than increased standardisation. Tamburrini's relativistic position leads him to conclude that, because athletes are submitted to different kinds of pressures, depending on the particular ethical landscape (sport), the sanctions should be 'culture-sensitive', dealt with on a case-by-case basis and generally more lenient for those with greater difficulty in abiding by anti-doping regulations. He believes that standardising doping sanctions treats non-similar cases similarly, and punishes equally: i) those who are able to successfully resist the temptation to dope; and ii) those who only could have done so at great costs for themselves.

In regard to fairness in competition, Tamburrini takes the unusual view that the unquestioned iniquitous effect of sponsorship and state support of national sport might at least partly be neutralised by letting non-sponsored athletes from developing countries catch up with their more privileged competitors through the intake of substances presently proscribed. Tamburrini argues that his proposal is not only fairer, in the sense that it implies dissimilar cases are treated according to the relevant dissimilarities, but also in another sense of fairness, namely that disadvantaged athletes might get an opportunity to equalise the initial conditions of competition by doping. Further, he thinks that this new fairer situation might even yield some desirable factual results, as it would probably contribute to the introduction of new actors in the sporting scene, thus adding to the excitement of sporting competitions.

In the chapter entitled 'Cultural Nuances: Doping, Cycling and the Tour de France' Angela Schneider argues that the key to understanding the Tour de France, its appeal and its connection to doping, is in understanding the core values of road cycling and the national psyche that has developed in France around the Tour itself. Given the types of values that are honoured in long distance road cycling, it is of little surprise that a culture of doping has emerged. The chapter contains a review of the research identifying the core values of road cycling as: endurance, perseverance, will power, competitiveness, survival instinct, loneliness, frustration capacity, overcoming struggles, sharing capacity and humility. It explains how human effort beyond its limits, and the human capacity of suffering without giving up, are essential parts of the sport. The athletes develop a mental capacity to fight, with little compromise, through their strength, effort and will power to overcome struggles. On a symbolic and psychological level only 'death' is proof that athletes have fought to their maximum with the fascination of going beyond their capacity, to test their strength. In road cycling there are no limits to human effort, it represents the ultimate motivation to achieve. Many believe that the road cyclist is the only true hero in the sports world as exhibited through pure will power.

The history of the Tour makes it clear that public opinion about doping does not always conform to the prohibitionist line on doping that is publicly embraced by many officials, and this in itself is a matter of real social significance. Schneider argues that this tacit acceptance of certain kinds of doping by ordinary people would certainly help to account for the problem. However, she claims that the deeper issue, which many have claimed is the cause of doping and the physiological severity of the Tour. The athletes, however, have rarely protested against their extreme suffering but they have protested against the medication they use to cope with stress. It is interesting from a public health perspective that there have been few calls for the reduction of the physiological severity of the Tour. The medical model is used to deal with this severity as it is noted that some team doctors see their athletes as patients requiring medical care.

It is also noted that worldwide physicians' organisations have taken a stance against the sport of boxing because of its health risks, but there is no such stance taken for cycling at the Tour de France. Instead, there seems to be an acceptance of a model of 'reduction of harm' to defend medical intervention rather than reduction of harm by reducing the physical stress requirements of the Tour. Schneider suggested that the Tour subculture may well have created the context for doping many years ago by accepting intolerable stress for business purposes. Thus, the reduction of harm argument comes at the point where intolerable physical stress appears to call for medical treatment, sometimes in the form of banned substances, to provide relief.

Another aspect of the Tour that is reviewed in this article is the fans' acceptance of doping as an accommodation to the stress of the sport. Schneider argues that the doping sub-culture sustains the required extreme performances, both of which can destroy the athlete's body. An important social and moral question is asked: 'Are the "special medical requirements" of the Tour justifiable, can they withstand outside criticism?' She argues futher that the logical inconsistency required on health issues regarding the question of whether professional cycling is abandoning the athlete's medical or health interests by leaving riders to fend for themselves. The chapter concludes that for change to really occur, the organisers and riders must come to believe that if doping is the answer for athletes to survive the Tour, we are asking the wrong question and the wrong things of them.

Sarah Teetzel's chapter 'On Transgendered Athletes, Fairness, and Doping', argues that the challenges created by the participation of transgendered athletes in elite sport, predominantly relate to, and are confused with, anti-doping issues. She claims that this stems from the perception that the transgendering process can provide an athlete with the same type of advantage that athletes gain from using substances and procedures banned under the World Anti-Doping Code (WADC). Teetzel identifies the relevant factors that one must address in working toward an answer of whether or not it is fair for transgendered athletes to be able to compete at the elite level. It is shown in this article that those who argue that allowing transgendered athletes to compete in sport is inherently unfair often appeal to hypothetical scenarios where male athletes with exceptional athletic talent annihilate women's competitions. Teetzel points out that these extreme examples fail to consider the effects that sex-reassignment surgery and years of hormone therapy would have on even the most gifted male athletes. A lack of information on transgender physiology, and misguided fears that border on discrimination, often make the transgendered athlete's experience in sport less than ideal and have up until recently prohibited transgendered athletes from competing at the highest level.

Teetzel notes that while there are conceivable advantages that an elite transgendered athlete might possibly possess, conclusive evidence based on long-term scientific studies has either not yet been carried out, or has failed to show any unfair advantages with any statistical significance. Teetzel draws on the scientific literature of performance enhancement and the transgendering process, the testimonials of transgendered athletes published in scholarly journals, newspapers and magazines, the arguments of athletes, medical professionals and sports officials published in similar sources, and recent developments in the policies established by international sports organisations such as the IOC and WADA.

The IOC's transgender policy mandates that ISFs cannot prohibit transgendered athletes from competing in their desired sex category at the Olympic Games if the athlete fulfills 3 requirements set out by the IOC. However, Teetzel claims that permitting transgendered athletes to compete does not ensure that they will not face violence and discrimination in sport from their competitors, sport fans and officials. She feels that education is needed to make sport more inclusive for transgendered athletes. More research on the effects of the transgendering process on athletic performance will help convince critics that transgendered athletes do not garner any unfair advantages in elite sport.

Throughout the article, Teetzel argues that it is inappropriate to liken transgendered athletes, who meet the IOC's requirements to compete at the Olympic Games, to athletes who use banned substances and methods to intentionally break rules and abuse therapeutic use exemption to excel at sport. While many of the most pressing issues involved in transgendered athletes' participation in elite sport are similar to doping issues, she notes a marked difference between using performance-enhancing drugs to increase athleticism, and using the same drugs as part of prescribed hormone therapy. However, she acknowledges that some still doubt the fairness of transgendered athletes competing in their desired sex category and much of this controversy comes down to what counts as fair and unfair in sport. Despite the assurance from endocrinologists that transgendered athletes are unlikely to possess any identifiable competitive advantages over their competitors, Teetzel predicts that allegations of unfairness will continue to surface periodically until irrefutable studies are complete.

Vassil Girginov looks at the problem from a sport management perspective using a case study from Bulgaria. In his chapter entitled 'Creating a corporate anti-doping culture: understanding the role of sport governing bodies', he addresses the issue of national sports governing bodies' role in interpreting and promoting anti-doping and draws on Garrett Morgan's notion of enactment of culture. It is claimed that organisations enact their environments as people assign patterns of meaning and significance to the world in which they live. Girginov supports the claim that we must attempt to understand culture as an ongoing and proactive process of reality construction. He argues that this perspective urges us to redefine the role of sport managers and officials and present them as reality constructors. They are seen as agents exercising important influences on an organisation's culture. Girginov employs the metaphor of sport organisations as cultures to develop an understanding of the challenges faced by the international sport movement in endorsing a global anti-doping policy. He explores the interpretations of the WADC in the Bulgarian Weightlifting Federation (BWF), which is one of the leading schools in this sport in the world.

Girginov argues that Sport Governing Bodies (SGBs) try to demonstrate their legitimacy in the public eye when they sign on to the WADC. This shows they are genuinely concerned about the integrity of sport, failing to do so would result in public disapproval, withdrawal of funding, and eventual suspension from national or international sport movements. He claims that employing a culture metaphor to study SGBs' interpretations of anti-doping policy helps to better understand some of the major challenges in implementing the WADC. Girginov argues that changing a SGB's policy, rules and procedures is not enough to appreciate how patterns of culture shape day-to-day action. SGBs also have to find ways of managing the new anti-doping culture.

A change in doping culture implies re-evaluation of some of those fundamental values and beliefs. It also means that the challenge of changing the doping culture is growing significantly with the rising number of governments and sport organisations who have signed the WADC. Girginov argues that organisations have a relatively fixed notion of who they are and are determined to sustain that identity at all costs. This motivates a SGB to overemphasise its importance and neglect the significance of the wider system of anti-doping relations. This system includes sports organisations, national governments, educational establishments, research institutions, individuals, and of course, international cooperation. Girginov concludes with the claim that while an acceptable level of agreement at the level of the *etics* of doping (universal approval of WADC) has been achieved, the real challenge to corporate anti-doping culture of getting the *emics* (SGBs' practices) in line with the *etics* remains.

Jim Parry's chapter on 'Doping in the UK – Alain and Dwain, Rio and Greg – not guilty?', is an attempt to explore the issue of doping in sport via applied ethics. It shows how complicated and messy individual cases can be, and how our judgements about them are coloured by a range of moral possibilities and intersecting contextual features. Parry claims that sometimes the sheer weight of competing considerations, together with the uncertainty of empirical determinations, overwhelms our ability to arrive at conclusions acceptable even to ourselves – sometimes there just aren't any clear-cut answers.

Parry addresses issues of the relation between theory, empirical evidence, background scientific assumptions, the ethics of sports and sports rules, and the context-dependence of our judgements. He also examines four recent cases involving British athletes: Alain Baxter (skiing), Dwain Chambers (athletics), Rio Ferdinand (football) and Greg Rusedski (tennis). These cases demonstrate very different, although overlapping, features that open up a wide range of issues for consideration. Parry explores the adequacy and morality of the actions of the athletes and their support teams and of certain rules, procedures, decisions, and judgments surrounding these cases. His outcomes are assessments of the relative innocence and guilt of each athlete in respect of a variety of factors.

Parry argues that sometimes we want the law to be clear-cut and evenly applied. Often, however, there is genuine complexity and difficulty in the context and detail of the particular case. Thus, the outcomes are often determined not just by the rule, but also in the interpretation and application of the rule, which requires reference to background moral principles. In turn, those principles can only themselves be applied with reference to empirical features of the case, and also to the facts of the matter. Mitigation, too, is almost wholly determined by context and by the features of the particular case.

There is no simple reading-off of the correct disposal of the case from the rules governing it. Parry thinks it is a matter of thoughtful judgment, the weighing of all the elements present and the bringing to bear of wider moral principles. He argues that if we carefully consider a range of cases, we can test both them and ourselves for consistency of approach and in application of principle, and thereby extend our capacity for thinking through cases and arriving at just disposals.

Yoshitaka Kondo looks at the doping problem from a Japanese perspective. In his chapter entitled 'Debate Surrounding the Doping Ban: Application of the Harm Principle', he points out that the imperative that 'doping is bad' is followed in Japan and, as a result, most violations have arisen from ignorance rather than intentional violations. He claims that only scattered cases of unintentional or inadvertent use by Japanese athletes has led to the view that they are generally considered as being relatively clean.

Kondo reviews the discussions of four Japanese scholars involved in the doping debate in Japan to provide context and background on how doping is regarded there.

He states that there are negative views of doping prohibitions, particularly those that ban the use of stimulants in sport. This skepticism seems to be based on conclusions that it is impossible to scientifically draw the line on the effects of stimulants, citing cases of ethnological findings. He also reviews a comparison of drug use in art and sport. He notes that the involvement of drugs in the creative activities of contemporary artists is a fact recognised also in the records left by the artists themselves. The natural endowments of athletes are assessed in a category different from those of artists. He claimes that there is a difference between the ethical assessment of artists and athletes that is demonstrated by his assertion that 'there is no room for the ideology of fairness in sports to be set within the ambiguous subjective realm of artistic creation'. Thus, the conclusion is that even if they have the same natural endowments, athletes and artists are assessed differently.

Kondo then presents two new choices to try to tackle the doping problem. The first is 'The future self as other'. He looks at the principles of inter-generational ethics to inform his interpretation. This is an important aspect of environmental ethics dealing with our ethical responsibility to future generations. He argues that ethical responsibility in this case means that passing on the burden of environmental contamination from the present generation, to future generations, is tantamount to harm. Therefore, arbitrary conduct that is environmentally destructive cannot be permitted. He sets up a hypothesis using present self and future self while referring to the concept of the ethical responsibility to future generations. He argues that when hypothesised in this manner the two selves are different persons. Kondo then applies this theory to doping in sport where there are concerns about athletes' health. He argues that the present self's right of self-determination is over ridden because doping is a behaviour that will adversely affect the health of the future self and thus the ethical responsibility to future generations should impede such conduct.

The second choice is '"Other" cannot be subjected to self control!' This is a method of hypothesising the 'other' within oneself where there is conduct one can control through his or her own will, and conduct that one cannot control this way. He claims that if we assume the existence of otherness within the self, in the sense of being uncontrollable, the scope of the right of self-determination becomes restricted and the prohibition of specific conduct becomes a possibility. Thus, doping could be prohibited within the framework of controllable conduct 'self' and uncontrollable conduct 'other'. This means one cannot decide on one's own to use illicit drugs since the self cannot control the body's biological reactions to illicit drugs. As long as the self cannot control the drug reaction as a rational, moral agent, who controls his or her own training programmes alone, it cannot be considered conduct subject to self-determination. Prohibition, consequently, is probably justifiable for Kondo on this view.

Kondo also examines the claim that the ban on doping inflicts damage on others. He claims that uncontrollable conduct like doping is deemed to be 'other' and beyond the scope of self-determination. In the case of ordinary training, the athlete would be reduced to a state of exhaustion if a given level were exceeded, which would render continued training impossible. If illicit drugs were used, however, it would become possible to exceed the self-controllable limits. Kondo concludes that doping conduct, which commits control to an uncontrollable other, corresponds after all to the infliction of harm and probably is beyond the scope of determination by the self.

In the chapter 'Doping and Anti-doping in Sport in China', Fan Hong analyses the factors that caused doping in sport in the context of Chinese history, culture and ethics and examines the Chinese government's anti-doping policy and practice from the 1990s. She claims that China does not have systematically state-run drug abuse sports programmes and that drug-use is not only a political problem, but also a moral, educational, economic, medical, social and cultural problem in the global society.

Fan Hong notes that Chinese people have a long history and culture of using herbs, animals and secret formulas to regenerate energy. It is natural for athletes and coaches to use some traditional Chinese medicine to achieve the desired transformation of their bodies in a magic way. She argues that Chinese medicine puts athletes' reputations in danger because Chinese medical materials originate from plant and animal sources that are neither under proper quality control nor well researched. Although, she notes there is a clear indication that some Chinese athletes were cheating to win, some Chinese athletes mistakenly misused medicine that is commonly available over the counter. There are heavy punishments for drug users by law in China, but there is no sufficient mechanism to protect those athletes who misuse drugs for health reasons, or to protect young athletes who are forced to take drugs.

In reviewing China's preparation of anti-doping programmes for the Beijing Olympic Games in 2008, Fan Hong points out that the Chinese Sports Authority has made great progress in the fight against drugs in sport. However, the desire to be the best in the world is still the dream for most of the Chinese and their Government. Many factors influence Chinese athletes in realising their dreams: a target number of medals at the Olympic Games; competitions are getting tougher; unethical practices are encouraged by some sports officials and coaches; huge financial rewards; the development of the national and international doping markets in China give sports administrators and athletes easy access to drugs, and there is a traditional Chinese culture of using drugs for transformation of the body. She argues that all of these factors probably still tempt some athletes, coaches and officials to take short cuts by using drugs. Drug-use in sport is not only a political problem, but also a moral, educational, economic, medical, social and cultural problem in China.

In 'Anti-Doping in Sport: the Norwegian Perspective', Runar Gilberg, Gunnar Breivik and Sigmund Loland give a view of the doping issue from Norway. In this chapter they attempt to describe and understand the Norwegian anti-doping work over the last decades with a particular emphasis on its preventive aspects. They discuss the ethical justification of the Norwegian anti-doping work, and whether anti-doping work has been successful with regard to attitudes as well as to the prevalence of doping among Norwegian athletes. They also comment on investigation into motives and reasons for Norwegian athletes using dope. Looking at the clear Norwegian guidelines against doping, they question whether they have been followed in action.

Given that Norway is a pioneer country in anti-doping work, and it has the goal of becoming the third best European nation in the Summer and Winter Olympics, the authors ask if this is setting the bar too high. They question the realism of the goal because in much of the Norwegian anti-doping material practically no conflict is raised between a clear 'no' to doping and a clear 'yes' to performance on a high level. Thus, they claim, one never escapes that at its core a choice of anti-doping is not a pragmatic, but a moral choice, that might have short-term costs and might go against narrow-term self interest.

Gilberg, Breivik and Loland conclude that Norwegian anti-doping work has been massive and complex. Along with controls and sanctions, considerable amounts of resources have been put into working on attitudes according to the authors. They note that some of the earliest campaigns gave the impression of propaganda. These had an exaggerated focus on adverse effects on health and attitudes compared to a modem perspective more centered on fair play and the disapproval of cheating. They refer to surveys to draw the tentative conclusion that the anti-doping information has reached its audience and made an impact. They found that among the general population, and more strongly among elite athletes, there are clear attitudes against the use of doping substances and methods in sport. However, they argue that this does not imply that doping is not used in Norway. They conclude with the belief that the anti-doping work has had a significant effect, and has been characterised by an impressive continuity and consistence.

Finally, Nellie Arvaniti provides us with a positive review on anti-doping and education. Her chapter, 'The Educational Perspective of Anti-doping', contains a review of what anti-doping education is and where it aims. Arvaniti characterises anti-doping education as an educational process based on scientific principals and methods, using programmed learning opportunities. This offers individuals support to turn down doping on the basis of sports ethics and respect for the athlete's health. She claims the basic objective of this is the social adoption of a negative attitude towards doping by all athletic agents involved. Arvaniti believes that through properly designed educational programmes and learning procedures, that apply indicative-quality programmes targeted on sports ethics and health, athletes can be provided with the necessary knowledge and information to develop critical, communicative and other capabilities that will lead to the conscious abstinence from doping.

Arvaniti reviews the understanding of sport as a game to help in dealing with the threats that challenge the Olympic spirit today. She feels the entire athletic system should be educated on anti-doping programmes i.e. athletes of all levels, sport agents, sport scientists, parents, journalists, sports executives, trainers, physicians, physiotherapists, etc. She argues that the entire school system should deliver such programmes and that it is necessary to include in the curriculum of physical education and sports science departments anti-doping programmes focusing on the ethical, medical, legal and educational issues. She believes that with their pedagogical capacity, and the proper formation, teachers can contribute effectively in the fight against doping.

Arvaniti asks whether it is possible that athletes completely stopped using performance-enhancing substances and methods that are illegal and dangerous to their health. The establishment of the WADA, and the cooperation of governments and athletic agents towards the adoption of a WADC (where the same weights and measures for all athletes will be in effect), constitute a turning point for the Olympic Movement. Arvaniti believes that Olympic champions and 'clean' high-level athletes, who are positive role models for the athletic family, will contribute substantially to the anti-doping movement. She also notes that great emphasis should be given to lower athletic categories, where sports have an amateur character and the athletes are younger. She concludes that athletes' health protection and the right to participate in 'clean' games are the duty and responsibility of the world athletic community.

Fair is Fair, Or Is It?: A Moral Consideration of the Doping Wars in American Sport

William J. Morgan

The Atlanta Olympic Games of 1996 were widely regarded, as one commentator colourfully put it, as 'a carnival of sub-rosa experiments in the use of performance-enhancing drugs'. This despite the fact that some 2,000 of the 11,000 athletes were tested for banned substances, and around $2.5 million was spent on such testing.[1] For all that effort and money, only two athletes tested positive and no medals were forfeited. The reasons why these testing procedures proved so ineffective are attributable to a number of factors, not least the infelicity of the tests themselves. But another important reason why these efforts were so spectacularly unsuccessful was due to an ambivalence on the part of the United States Olympic Committee (USOC) and the International Olympic Committee (IOC) themselves about catching violators, owing to the fear that if they turned up too many athletes using performance-enhancing drugs the public would be reluctant to support Olympic sports any more.

By contrast, in the just-completed 2004 Athens Games a record number of positive drug tests were reported. These results reflect, among other things, improvements in the drug tests themselves (though it is still relatively easy for the slightly sophisticated and wily to get around them), and perhaps most of all a greater will and resolve on the part of the USOC and the IOC to catch violators of the drug ban.

But does this newfound will to catch athletes using these drugs constitute real moral progress or not? I am inclined to think not, even if it must be granted that it did at least address the hypocrisy of the USOC's earlier half-baked efforts to stem the flow of drugs into American sports. My scepticism here is that the sort of hunter-hunted struggle this technical testing approach set in motion to expose and punish violators of the performance-enhancing drug ban, had little if anything to do with what could reasonably be called moral efforts to level the playing field, despite pronouncements to the contrary, and almost every thing to do with morally questionable efforts to get athletes to tow the company line at any cost. More precisely, I regard the USOC's greater determination to catch drug users by, among other things, lowering the standards of what constitutes reasonable evidence of such use, as a breach of fairness as morally egregious as the unfair use of performance-enhancing drugs by athletes that it was supposed to discourage, if not stop.

My argument for this, somewhat controversial, claim will proceed as follows. I begin by highlighting the sense in which the notion of fair play speaks not just to a moral feature that is widely thought pivotal to the conduct of sport, but widely thought pivotal to the conduct of American life in all its various forms – which goes a long way toward explaining why sport has the strong hold on the American national psyche that it does. I next offer an analysis of fair play in which I distinguish and discuss two of its most important strands, namely, fair play as a reciprocal regard for the interests of individual participants in sport, and fair play as what Butcher and Schneider aptly call 'respect for the game'.[2] I then try to show how the current anti-doping strategy adopted by the United States Anti-Doping Agency (USADA), following the lead of the World Anti-Doping Agency (WADA), undermines these two moral principles of fair play, and so is as morally blameworthy as the unfair doping strategy pursued by athletes obsessed with winning – does the old saw 'two wrongs don't make a right' sound familiar? Finally, I will close by arguing that if we are really morally serious about dealing with the doping problem in sport, then we will have to look for a moral solution to what is at bottom a deep moral malaise, and not, as is customary in contemporary America, seek a technical solution for what is wrongly perceived to be essentially a technical problem. At the very least, that means taking a hard moral look at the great emphasis we place on winning in sport as evidenced by the outsized economic rewards we attach to it.

Fair Play and American Culture

My focus on fairness in this regard is not an autobiographical quirk but a national and cultural one. By that I mean that the ideal of fairness in its many iterations (for example, fair play, fair dealing, fair outcome, fair trial, et cetera) is a way of moral thinking Americans almost instinctively entertain when they reflect on their characteristic social practices and institutions, though one they share with the members of other English-speaking nations. What is more, it is also a characteristic feature of American sporting life, which is why most Americans get their first lessons on how to treat one another fairly early on in their sporting lives, and continue to draw inspiration from, and be guided by, its moral prescriptions well into their adult sporting lives, both as participants and spectators. It is little wonder, then, why sporting metaphors figure so prominently in spreading the moral message of fair play to other spheres of American life, perhaps most notably to the political realm. As George Fletcher thus opines, it 'is a striking feature of English and American culture [that] we cannot think about human relations without thinking about sports and the idiom of fair and foul play'. As he goes on to observe, 'this is not true in French, German, Russian, Italian, or any other major language or culture of the West', which explains further why when the concept of fair play does manage somehow to find its way into the moral vocabularies of other peoples, the Israelis and the French to be precise, it is accounted as an 'untranslatable American idea'.[3]

So the moral, cultural and linguistic roots of fair play are unmistakably American ones, and equally unmistakably bound up with its rich sporting culture. It is for this reason that Progressive populist intellectuals and social reformers at the turn of the twentieth century seized on sport and its emphasis on fair play as a moral antidote to what they strenuously objected was an unfair distribution of wealth wrought by American industrial society in which a precious few became wealthy beyond their dreams and far too many of their countrymen were forced into poverty. In fact, sport's commitment to fair play cut to the very moral centre of America itself, to its conception of itself as a moral commonwealth in which its democratic experiment to wean itself of the patrician manner and class-driven social hierarchy of the motherland, England, was widely regarded as its defining feature. For if political power is to be invested in the people, as it must in any true democracy, then the people must prove equal to the task socially, politically and, especially, morally. Democracies only work, in other words, if they are peopled by informed, conscientious citizens, who can be counted on to wield the power entrusted to them fairly. This is, to reiterate, what led Progressives to take a serious look at the fair play on display in sport, at what William James called 'the fixed machinery of conditions' (rules) that ensure the equal treatment of all of its participants, and to claim boldly that sport offers us a 'glimpse of what the "real" world ought to look like'.[4]

Two Principles of Fairness

That arguments both about athletes using performance-enhancing drugs and being tested for them in the United States have typically, but, of course, not exclusively, targeted their alleged fairness is no accident then, but a justificatory gesture most Americans naturally make when they want to assess the moral character of just about any social practice. This is especially the case in practices like sport where competition plays such a central role in determining athletic excellence. But it is important to understand how the concept of fairness is being understood and used in the present case in order to grasp the arguments made in its name. With this in mind, I want to argue that the sense of fairness at issue here is principally grounded in two principles of conduct: first, what I call, after Rawls, fairness as reciprocity among individuals involved in a joint, cooperative activity; and second, what Butcher and Schneider call 'fairness as respect for the game'.

Let's begin with the notion of fairness as reciprocity, which in sport has to do with how others in the competition should be treated in their respective bids for athletic distinction. There are two important features of fairness in this regard that need to be discussed.[5] The first is a straightforward insistence on the impartial observance and application of the rules that define the fundamental character of sport and how it is to be conducted. In this respect, fairness means 'equality of conditions' in which similar cases, as determined by the rules of the practice itself, should be treated similarly. The 'structure' of a practice, then, is fair if, and only if, it reflects a 'proper share, balance, or equilibrium between competing claims'.[6]

The second feature of justice as reciprocity sets out what counts as justified inequalities in practices like sport. For while fairness in and outside of sport requires 'equality of conditions' it does not require 'equality of results', which simply means that the benefits and responsibilities that accrue from participation in sport do not have to be apportioned in the same (identical) amount to each participant in order to be considered fair. Another way of saying this is that all 'arbitrary' distinctions between and among participants in sport that advantage one or more participants at the expense of other participants in the awarding of these benefits and responsibilities should be eliminated. For Rawls, distinctions and the inequalities that follow in their wake are arbitrary if they do not work out to the advantage of all members of the athletic practice community, and/or if the roles and positions with regard to which benefits and responsibilities are meted out in sport are not open to all according to their talents and capabilities.[7] On this second feature, therefore, a sport practice is fair if the goods and responsibilities gained by participants in it are reciprocally advantageous to all concerned, that is, mutually enhance the goods and qualities particular to the practice that make it so attractive to participants in the first place, and if the opportunity to engage in sport and partake of the goods it provides is open to everyone based on their relevant capabilities as determined by the rules and norms of the practice itself.

If we join these two strands of fairness as reciprocity together, it becomes clear that fairness in sport demands that everyone in sport be treated equally, in other words, that the rules of sport apply to all in relevantly similar ways, and that the distribution of benefits and responsibilities in sport be determined by a competition open to all on the basis of the relevant talent and capabilities of would-be participants and in such a way that does not diminish the goods that sport delivers that draws people to them. Dworkin's distinction between the right to equal treatment, 'which is the right to an equal distribution of some opportunity or resource or burden', and the right to treatment as an equal, which is the right 'to be treated with the same respect and concern as everyone else', is instructive in this regard. For equal respect and concern do not entail the identical distribution of some good in sport, for example, who gets to start or play a certain position in a game, so long as those goods are open to all based on considerations of merit.[8] Of course, ignoring this important distinction between equal respect and the identical distribution of some good in sport would itself be arbitrary and so manifestly unfair, since it would undermine the competitive quest for athletic excellence that makes sport the vital and engaging practice that it is, and, therefore, would prove mutually disadvantageous to the members of the sporting community.

Now, it is important to make clear that fairness as reciprocity in both of its key senses above presumes that participants in sport will, at least in part, act as self-interested parties seeking their own particular advantages in and through it. Indeed, seeking such advantages is one of the driving forces of competitive sport itself, since competitors will, in their respective efforts to achieve athletic excellence, attempt to frustrate and deny their competitors' desires and efforts. This suggests that the importance of fair play in competition is to ensure that that self-interested pursuit does not get out of hand, that participants restrain their self-seeking ways out of regard for the fairness of the competition. And that regard is to be accounted as a distinctly moral one, which explains why fair play should be accounted as a genuine moral principle. For as Rawls aptly observes, a person 'whose moral judgments always coincided with his interests could be suspected of having no morality at all'.[9] So when participants in sport agree beforehand to abide fairly by the rules and relevant conventions of sport and not to tailor them to their own idiosyncratic interests and concerns, in other words, to apply those rules and conventions impartially to themselves as well as to their fellow competitors, they are acknowledging that the interpersonal relationships that bind them to one another in competitive sport are indeed moral ones they are mutually obliged to observe.

The moral reasons one has to curb one's self-interests in sport that are particular to fair play are, therefore, a species of what Scheffler calls 'relation-dependent' reasons.[10] That is, just as a relationship like friendship commits one to treat one's friends differently from the way one treats, say, strangers, so a competitive relationship in sport commits one to treat one's fellow competitors differently from the way one treats, say, strangers. Everything here, of course, hangs on what is meant by 'different treatment'. One thing it definitely does not mean is that whereas one is always free to treat strangers as mere means rather than as ends-in-themselves, one is not similarly free to treat friends or competitors as simple instruments of one's own egoistic gratification. For treatment of someone as an end, which is synonymous with treating them with equal respect, is something not only owed to strangers but to any moral agent properly so-called. Rather, different treatment in this instance means that in one's relationships to friends and competitors in practices like sport, though certainly not competitors in the market, one incurs special and rather robust responsibilities to significant others by virtue of the relationship in which they stand to one another that does not obtain for outsiders. For being someone's friend just means that one can ask of such a person, and, of course, they can ask of you, something one would neither be comfortable nor justified in asking of a stranger, for example, to lend you a substantial sum of money, or to make a far-reaching request, or to listen compassionately and as long as it takes to some sad event that has befallen you. Similarly, to be someone's competitor in sport means that you can ask of them, and once again, of course, they can ask of you, something that would neither be appropriate nor justified to ask of a stranger, namely, to take the competition as seriously as you do, to push you to achieve a level of excellence that may well be nigh impossible to achieve outside of the competitive encounter, to train hard, and so on. Of course, there are limits even to what we may legitimately request of friends or athletic competitors, but those limits go well beyond the range of what would be appropriate to request of strangers precisely because we do not incur the same moral responsibilities to strangers that we do to these significant others because we stand in no significant interpersonal relationship to them. So even though strangers should always be treated with equal respect, they are not entitled to the same moral consideration as our friends and athletic competitors are. That said, what goes for our friends and athletic competitors goes as well for the friends and athletic competitors of others with whom we have no connection and from whom we receive no out of the ordinary consideration, which we must, on pain of contradiction, reciprocally acknowledge as constituting special responsibilities that are as morally compelling and substantive as ours.[11] This is why in acknowledging the special responsibilities that flow from our most important relationships and that furnish us with good reasons for constraining our self-interests we are not violating the sacrosanct moral principle regarding the equal worth of all persons, the silly and morally dangerous idea that some people are more valuable than others.

Just how reciprocity figures in the principle of fair play should by now be fairly clear. For it is the notion of reciprocity that explains why individuals who possess no moral authority over one another and are engaged in a joint activity are themselves the ones who set the rules and norms that both shape their conduct and determine what is a fair share of the goods and responsibilities that flow from such cooperative activity.[12] Crucial to the very idea of reciprocity, therefore, which by the way does not require 'a deliberative performative act' such as the making of a promise but simply knowing participation in a practice,[13] is that whatever reasons participants in a practice agree on to restrain their self-interests must be mutually acceptable to all members of the practice fraternity, if such restraint is to be accounted as fair. For only if there is mutually acceptable determination of and acknowledgement of principles of fair play can we reasonably expect participants to be morally committed to them, and can we expect there to be 'true community between persons in their common practices'.[14] Consequently, in the absence of such mutual determination and acknowledgement, we can not reasonably expect participants to commit morally to the rules and norms of sport or to the rules and norms of any other social practice, since in doing so they would have to accept arbitrary distinctions that single them out for what they rightly regard to be unfair treatment. Righteous indignation, therefore, would be the most likely outcome of participants yielding to principles that are not mutually acceptable to all, since the price to be paid for lack of reciprocity in our practical reasoning with our fellow practitioners is fairness itself.

There is, as noted, another sense of fairness that is related to, but goes beyond, Rawls's notion of fairness as reciprocity, and that is specific to social practices like sport. This is Butcher's and Schneider's idea of fairness as respect for the game, which requires that participants in sport do more than observe and follow its rules and norms that owe their moral force, as just noted, to the mutual acceptance of them by all parties concerned, but that they additionally esteem and value the form of life embodied in sport. In particular, this means a commitment to athletic excellence and the qualities of action, or better, virtues, they demand. A minimalist account of such athletic virtues would include recognition of 'what is due to whom' in the pursuit of athletic excellence, a willingness to take whatever risks are compelled by such pursuit, and the capacity to acknowledge our own inadequacies and to correct them by considering carefully and thoughtfully what game authorities tell us are our shortcomings with regard to such pursuit.[15] In short, the virtues of fairness, courage and honesty are minimal requirements that follow when one morally values practices like sport, that is, when one takes to heart the sort of life it makes possible and exemplifies.

The sense of fairness at issue here reveals a different sort of moral reason for conducting oneself fairly in sport, one that is parasitic on the game itself and on the kind of excellence it seeks. The moral reasoning introduced by this latter notion of fairness concerns what Scheffler calls 'project-dependent' reasons,[16] and what I prefer to call instead 'practice-dependent' reasons. What distinguishes practice-dependent moral reasons from other kinds of moral reasons for action is that, as their name implies, they take their point of departure from the forms of life specific to social practices, such that, whatever meaning and value these practices possess can be read directly off of the forms of life they sanction. That means that when one morally values a practice one can be understood as, first, acknowledging that among the various reasons one might have for engaging in it one's primary, but, of course, not only, reason for doing so is to further the goods internal to it; and second, as committing oneself to the social relations crucial to the flourishing of this way of life and of the practice-based goods it puts in play. Fairness from this practice perspective is, therefore, unlike fairness as reciprocity since participants who act first and foremost out of regard for the practice itself, that is, who find the way of life it instantiates compelling in its own right, do not act as self-interested parties seeking their own good but as partners in a common enterprise seeking a common, shared good. In the first instance, fairness requires that individuals reciprocally curb their self-interests as a sign of equal respect for one another, whereas in the second instance, fairness requires those who engage in the practice to recognize and act on the built-in cooperative character of the practice itself as a sign of their moral respect for it. For when one takes up a practice because one morally values the way of life it makes available that can only mean, as we have seen, that one regards the aims, goals and goods specific to that practice as one's very own aims, goals and goods.

In the specific case of sport, that means when one values the perfectionist life sport is all about one can be understood as, first, acknowledging that the primary, but again not only, reason one engages in it is to realize the goods internal to it, which are all bound up in one way or another with the kinds of bodily excellence on display there, and second, as committing oneself to the cooperative social relations that underlie and guide the competitive pursuit of such goods. This rules out any amoral instrumental regard for both the game and those who play it. It rules out the former because respect for the game itself requires that we recognize that the challenges it puts in our way to excite the distinctive kinds of excellence it is known for are created by placing limits on certain highly useful and efficient ways to achieve its goal. It is, for example, useful but proscribed to trip one's opponent in a footrace or to use a catapult to clear a high jump bar.[17] It further rules out as morally objectionable treating one's opponents as mere instruments to get what one wants in sport, because unless practitioners cooperate in their mutual effort to achieve excellence in certain prescribed ways, which overlays and thus regulates their competitive pursuit of individual advantage, none can achieve excellence in sport. In short, because the goals and goods of sport are at bottom shared ones, because it is their being-for-us rather than their being-for-me-and-for-you that accounts for their distinctive rationality and normative force, one cannot without distortion separate one's ends and goods from either those of the game or those who engage in it. And if one cannot individuate one's goals and goods in this fashion, one cannot, again without distortion, use either the game or its participants as instruments to satisfy one's egocentric preferences. Indeed, since such egocentric ends and goods are, as a precondition of one's very involvement in a common enterprise like sport, subordinated to those of the game, how else to make the ends and goods of the game one's own ends and goods, they have, and can have, no important rational or normative standing within it.

Fairness, Doping and Anti-doping Measures

We should now be in a position to examine the fairness of doping as well as anti-doping attempts to stem it by the USOC and the USADA. I want to begin with doping itself to establish that it is indeed an unfair practice, and thus that the USOC and USADA are morally justified in trying to stop it. This will show that my gripe with both of these sport organizations is not that they take anti-doping efforts seriously, but rather that the way they have chosen to carry out these efforts is itself unfair, and, therefore, puts in serious question the professed aim of their anti-doping programme to safeguard the moral integrity of sport.

Now, if as I have already argued considerations of fairness are indigenous to the way most Americans think about ethics no matter what the issue, then it should come as no surprise that the rationale a great majority of American athletes rely on to justify their use of performance-enhancing drugs similarly takes its point of departure from the notion of fairness. So claims that using these drugs somehow levels the playing field in sport trip naturally off the tongues of elite athletes as the words of the following world-class cyclist attest, 'Is it cheating', this athlete pointedly asks, 'if everyone does it?' The same athlete muses further in a similar vein, 'you start to think if you don't take something, you're going to lose. And who's going to cheer for someone who finishes last in a heat.'[18] Typically, such justificatory gestures are often confusedly mixed in with claims that athletes are forced to take these drugs if they are to remain competitive, but their main claim is that since most athletes are already using these drugs any unilateral decision not to use them would put one at a considerable competitive disadvantage. When we further factor into the equation the great discipline and sacrifice it takes to be an Olympic athlete, and the great rewards allocated to winners, it is easy to see why fairness figures so prominently in athletes' decision to take performance-enhancing drugs.

The first thing that should be said about this argument is that it is not absurd on its face. For it raises the interesting and important issue of what fairness entails when individuals in a social practice systematically fail to comply with its rules, when non-compliance with certain of its rules is so widespread that it is plausible to wonder whether it even qualifies as a genuine rule any more, let alone as a moral one. That is to say, cases like this suggest that it is not just the rules that allegedly govern our interactions with one another that must be accounted for when considering our moral obligations to one another, but as well the behaviour of others. It suggests further and more strongly, that in some instances, namely, when non-compliance is rife, how others behave toward us trump the explicit rules that are supposed to dictate such behaviour thereby attaining the status of rules themselves, albeit implicit ones. This is the very point Carl Elliot is getting at when he argues that the vilification of athletes who take substances to improve their performance is hypocritical when we consider that ordinary Americans consume with impunity drugs like Viagra to improve their sexual performance, Paxil to boost their social confidence and performance, and low doses of testosterone from their family doctor to enhance their overall well-being and physical performance. The different way we treat these latter drugs that are aimed at underperforming average citizens, Elliot sardonically remarks, is owed to the fact that 'we [Americans] have simply changed the rules' for ourselves to exculpate our drug-taking, but adamantly, and I would add inexplicably, deny that the rules of sport have similarly changed thereby allowing us to inculpate athletes' drug-taking'.[19] If the actual behaviour of athletes in top-level sport is any indication, however, it looks as if the rules of sport regarding drugs have indeed changed and, therefore, that the public's browbeating of them for disregarding these rules is unwarranted.

Hence, when athletes cite the non-compliance of their fellow competitors regarding rules against these drugs as a reason for paying them no mind, they cannot be curtly dismissed as being morally irresponsible. In fact, there seem to be at least two principles at stake here, not one as I just intimated. The first, and one that has so far gone unremarked, is Hobbes's 'principle of self-preservation', which holds that our consent to follow the rules of some practice is conditional on others doing the same. Hence, if others fail to observe the rules I am not morally bound to do so either in order to protect myself from the harm caused by such transgressions. The second moral principle is, of course, fairness, which in this case is a simple matter of conceding the obvious, that very few, if any, athletes are observing the rules that prohibit taking performance-enhancing drugs, and drawing the correct inference, that these rules therefore have no morally binding force. Indeed, the idea that these rules should never be enforced in sport is pretty much the only thing, or so the claim goes, that athletes could be said to mutually agree on when non-compliance is this widespread. What is more, since athletes' non-compliance in this case is selectively targeted to rules against drug use, and not summarily to other rules that govern sport, their claim that these rules should be suspended so that they disadvantage no one is neither irrational nor morally reckless. It is not irrational since rationality here is keyed to consensus, and the consensus in this case is evidently on the athletes' rule-breaking side, not against it, and it is not morally reckless because it allows for something like Kavka's distinction between 'offensive' and 'defensive' rule violations. Offensive rule violations are ones in which an agent breaks a rule that others are complying with so as to gain an advantage over them, whereas defensive rule violations are ones in which an agent breaks rules so as not to be disadvantaged by the fact that practically everyone else is breaking them as well.[20] While the first kind of offensive rule violation is morally defective because its unilateral suspension of the rule makes it unfair, the second, defensive rule violation is morally sound because its mutual suspension of the rule, which by the very fact of its mutuality suggests it is a suspect rule, remedies what otherwise would be an unfair outcome. And because it seems uncontroversial that elite athletes' violation of drug rules in sport fall into the defensive category, their behaviour must be adjudged morally permissible.

Or should it? After all, it is one thing to say that breaking rules against performance-enhancing drugs in order to level the playing field is not absurd on its face, and another to say that it is a persuasive argument for regarding such behaviour as morally permissible. In point of fact, however, I do not find this to be a persuasive argument for essentially two reasons.

The first and main problem with this argument is that it is not a moral argument at all. That is to say, the point of this argument is plainly to protect the individual interests of athletes from the self-serving actions of their rule-breaking competitors by giving them a free pass to do the same, which suggests that it was never intended to convey any idea that individuals should curb their own self-interests so that the interests of others be given fair consideration. On the contrary, it merely presumed from the outset that since evidently everyone is violating the prescriptions against performance-enhancing drugs in sport, no one has any reason, moral or otherwise, not to do likewise, not to get caught up in this orgy of rule-breaking. What we have here, then, is more so reminiscent of Hobbes's famous state of nature in which all moral bets are off because all moral obligations to others have been suspended, than it is of Rawls's moral ideal of fairness as reciprocity which mandates that we take into account the interests of others and treat them fairly. Simply put, that means any prior commitment to abide by these rules and apply them impartially both to myself and to my fellow competitors goes out the window when non-compliance is this widespread. And as Rawls himself forewarned us, when athletes' moral judgments always coincide with their self-interests, as they so transparently do in this instance, they can justifiably be accused of having no morality at all.

A second, and for my purposes a final, problem with this argument lies with its premise that everyone is already breaking the rules forbidding use of substances like steroids. The idea that everybody is already doing it and, therefore, I am justified in doing it as well often has a cavalier, if not adolescent, ring to it because it is often difficult to substantiate, and because those making the claim not only seem too quick and eager to make it but also appear to rely on its problematic evidentiary status to confound any would be interlocutor – that is, like interlocutors who claim that what they say has divine backing, which makes further conversation pointless, interlocutors who claim that everybody is doing something others want to brand as morally objectionable also make further conversation pointless; which if the truth be told is their real aim rather than winning the point that touched off the conversation in the first place. In the case of the alleged use of steroids and such, this is especially the case since it is very difficult to pin down just how many athletes in fact imbibe or shoot up these substances. Part of the problem, of course, is that this sort of drug-use is illegal and very few athletes are willing to subject themselves to criminal prosecution by disclosing what illicit substances they are taking. So it is pretty much anyone's guess what percentage of athletes we are talking about here. I have seen estimates of drug use by elite athletes as low as 5 per cent to as high as 95 per cent. I am incredulous about both of these numbers, particularly the lower one, but I hesitate to make a guess myself.[21] But one thing I do feel much more confident in saying is that clearly not all elite athletes are using these performance-enhancing drugs. And that means claiming that everybody is using them to justify one's own drug use is bound to put some goodly number of one's competitors at a significant disadvantage. In other words, the casual use of this claim to exempt one from any moral obligation to follow these rules gives one a decided unfair advantage over those who do observe them. What is more, as Holley astutely notes, 'Suspicion of the untrustworthiness of competitors is likely to lead to exaggerated judgments of the extent of violations, and assessments of the possibility that this violation may significantly contribute to a downward spiral of rule violations are likely to be minimized.' So this breach of fairness in sport is no small matter, which is why I further concur with Holley's conclusion that arguments of this sort which condone rule-breaking are a 'recipe for destroying mutually beneficial systems that depend on conformance to rules'.[22]

What about the other, anti-doping side then, about the USOC's and USADA's efforts to put an end to this self-serving resort to performance-enhancing drugs? From what has been said thus far, it certainly seems that they are on the morally right side of this fairness issue. And in one sense they clearly are. For it seems that fairness itself dictates that athletes who use these drugs should be weeded out and punished for their rule-breaching ways. Further, reliance on drug tests and other similarly objective non-analytic measures seem to be a fair and thus properly impartial method for catching rogue athletes. But as the old saying goes, the devil is in the details, and a closer look at some of these details casts a different, not so morally auspicious light on these measures and the USOC's and USADA's efforts to enforce them.

The main staple of anti-doping programmes is, of course, drug tests. As I have said, they seem to be eminently fair since they provide an objective, impartial way of finding out which athletes are thumbing their noses at the rules. The well-noted problem with them, however, despite the fact that the tests are getting better – in part because they have become more invasive as evidenced by the recent introduction of blood-tests to uncover use of human growth hormone and Erythropoietin (EPO) – is that they are still relatively easy to defeat, which is why the significant number of false negatives they typically generate is something of a joke in elite athletic circles. Getting around the tests is as simple as, for example, buying a commercially available steroid and tweaking the trace signature that would normally show up in the athlete's urine, which, abracadabra, yields a brand new steroid that is for all intents and purposes undetectable. What is more, it does not take an expert chemist to create new drugs like this, as the authors of a *Sports Illustrated* article recently demonstrated when they solicited a third-year college chemistry student to doctor a steroid they gave him that would not be traceable in a urine test, which he had no trouble in doing.[23] So the only athletes likely to be caught by such tests are careless or clueless ones, or, as the recent case of a syringe filled with a new drug sent anonymously to the USADA that was subsequently discovered to be Tetra Hydrogestrinone (THG) attests, unlucky ones.

Understandably frustrated by their inability to catch elite athletes with the will and resources to beat their best drug tests, the WADA and USADA have started to rely more extensively on non-analytic methods. Such measures include circumstantial evidence such as used IV bags and calendars with apparent coded notations about what drugs to take and when to take them seized in criminal investigations, and personal testimony from those that administer and distribute such drugs. The most noted success of this latter approach was the USADA's involvement in the highly publicized criminal investigation of the BALCO steroid scandal, the Bay Area Laboratory Co-Operative founded by Victor Conte, which relied almost entirely on materials gathered by federal authorities armed with search warrants. And the recent eight-year suspension by the American Arbitration Association of the 2003 World Indoor 200 Metres sprint champion, Michelle Collins, who never failed a drug test during her career but was implicated in the BALCO investigation, was an important validation of this new non-analytical strategy by the USADA.

In taking this non-analytic step to bolster their anti-doping efforts, the USADA was lauded by authors Steven Ungerlieder and Gary Wadler for finally facing up to the fact that the old 'principle of strict liability', the idea that 'if it's in your body, you're guilty',[24] was unworkable because it left too many guilty athletes off the hook. No doubt, they are right about this, and are right as well for applauding the recent resolute efforts by both the WADA and USADA to track down drug-users and distributors in sport, which, to reiterate, is a welcome change from their past irresolute efforts, and for their successful efforts to standardize rules regarding drug use in sport, which have been adopted by the IOC, 33 international sports federations, 195 national Olympic committees (including the USOC) and 110 governments (including the US). But when they go on to claim, in a fit of hyperbole, that such expanded efforts herald 'a new world order in elite sports, one committed to fair play and ethical values',[25] I must strongly demure. On the contrary, I believe this new expansion of WADA's and USADA's efforts to detect use of these substances raises some grave moral concerns of its own. In particular, there are two moral problems I have with their new anti-doping regimen, both of which bear on the issue of fairness.

The USADA's reliance on circumstantial evidence to finger drug-users in sport is, as I have already conceded, morally unimpeachable, not to mention practically sensible. However, its attempt to change the standard of what counts as proof of non-compliance in cases like this is morally impeachable, not to mention highly morally offensive. So my first problem with the USADA's 'new and improved' anti-doping strategy has to do with its effort, following a similar initiative by WADA and the International Association of Athletics Federations (IAAF), to change the standard of proof for doping offences from the customary criminal standard of 'beyond a reasonable doubt' to 'comfortable satisfaction'. Lawyers defending athletes against such offences were upset by this effort for two reasons. First, because it was supposedly implemented before the USADA initially said it would take effect, which one lawyer likened to 'the classic case of moving the goal line in the middle of the game',[26] and second, because it was hopelessly vague. Both of these charges seem to have merit. But even if the date of its implementation were the same one as the USADA initially announced, and even if it were somehow, per impossible, rendered clear, it would still be morally objectionable on grounds of basic fairness. That is because creating a separate, special standard of evidence for suspected doping violators that is significantly less stringent than the standard of 'beyond a reasonable doubt' employed for suspected legal offences by ordinary Americans is a paradigmatic case of unfairness, of making an arbitrary distinction of athletes that puts them at a considerable disadvantage to everyone else. In short, this is a classic case of treating similar cases dissimilarly, a violation of the reciprocity that Rawls and others have persuasively argued goes to the very heart of our conception of fairness. For demanding athletes consent to be governed by a weaker evidentiary standard like 'comfortable satisfaction' is requiring them to do something that is manifestly unfair because it is not anything they could reasonably agree to, that could meet with their mutual agreement.

So requiring athletes to comply with such a standard is only likely to sour their relationships with governing athletic institutions, not to morally uplift or solidify them. In other words, the USADA's efforts to enforce the 'comfortable satisfaction' standard will, with good reason, be seen by athletes as openly taking advantage of its authoritative position to strong-arm them into complying with something that they rightly regard as fundamentally unfair. This can only breed mistrust, resentment and retaliation, the very features that need to be expunged from elite sport if we are to make any moral progress on this front. Fortunately, the American Arbitration Association has so far resisted the USADA's insistence that all doping violators be tried according to the less demanding standard of 'comfortable satisfaction' and, therefore, continues to use the more rigorous standard of 'beyond a reasonable doubt'. How long such arbitration panels will cling to this latter standard is anyone's guess, but at least for now it has blunted some of the athletes' resentment and mistrust of the USADA and USOC. The same, I am afraid, cannot be said for the second moral problem I see with the latter's more muscular approach to anti-doping.

Now, in one sense, as already noted, the USADA's expansion of its anti-doping initiatives beyond drug testing to constructing circumstantial cases against doping cheats, which, as the BALCO case so clearly showed, opens up a new, cosy working relationship between athletic regulatory agencies and local and federal criminal authorities, is on its face morally unobjectionable and practically sensible. But in another sense, it is morally treacherous, especially in light of the morally noxious environment in which elite sports are practiced today. That is to say, given the widespread mistrust that already poisons social relationships in the athletic community today (which as we have just seen the USADA and other regulatory institutions have only made worse), in which athletes are always looking for a competitive edge and are unsure whether they can trust their friends let alone their competitors, and in which the economic stakes are so high, it is not hard to see how good faith efforts to construct circumstantial cases of doping can easily degenerate into morally offensive cases of score settling. In other words, in strengthening their efforts to catch drug cheaters by marshalling circumstantial evidence against them without at the same time trying to do something about the morally unhealthy setting in which elite sports presently find themselves, athletic institutions like the USOC and regulatory arms like the USADA only make sport more not less vulnerable to moral jeopardy in which even explicit appeals to fairness can no longer be taken seriously. Let me explain.

Or better, let journalists Longman and Fressenden explain, for they anticipate the critical point I want to make here when they note how the USADA's strategy to get circumstantial evidence on suspected dopers sets in motion a morally unseemly chain of events that closely approximates what happens when legal authorities try to get circumstantial evidence on street drug users. More specifically, what they noticed is that the way performance-enhancing drug cases play themselves out when athletic authorities adopt this quasi-criminalistic strategy starts to look more and more like the way street drug cases play themselves out with one important twist: whereas street drugs rivals kill off one another, steroid drug rivals 'rat off one another'.[27] Put more bluntly, once athletes realize that casting suspicion on their opponents' alleged drug habits provides them yet another opportunity to get a leg up on their competitors, the already morally foul atmosphere in which elite sports operate is only likely to become that much fouler. For in this kind of cut-throat, do-whatever-it-takes-to-win atmosphere, the chance to smear one's opponents, to destroy their athletic reputations and fortunes by carefully crafted allegations of drug use, will, no doubt, prove too tempting for today's jaded elite athletes to pass up. That is why we should be especially chary of appeals to fairness in this context, since in this Hobbesian setting such appeals are more likely to be employed as rationalizations to justify their backstabbing, double-crossing behaviour than as moral deterrents to such crass behaviour. A couple of real-life examples should suffice to make the point.

Consider first the main villain of the BALCO investigation, its founder Victor Conte, who in a recent national television interview incriminated himself by admitting that he did, in fact, supply designer drugs and Human Growth Hormone (HGH) to prominent American Olympic athletes like Marion Jones. The fact that he did so without the guarantee of a plea agreement baffled most observers. So the obvious question is, why did he do it? Was it an act of supreme contempt aimed at the USADA? Or was it part of a risky legal ploy to get leniency? Or did he do it to take down others given the overwhelming evidence against him? Or perhaps he chose to morally sacrifice himself for the greater moral good of sport, specifically in order to create a more level playing field?[28]

The same sort of questions are prompted by my second example, the previously mentioned case of the anonymous, and supposedly high-profile, track coach who sent a syringe filled with what was later found to be THG to the USADA. Did the coach decide to take this bold step because athletes he did not coach who used these substances threatened his livelihood, or because he feared his athletes might defect to coaches who encouraged and had the wherewithal to get such substances? Or did he do it out of moral concern for the fairness of sport, which he thought was being compromised by use of these drugs?

Of course, no one can say for sure why Conte outed himself or the unknown coach decided to turn the syringe over to athletic authorities. And it would be foolish to discount the possibility that their motivation was complex and involved all or several of the reasons offered above – though it is tempting, at least in Conte's case, to suspect the worst, even though he claims to have acted out of the highest moral motives and offered his expertise in concocting designer-drugs to athletic authorities to help clean up sports.[29] But all of this is in one important sense quite beside the point. For the point here is not to divine their motivation for doing what they did, but to underscore how the USADA's quasi-criminal strategy in pursuing drug cheats in this way exposes both sports and the athletes who play them to further moral harm. It does so because it worsens the moral distrust that already permeates sports, and that encourages many athletes to adopt motives and engage in actions that are not morally conducive to them – that it further gins up disdain for regulatory organizations such as the USADA goes without saying. Of course, I am not suggesting that the USADA or any other athletic body should simply trust athletes to do the right thing when it comes to performance-enhancing drugs, after all, it was their untrustworthiness that prompted them to take this circumstantial route in the first place. But I am saying that whatever measures they do take to staunch the flow of drugs into sports should do no additional moral harm, and that by this standard they have missed the mark by a wide margin because they have, to reiterate, exacerbated the mistrust that is rife in sports today and that is responsible for much of the moral mischief that goes on there. All of which suggests that Ungerlieder and Wadler could not have been more wrong when they exclaimed that this new resolute chapter in the USOC's efforts to crack down on drug offenders in elite sport heralds 'a new world order in elite sports, one committed to fair play and ethical values'. On the contrary, as I have been arguing, such a new world order can dawn in sports if, and only if, athletic bodies like the USOC turn their main attention away from things like drug tests and criminal investigations and instead address the more complex and vexing reasons why athletes take these substances in the first place and endeavour to find a moral remedy to override them.

Of course, there is another, easier fix, which claims to solve the fairness issue without so much as lifting a moral finger. I am speaking here of legalization, of simply dropping the rule against these substances. That way anyone and everyone would be free to use these drugs as they see fit without worrying about being accused of cheating, of taking unfair advantage of others. But legalization isn't the cure-all that many make it out to be since it raises a different kind of fairness problem that implicates the second sense of fairness discussed above, namely, fairness as respect for the game.

It will be remembered that the idea of fairness as respect for the game is a morally stouter notion of fairness because it enjoins not only that we follow rules that are mutually acceptable to all, but further that we value the form of life particular to sport. That is why fairness so understood requires a fundamental commitment by its participants to the standards of excellence and goods that define sport, and to the qualities of action or, better, virtues, necessary for realizing those standards and goods. Hence, when one makes the aims and goods of sport one's very own, which is just another way of saying that one values the form of life sport makes available to us, one morally rules out treating either the game or those with whom one plays it as instruments of one's own egoistic gratification.

The problem with legalizing doping in sport, then, is that it introduces an alien instrumental regard into sport that undercuts the perfectionist form of life it stands for and the social relationships that are crucial to the flourishing of that life. So the legalization of doping is a morally flawed idea that should not see the light of day, or so I want to argue in what follows.

What, then, is this alien instrumental standard that legalizing doping supposedly puts in place and in what sense does it disrespect the form of life specific to social practices like sport? An important part of the answer to this question has to do with the fact that the practice of doping is itself intimately bound up with a professional conception of sport, one in which winning is both separated from the play of the game and valued above all else that takes place within it.[30] To see how doping is implicated in this professional conception of sport, I need first to say something more about in what sense this winning-at-all-costs ethos subverts the basic character of sport itself.

Let us begin with relatively uncomplicated sports like foot racing or golf.[31] The goals of these sports turn out, under closer inspection, to be rather more complex than they might originally seem. For the aim of foot racing is not just to cross the finish line first, but to do so by, among other things, running around the track, and the aim of golf is not just to put the ball into the hole, but to do so by using the fewest number of strokes. In other words, the goal in both games is a compound one that inextricably links the outcome sought to the play that leads up to it by including within it both a specification of the state of affairs to be achieved as well as a specification of the manner in which it is to be achieved. Under a professional understanding of these games, however, in which winning is the paramount concern, a not-so-subtle shift in their respective aims is effected, such that, the goal of foot racing becomes the more uncomplicated one of crossing the finish line first and of golf of putting the ball into the hole. What were formerly compound goals, then, in which rules, ends and means stand in an organic, inseparable relation to one another, are made more discrete and compact by breaking them apart from one another, such that winning can be detached from the play of the game that leads up to it and, therefore, isolated and valued as the stand alone outcome of athletic activity.

While this shift in the aims of sport might at first seem inconsequential, its actual effects are anything but. For once sports are turned into essentially instruments for attaining stripped-down goals like those just described, the main problematic of sport ceases to be trying to achieve goals that rule out certain useful ways of attaining them, to achieving goals by using any and every useful means available to players. That means that it is the very utility of, say, tripping one's opponent in a foot race or of, say, grounding a club in golf that matters most in trying to come out on top in sports like these, in winning, and that prescriptions against their use figure only in a technical rather than a moral sense, that is, only in the sense that if such actions are not done cleverly they may not be so efficient after all in attaining what it is that we so single-mindedly seek in sport so conceived, namely, the coveted victory.

Now, while it may be easy to see how tripping an opponent in a foot race is illustrative of this morally-challenged professional conception of sport in which the accent is placed entirely on winning, it is not so easy to think of doping in these terms. But if we reprise my previous point that the goal of foot racing, rightly understood, is to cross the finish line first by, among other things, going around the track, and render the phrase 'among other things' to mean that one is to rely principally upon one's athletic talents and skills in getting to the finish line first, then how doping figures in this professional conception of sport should be less difficult to divine. For as Simon has persuasively argued elsewhere, when one's winning of a foot race or any other sport is owed in some significant measure to how one's body contingently and favourably responds, say, to a steroid, that win is compromised by the fact that how one's body happens to respond to a drug is not a bona fide athletic talent or skill because it has nothing important to do with what an athletic test is supposed to be about.[32] So taking certain substances to boost one's performance in sport is morally objectionable for the same reason that tripping one's opponent in a foot race is: both violate the perfectionist point of sport by using highly efficient, what Suits sometimes calls 'ultimate means', that have nothing essential to do with what the athletic purpose of sport is.

In a nutshell then, legalization of doping in sport is morally repugnant not because, as is commonly thought, it undermines human agency, the idea that when athletes dope we are no longer able to attribute their performance to them but only to the drugs they took, but that it inflates human agency in an instrumental way that makes a mockery of the form of life sport is emblematic of. Something very much like this is what Sandel had in mind when he agued that the main problem with drug enhancement, both in and outside of sport, is that it 'represents a kind of hyperagency – a Promethean aspiration to remake nature, including human nature, to serve our purposes and satisfy our desires. The problem is not the drift to mechanism but the drive to mastery.'[33] Sandel goes on to suggest that the moral danger of this drive for perfection is that it severely erodes our appreciation of what he calls the 'gifted character of human powers and achievements', the fact that they are not 'wholly of our own doing.'[34] But I think the more worrisome moral danger that this drug-abetted quest for mastery poses for social practices like sport is that it undermines our understanding and appreciation of its unique aesthetic and moral character, of the distinctive kind of excellence it exemplifies and excites by purposely ruling out certain useful means in which its goals can be achieved and of the moral virtues it puts in play by making those rule-based limitations an essential feature of those goals themselves. Thus, it is the capacity of sport to rouse our aesthetic sensibilities, to induce in us what Kant calls a feeling of sublimity by providing glimpses of unimagined bodily perfection, and to provoke our moral sensibilities by teaching us respect for things like basic fairness, that is jeopardized by such a Promethean aspiration to succeed no matter what. What is at stake here, therefore, leaving aside the aesthetic side of the equation for the moment, is nothing less than the moral integrity of sport itself and, more pointedly, the moral insinuation conveyed by its peculiarly non-instrumental manner of proceeding that calls into question one of the main pillars of our increasingly instrumentalist culture: namely, the morally-pernicious technological idea that if something can be done, that if we have figured out how to do or make something, be it a cluster bomb or a way to prolong or enhance life in all its various forms, it should be done. For if sport teaches us anything of a moral sort, surely it is that not every thing we human agents do should be turned into a means to satisfy our every desire.

So the athletic establishment's opposition to the legalization of doping is, once again, morally sound. But as before, the recognition that dropping all prohibitions against doping is unfair because it disrespects the game also places definite moral limits on the manner and extent to which it should be stemmed. That is to say, it suggests that the USADA's mostly one-sided technological approach to doping is itself morally suspect for at least two reasons. First, its concerted effort to perfect drug tests and upgrade investigative procedures in order to track down and punish dopers is suggestive of the very same hubris that prompted athletes to enlist tactics like doping in their determined effort to achieve athletic supremacy. This pitting of the technical ingenuity and grit of anti-dopers against the technical ingenuity and grit of dopers, no doubt, has a certain psychological resonance for the former in their struggle not to be outdone and outsmarted by the latter, especially since athletes have up until recently held a clear edge in this battle of wits, but it has no moral resonance to speak of since its actions in this regard betray any claim on its part to be concerned foremost with the moral health of sport. Second, and in a related vein, the USADA's anti-doping programme falls morally short because it treats only the symptom rather than the cause of this athletic will to power, and, therefore, falsely presumes that the problem is drug-taking and the solution drug-testing and kindred technical measures. But the cause of doping and the problem it raises is fundamentally a moral one, and one that involves, as noted, a profound disrespect for the game itself and all it stands for. That means, of course, that the solution must be a moral one as well, and the daunting one of finding some way to inculcate moral respect for the kind of perfectionist life sport, rightly understood, requires.

Conclusion

To sum up, I have argued that the USOC and the USADA are well within their moral rights to oppose doping in sport and to take appropriate steps to deter its use. But I have also argued that its anti-doping programme is morally flawed because it has overstepped the boundaries of fairness by seeking to impose a lower standard for what counts as evidence of such drug use by athletes and for instituting criminal-like procedures that only contribute to the morally noxious environment in which elite sports are played today. More generally and fundamentally, I have accused these athletic bodies of being morally insensitive both in their basic understanding of the doping problem and in their overall response to it, which explains their misguided effort to seek a technical solution for what is a moral problem bordering on a full-blown moral crisis. I have deliberately refrained, however, from offering my own moral remedy in this regard, partly because such an effort would require a paper in its own right. But I did earlier suggest a tentative step in this direction when I said that any possible moral remedy should begin with the question why athletes dope in the first place. I would now like to close by giving my short and hardly daring or controversial answer to this question: money. That is, it is mainly because elite sports are played for such large economic stakes nowadays, as I see it, that athletes are prepared to do just about anything to win, including doping, and that athletic regulatory institutions are prepared to do just about anything to catch them in order to safeguard their brand name. If I am right about this, then we have good reason to worry not just about the fate of any proposed moral reform of sport but whether any such reform is even in the offing. For when the IOC sometime in the 1980s or so, under Samaranch's leadership, decided to sell its logo, and in the process, I am convinced, its soul, to the highest corporate bidders, which in short order transformed it from a poor, cash-strapped organization to a wealthy one with more cash than it knew what to do with, it firmly cast its lot with the very professional conception of sport that is, I believe, the root of most if not all of the moral problems like doping that plague sport today. Since I see not one shred of evidence that the IOC or any of its regulatory bodies, or, for that matter, athletes themselves, are prepared to do anything to staunch this flow of money into sports, I am not, therefore, sanguine about the moral future of elite sports.

Notes

[1] Bamberger and Yaeger, 'Over the Edge', 62.
[2] Butcher and Schneider, 'Fair Play as Respect for the Game', 21–48.
[3] Fletcher, 'The Case for Linguistic Defense', 331–2.
[4] Dyerson, *Making the American Team: Sport, Culture, and The Olympic Experience*, 11.
[5] My account of this first version of fairness as reciprocity is primarily drawn from John Rawls's seminal essay, 'Justice as Reciprocity', 190–224. I should also note in this regard that, for Rawls, justice and fairness are closely related concepts that both share the central feature of reciprocity. What distinguishes them for Rawls is that whereas justice covers practices that individuals have no option of whether to engage in them or not, fairness covers practices, what he in other places calls voluntary associations, where individuals always have an option to engage in them or not. But this distinction is not as firm as it might at first seem, since once one does engage in an optional practice like sport and so makes a firm commitment to abide by its rules, one doesn't have the option to violate those rules or the special responsibilities to others that follow from their acceptance of them. More about this later.
[6] Rawls, 'Justice as Reciprocity', 191.
[7] Ibid., 193.
[8] Dworkin, *Taking Rights Seriously*, 227. For an excellent analysis of Dworkin's distinction as it applies to sport see Simon, *Fair Play: The Ethics of Sport*, 31–4.
[9] Rawls, 'Justice as Reciprocity', 202.
[10] My argument in this paragraph borrows liberally from Samuel Scheffler's illuminating essay, 'Projects, Relationships, and Reasons', 247–69.
[11] Ibid., 249.
[12] Rawls, 'Justice as Reciprocity', 208.
[13] Ibid., 210.
[14] Ibid., 209.
[15] The account of virtue as an 'acquired human quality' and of a minimalist account of such virtues as comprising justice, courage and honesty, comes from Alasdair MacIntyre's important book, *After Virtue*, 191.
[16] Scheffler, 'Projects, Relationships, and Reasons', 247.
[17] Suits, *The Grasshopper: Games, Life and Utopia*, 29–30.
[18] As quoted in Juliet Macur, 'Seeking Her Way Out of Infamy', *New York Times* (10 Aug. 2004), C17–8.
[19] Carl Elliot, 'This Is Your Country on Drugs', *New York Times* (14 Dec. 2004), A31.
[20] As quoted in Holley, 'Breaking the Rules When Others Do', 160.
[21] As Holley pointedly shows however, making some such guess is crucial if we wish to wield Kavka's distinction between 'offensive' and 'defensive' rule violations to good effect. That is because what counts as an offensive or defensive rule violation itself depends on the extent of non-compliance in question. As he writes, 'If I shoplift when 30% of other shoppers are doing so, am I an offensive shoplifter or a defensive shoplifter?' Ibid., 161.
[22] Ibid., 161.
[23] Bamberger and Yaeger, 'Over the Edge', 64.

[24] Steven Ungerleider and Gary Wadler, 'A New World Order in Elite Sports', *New York Times* (20 June 2004), 7.

[25] Ibid., 7.

[26] Liz Robbins, 'Lower Standards Angers Athletes and Lawyers', *New York Times* (20 June 2004), C23.

[27] Jere Longman and Ford Fressenden, 'Rivals Turn to Tattling in Steroids Case Involving Top Athletes', *New York Times* (11 April 2004), 4.

[28] Jere Longman, 'In Conte's "20/20" Remarks, Legal Experts See a Risk', *New York Times*, (11 Dec. 2004), B20.

[29] Ibid., B20. Despite Conte's outsized ego, and the strong possibility that he has not the slightest moral interest in cleaning up sport, in other words, that he is a moral scoundrel not to be trusted, the USADA has expressed great interest in talking to him. Their reason, which comes directly out of the mouth of their director of legal affairs, Travis Tygart, is because 'He could provide additional information regarding athletes and others involved in it'. Of course, I'm not surprised they want to talk to Conte, since he is, after all, a well-placed and evidently loose-lipped snitch. But the fact that they seem so eager to talk with an admitted felon like Conte just goes to show how little of their crackdown on doping has to do with moral efforts to reform this practice and how much it has to do with establishing the criminal culpability of suspected dopers.

[30] My claim that doping is essentially linked to a professional conception of sport is a somewhat controversial one. For an alternative view, see Brown, 'Paternalism, Drugs, and the Nature of Sport', 130–41. Brown argues that doping can also find a home, and an ethically justified one, in an experimental conception of sport that puts the entire onus on seeing what individuals can accomplish when they use every technical means at their disposal. I don't think he is right about this, but trying to make a case for this point would take me too far afield for present purposes.

[31] My analysis here, as before, is indebted especially to Chapter 3 of Suit's book, *The Grasshopper: Games, Life and Utopia*.

[32] Simon, 'Good Competition and Drug Enhanced Sport', 126.

[33] Sandel, 'The Case Against Perfection', 54.

[34] Ibid.

References

Bamberger, Michael and Don Yaeger. "Over the Edge." *Sports Illustrated* 86 (14 April 1997): 60–4.

Brown, W. M. "Paternalism, Drugs, and the Nature of Sport." In *Ethics in Sport*, edited by William Morgan, Klaus Meier, and Angela Schneider. Champaign, IL: Human Kinetics, 2001.

Butcher, Robert and Angela Schneider. "Fair Play as Respect for the Game." In *Ethics in Sport*, edited by William Morgan, Klaus Meier, and Angela Schneider. Champaign, IL: Human Kinetics, 2001.

Dworkin, R. *Taking Rights Seriously*. Cambridge: Harvard University Press, 1977.

Dyerson, M. *Making the American Team: Sport, Culture, and The Olympic Experience*. Urbana and Chicago: University of Illinois Press, 1998.

Fletcher, George. "The Case for Linguistic Defense." In *The Morality of Nationalism*, edited by Robert McKim and Jeff McMahan. New York: Oxford University Press, 1997.

Holley, David. "Breaking the Rules When Others Do." *Journal of Applied Philosophy* 14, 2 (1997): 159–68.

MacIntyre, Alasidair. *After Virtue*. Notre Dame: University of Notre Dame Press, 1984.

Rawls, John. "Justice as Reciprocity." In *John Rawls: Collected Papers*, edited by Samuel Freeman. Cambridge, MA: Harvard University Press, 1999.

Sandel, Michael. "The Case Against Perfection." *The Atlantic Monthly* 293, 3 (2004): 50–62.

Scheffler, Samuel "Projects, Relationships, and Reasons." In *Reason and Value: Themes from the Moral Philosophy of Joseph Raz*, edited by Philip Pettit, Samuel Scheffler, Michael Smith and R. J. Wallace. Oxford: Clarendon Press, 2002.

Simon, Robert. "Good Competition and Drug Enhanced Sport." In *Ethics in Sport*, edited by William Morgan, Klaus Meier, and Angela Schneider. Champaign, IL: Human Kinetics, 2001.

Simon, R. *Fair Play: The Ethics of Sport*. Boulder, CO: Westview Press, 2004.

Suits, Bernard. *The Grasshopper: Games, Life and Utopia*. Toronto: University of Toronto Press, 1978.

Are Doping Sanctions Justified?
A Moral Relativistic View

Claudio Tamburrini

Certain performance-enhancing substances and training methods are forbidden by the International Olympic Committee (IOC), the World Anti-Doping Agency (WADA) and other international sport organizations. Although banned substances differ in efficiency and are differently harmful for users, they all go under the denomination of 'doping'. Today, the doping list includes several hundred proscribed drugs and methods and the list expands steadily. Many of the items included in the list are neither performance-enhancing nor dangerous. However, they are nonetheless forbidden, as they can be used to conceal the use of other doping substances.

The reasons usually given by ruling sports organizations to ban doping can be summed up as follows:

(i)   Doping is *harmful* to athletes' health.
(ii) Doping is *unfair* because athletes who are reluctant to use it do not have a fair chance when competing against doped athletes.
(iii) Doping *runs counter to the 'nature'* or *the 'spirit' of sport*, which is said to be to strive for victory by exhibiting natural physical skills and excellence of character without the help of any artificial products.

In recent years, particularly after the creation of WADA in 1999, further steps have been taken in the so-called fight against doping. Succinctly, WADA's initiatives aim to: (1) increase the risk of catching athletes who dope; and (2) standardize the different anti-doping regulations and sanctions for doping use [1].

This first aim is expected to be achieved mainly by (a) conducting more in- and out-of-competition doping controls; and (b) introducing non-analytical, judicial methods (for instance, gathering circumstantial evidence for doping use, like syringes and other material, in suspected laboratories, training camps or in connection with custom controls). Related to this latter strategy is the proposed acceptance of a separate standard for doping liability based on 'comfortable satisfaction' with circumstantial and technical evidence, thereby putting aside the customary criminal law standard of 'beyond reasonable doubt'.

In the literature on doping, the discussion has been mainly concentrated on (a) above. Thus, some authors have criticized doping controls for being invasive and for violating athletes' privacy [2]. Furthermore, in this volume, William J. Morgan addresses (b) and attacks the lowering of legal guarantees that the new liability standard for doping offences implies [3].

However, very few sport scientists and philosophers have overtly defended the right of athletes, if they so wish, to resort to doping as part of their technical preparation and training [4]. And even fewer have discussed issue (2) above, that is, the on-going standardization of doping regulations and sanctions attached to doping offences.

In this essay, firstly, I will argue, contrary to (iii) above, that doping is not only compatible with, but also incarnates, the true spirit of modern competitive elite sports. This supports the case for doping in sport at an elite professional level. This standpoint, which has to be underlined, should not be understood as an exhortation to athletes to violate current bans on doping, but rather should be considered as a proposal to lift the current ban. To substantiate my first claim, I will start my discussion from Morgan's already quoted essay in this volume, where he, following Butcher and Schneider, casts the idea that doping violates the spirit of sport in terms of fairness, understood as 'respect for the game'[5].

Secondly, I will also argue, contrary to (ii) above, that, if the doping ban is kept, fairness (understood as equality of the relevant competitive conditions in a sport contest) demands more fine-tuned doping regulations and sanctions rather than increased standardization. This criticizes the IOC and WADA's current efforts to enforce general standards to punish doping violations, as their current policy fails to consider the social and sport-ethical particularities of the different communities from which dopers come.

In this essay, I will not discuss argument (i) above, which states doping should be banned because of its harmfulness, for two reasons. First, I have already addressed that objection elsewhere [6]. Secondly, I believe that argument will be isolated from the other two and be left behind in the doping debate relatively soon. It is not a question of whether, but rather of when, performance-enhancing effects similar to those achieved at present by (harmful) doping practices will be attainable using substances that are relatively harmless or at least no more harmful than current elite training techniques. Thus, as the harmfulness argument is dependent on the contingent development of medical science and sport medicine, it is not solid ground for the prohibitionist case to rest upon. I think it is fair to abstain from gaining support for my position by attacking a rather weak factual argument for the opposite side. I will summarize this view below.

Is Doping Contrary to the 'Spirit' of Sports?

According to William Morgan, 'doping itself . . . is an unfair practice', hence 'the USOC and the USADA are morally justified in trying to stop it' [7]. Accordingly, he opposes the legalization of doping based on the argument that

> taking certain substances to boost one's performance in sport is morally objectionable for the same reason that tripping one's opponent in a foot race is: both violate the perfectionist point of sport by using highly efficient, what Suits sometimes calls 'ultimate means', that have nothing essential to do with what the athletic purpose of sport is [8].

It is not easy to grasp why doping would be contrary to 'the athletic purpose of sport'. Morgan gives us a hint of what he seems to have in mind by referring to Michael Sandel's argument that drug enhancement, both in and out of sport, 'represents a kind of hyper agency – a Promethean aspiration to remake nature, including human nature, to serve our purposes and satisfy our desires. The problem is not the drift to mechanism but the drive to mastery' [9]. I must confess I have a hard time trying to make good sense of this kind of demagogic argumentation. As it is stated, the present objection questions the scientific attitude itself, which, no doubt, aims at 'remaking' nature to satisfy human desires. Is 'a Promethean aspiration' not perhaps trying to unveil the causes of natural phenomena, for instance, diseases, in order to find a cure for them, or at least to alleviate suffering? It is true that the objection is cast in terms of *hyper* agency. When we are not provided with a clear delimitation of where to draw the line between reasonable strivings to modify nature and intrusive instrumental interventions in the natural chain of events, this kind of argumentation is only tantamount to empty rhetorical fireworks [10].

Perhaps Morgan could give us a more precise meaning of the 'Promethean aspiration' as exclusively referred to sport? In his view, doping is intimately related to a professional conception of sport in which the search for victory is separated from the play of the game and valued above everything else. He writes, with reference to Robert Simon,

> When one's winning of a foot race or any other sport is owed in some significant measure to how one's body contingently and favourably responds, say, to a steroid, that win is compromised by the fact that how one's body happens to respond to a drug is not a bona fide athletic talent or skill because it has nothing important to do with what an athletic test is supposed to be about [11].

The central core of this argument seems to be that a sporting performance violates the spirit of sport when it (wholly? mostly? to a great extent? even minimally?) is affected by the way the athlete's body reacts to a *drug*.

Several questions can be raised on this stance. One could, for instance, ask why we should accept such anti-drug fundamentalism. The answer cannot possibly be that a drug is an *external* factor modifying the body. Unless athletes were capable of training by meditation, all kind of sports preparation for a competition require letting one's body be affected, directly or indirectly, by external factors, for instance, diet, coaching and even sponsorship.

Perhaps what the argument above tries to express is the fact that banned drugs, unlike diet, are not a necessary (what could be called *natural*) component of our daily life. So, it could be argued that, even if you are an athlete, you need to eat, but you don't need to dope. Eating is a natural thing to do, whereas doping is artificial. We may not deny that eating is a natural need. But the same does not apply to additional dietary products regularly consumed by elite athletes.

Furthermore, within the framework of the present argument, it is not easy to understand why the sports community accepts surgery performed to achieve performance enhancement in sport. Such an intervention goes, no doubt, beyond what might be considered necessary for restoring 'natural' bodily function. Some years ago, Tiger Woods underwent eye surgery, which gave him a competitive advantage over some of his opponents. A few journalists raised the issue of whether this intervention should not be seen as an illegitimate performance-enhancing measure [12]. There was, however, no official reaction from sport establishments or other prominent doping opponents. It is difficult to get rid of the impression that provided you don't mix with drugs everything else is acceptable in the world of sport.

But is it really so that drugs are incompatible with the spirit of sport, in the same way as tripping someone's foot in a foot race is? Tripping an opponent's foot is proscribed by the constitutive rules of foot racing, as it amounts to introducing a factor alien to the skill the sport discipline in question is thought to measure, a factor which would now be deciding the outcome of the contest. If doping were legalized, we would just be introducing some new techniques and substances to the repertoire already used by elite athletes. Or is there perhaps a morally relevant difference between creatine and hypoxic air machines on the one hand, and anabolic substances and Erythopoietin (EPO) on the other?[13].

Rather, what seems to be the case is that sport has evolved into a highly competitive, professional activity in which agents try their best to perform at their highest possible level. Unlike recreational sports – whose main traits (to have a good time and promote health) still marked competitive sport at the beginning of the twentieth century – professional sport is now driven by a desire to expand the boundaries of what hitherto was considered to be humanly possible, even by jeopardizing one's own health. In that sense, professional elite sport does not differ from other professional activities in which individuals are granted the right to freely choose the level of sacrifice and risk-taking they are willing to accept in order to achieve success. Why should professional elite sport be any different?

Banned doping substances and techniques are therefore obviously in accordance with the 'spirit' of today's crudely competitive, highly technified sports world, as they have everything to do with the essential purpose of the athletic contest: to expand the limits of our capacities. In that sense, sport is no more inhuman than any other competitive activity, for instance, philosophy, in which individuals compete with each other at high costs to themselves (both in terms of physical, psychological and social health) as a consequence of their competitive endeavours.

Are Standardized Doping Sanctions Fair?

In this volume, Morgan questions the IOC and WADA's attempt to lower the present standards for assessing legal responsibility for a doping infraction. In his view, replacing the well-established 'beyond reasonable doubt' with 'comfortable satisfaction' with circumstantial evidence 'is morally impeachable, not to mention highly morally offensive'[14].

Morgan's reasons for opposing this development are not jurisprudential ones, at least not directly. Thus, he does not formulate his reluctance to accept the new standards for judging circumstantial evidence in terms of 'jeopardizing legal security' or 'increasing the risk of penalizing the innocent'. Instead, he chooses to criticize the new evidential standards in moral terms, as contrary to the ideal of fairness (and notions derived from fairness, such as fair play and a fair trial).

According to Morgan, the strategy adopted by the USADA and WADA is unfair, mainly on two grounds. First, it implies treating similar cases alike, thus 'making an arbitrary distinction of athletes that puts them at a considerable disadvantage to everyone else'[15]. Secondly, it contributes to a morally foul(er) attitude between competitors, as it introduces a chance to smear one's opponents by carefully crafting allegations of their drug use [16]. For these reasons, Morgan concludes that the USADA and WADA's mostly one-sided technological approach to doping is itself morally suspect because 'the cause of doping and the problem it raises is fundamentally a moral one ... That means, of course, that the solution must be a moral one as well' [17].

Although Morgan seems to propose a general solution to the doping issue, his criticism is not cast in moral objectivistic terms. There is, in his argumentation, a cultural relativistic element, as he attributes the notion of fairness to English and American tradition. Thus, he writes:

> the notion of fair play speaks not just to a moral feature that is widely thought pivotal to the conduct of sport, but widely thought pivotal to the conduct of American life in all its various forms [18].

Morgan further argues:

> By that I mean that the ideal of fairness in its many iterations (for example, fair play, fair dealing, fair outcome, fair trial, etc.) is a way of moral thinking Americans almost instinctively entertain when they reflect on their characteristic social practices and institutions, though one they share with the members of other English-speaking nations [19].

One might be tempted to call into question Morgan's exclusive attribution of the ideal of fairness to American values. Is it really the case that fairness is simply absent from cultural settings other than the Anglo-Saxon? I doubt it. However, I do not intend to take issue with him on that. Rather, I will assume he is right in his description of the incidence of the ideal of fair play in American institutions and sports activities and, starting from that, I will argue that an appropriate interpretation of that ideal requires locally-adapted sanctions for using doping substances and methods, rather than the standardized penalties that WADA and other international sport federations want to submit doping transgressors to at present. Thus, my argument might be put in moral relativistic terms, as stating that sanctions for doping ban violations should be made relative to the particular context in which the transgressor has been raised as a sportsperson and to the particular sport cultural pressures put on him/her by the athlete's society and sporting community. In my view, it is precisely this cultural relativistic ingredient that gives rise to the most powerful criticism to WADA's new anti-doping policy. But before unfolding my arguments against standardized doping sanctions, I will outline the central tenets of ethical relativism.

In short, ethical relativism is the thesis that normative principles or statements are to be judged in light of the values of the group or culture in which they are uttered. For relativists, the fact that different cultures have different moral codes constitutes a key to understanding morality. For them there is no objective truth in ethics. All that exists is the varying customs of different groups or societies and these customs cannot reasonably be said to be right or wrong from an objective point of view. To be able to pass that judgement, we would need to be in possession of an independent standard by which these different stances may be judged. However, relativists affirm, there are no universal moral standards that can be universally applied to all peoples at all times. The only moral standards against which a society's practices can be judged are its own. Every attempt to judge other cultural and moral traditions is culture-bound. An individual's behaviour can then rightly be judged only within the moral framework in which it takes place.

In the realm of elite, professional sports, we find the co-existence of different views regarding doping and its supposed wrongness. There also seems to be radical divergence regarding what to do about athletes who dope.[20] These differences appear both at a national level as well as within sporting communities.

At the national level, at least if we are to accept Morgan's arguments, we have the Anglo-Saxon view, which rests on the supposed unfairness of doping. In Scandinavia, particularly in Sweden, we find perhaps the strongest opposition to softening the doping ban, and many people in Sweden would like to see life-long sanctions enforced even for first doping offences.

In other sports latitudes of the world, however, people who are interested in sport seem to have a more relaxed attitude towards doping. They simply do not appear to be so obsessed with 'winning the fight against doping', one of WADA's slogans. Does it mean that these sport communities lack a sense of fairness, or that they believe that everything goes in competitive sport? Not necessarily. Their normative attitude towards doping might depend on other factors that also deserve to be taken into consideration. Sport audiences in some Third World countries, for example, probably consider that the money invested in sport infrastructure, training techniques and sport medical investigations in developed countries give athletes of the First World an almost insurmountable competitive advantage not obviously related to the sort of physical and character skills a competition is supposed to measure. So, they might reason, why should one get so excited about doping? Furthermore, in other countries (for instance, China and some African nations), striving to win sport competitions might be seen as part of a programme for national affirmation, and a goal that *in their view* might justify using forbidden performance-enhancing substances. On what grounds could we dismiss the argument, which might be cast in communitarian terms, that 'for us, in our society, we don't distinguish in terms of wrongness as sharply as you (Americans, Scandinavians, and so on) do between permitted performance-enhancing substances and what has been labelled as "doping"'? To reject that stance, we would need to resort to ethical objectivistic reasons, that is, to be able to point out a moral standard valid in all cultural and ethical settings across the world. This, however, is obviously not an easy task to undertake. It could be rebutted: 'What does ethical relativism have to do with anti-doping regulations? There is a universally valid normative framework enforced by ruling sports organizations, according to which it is forbidden to dope. So, the fact that in some sports cultures doping is not so harshly criticized, or that it is even tolerated, has no bearing at all on the question of whether, and how, dopers should be sanctioned. They should be sanctioned as it is established in the anti-doping regulations. And that's all that matters.'

I find that argument unconvincing. It simply says that whoever wishes to be a part of a competition is compelled to comply with the regulations enforced by the sports establishment. This is not an ethical argument, but a political one. This kind of argumentation is particularly problematic because of the non-transparent, undemocratic structure of the international sports organizations charged with the task of setting the rules of sport. So, even as a political argument, the statement above lacks legitimacy and is therefore morally void.

But is it really the case that, provided a sports community accepts doping, the rest of the world is not entitled to criticize that stance, no matter how wide-spread the opposition to doping might be? After all, ethical relativism is a highly questioned meta-ethical position.[21] Could we not affirm that universal moral standards still exist, even if moral practices and beliefs vary among cultures? Apartheid in South Africa and the Holocaust in the Third Reich were morally reprehensible, regardless of the moral beliefs of the South African and Nazi societies. Could doping not be seen as another instance of those 'morally reprehensible' practices, regardless of the (sport) ethical beliefs of the particular society in which it might be tolerated?

I doubt it. In the previous section, I have argued that doping in fact is a part of today's elite professional sport. While Apartheid and the Holocaust have been submitted to the irrevocable verdict of history, the direction in which sport is evolving at present suggests the public will increasingly accept doping. There are reasons to suppose current developments in general medicine and genetic technology in particular will facilitate this acceptance. Sport is a field of special interest in the discussion of human enhancement. This notwithstanding, within sport there exists a very strict ideology that repudiates methods of human enhancement widely accepted in other areas of society. For example, while the use of beta-blockers is permitted among musicians, it is forbidden among athletes. What seems to trouble people is the use of drugs by healthy people.[22] However, the new genetic technologies might come to erode this opposition sooner than we can imagine, for instance, with the onset of germ-line genetic engineering. When a person genetically designed to be a winner excels, it is not because he or she used drugs. Furthermore, by winning, the genetically-designed person expresses his or her true genetic nature. This can hardly be called cheating, can it? How could the strict anti-doping ideology that still prevails in sport possibly resist the irruption of the new technologies in society?

But, it could be objected, whatever the impact of technological developments on sport might be, it is a fact that most philosophers reject ethical relativism. For them, ethical relativism fails to recognize that some societies have better reasons for holding their views than others. (Recall, again, the way political institutions work in a democracy and how they worked during the Apartheid or the Third Reich.) Besides, these objectors claim, while the moral practices of societies may differ, the fundamental moral principles underlying these practices do not. We might have different ways of promoting the same central values. If we take the time to look under the surface, we will notice that all societies at all times strived to further certain central goals for human flourishing. Finally, if the rightness or wrongness of an action depends on a society's norms, then it follows that one must blindly obey the norms of one's society, as doing otherwise would, by definition, amount to acting immorally. Thus, for instance, a member of a society in which racist or sexist practices are accepted is compelled to accept those practices and live according to them. This view, however, promotes social conformity and leaves no room for moral reform or improvement in a society.

I will not extend myself in this criticism of ethical relativism. It should be obvious by now that, in spite of its usefulness as a reminder that our beliefs are deeply influenced by culture, ethical relativism is far from being free from objections. How does this fact affect my opposition to the standardization of doping sanctions beyond and across sports cultural diversities?

Not much, I believe. To sustain my case, I don't need to postulate the truth of ethical relativism as a meta-ethical or normative theory. It suffices simply to ascertain its accuracy as a factual description of how things look on the moral map of the world. Our moral beliefs, among them our intuitions regarding sport ethical issues, actually differ. From that it follows that if an individual belongs in a sport cultural milieu in which doping is promoted and/or tolerated, he or she will have a much harder time abiding by doping regulations. There might be several reasons for this.

One reason might be social pressure. The doped athlete could have been raised and educated as a sportsperson in a social and sporting reality in which it is expected that he or she will dope. After all, not all athletes are lucky enough to grow up in an American tradition of fairness! In such a sports cultural setting, not doping might be seen as failing to try one's best to succeed, which is a shortcoming we normally associate with weakness of character.

Athletes might also decide to dope for economic reasons. Particularly in poor countries, the prospect of attaining sports success might be the only option available to overcome poverty. Political pressure can also motivate the decision to dope. In the context of a political reality (think, for instance, of Cuba or China) in which sports victories are demanded from athletes as repayment for the benefits they have been granted by society (in terms of economic resources and social privileges), athletes might simply be in too weak a position to refuse to dope.

What these examples illustrate are situations in which athletes face such extreme pressure that it is justifiable for them to speak of diminished responsibility for the doping offence. The on-going standardization of doping sanctions, however, allows for no gradations in guilt. In WADA's view, a doped athlete from a poor country with a doping tradition, ruled by a totalitarian government that demands athletes sacrifice themselves for the national cause, is equally as guilty as an athlete from a rich Western democracy with no tradition of supporting doping (or, as in Sweden, with a powerful official anti-doping policy), where individual athletes are submitted to no pressure at all when deciding how to prepare themselves for a competition. Is this really fair?

I don't think so. *Fairness suggests that the harder it is for an athlete to comply with current doping regulations, the lesser the athlete's moral guilt (and corresponding liability) for the doping offence.*[23] Accordingly, an athlete should not be sanctioned with the same harshness as other athletes who can comply more easily with the rules.

Let me now sum up my conclusions. Given the fact that athletes are submitted to different kinds of pressures depending on the particular (sport) ethical landscape in which they act, it is only fair that leading sport organizations adopt differentiated, 'culture-sensitive' sanctions for doping offences, to be meted out on a case-by-case basis. Standardizing doping sanctions ends up treating non-similar cases similarly, and results in punishing those who are able to successfully resist the temptation to dope and those who only could have done that at great costs for themselves, equally harshly.

To this it might be objected: 'Although it might be fair(er) to punish people according to how difficult it was for them to abide by current regulations, it is (in another sense) unfair to let some dopers go along with doping, or even sanction them more leniently than other doped athletes. The reason is that, if we did that, then some athletes will get advantages over others, depending on how much doping is tolerated in their national communities.' Or so opponents of culture-sensitive doping sanctions would probably say to try to support their case.

However, whether or not letting some athletes dope (or sanctioning them more leniently) is unfair to their competitors will certainly depend on how disadvantaged the athletes were from the start in relation to their competitors. If, for instance, an athlete of a poorly represented country gets a punishment reduction after a doping offence, then this advantage might be seen as an equalizing factor in sports competitions. Fairness (understood as equality of opportunities in competition) suggests we should enact harsher sanctions upon, for instance, American athletes (as they already are quite advantaged technologically and have great training resources at their disposal), and more lenient sanctions upon athletes who come from disadvantaged Third World countries.

Objectors might argue: 'If we do that, then unpredictability would prevail. No one could possibly know in advance what he or she will be risking as a sanction, if (culturally and individually) differentiated penalties for doping offences were enforced.'

I cannot see a problem here. Unpredictable punishments no doubt deter more than predictable ones do. If I know in advance that if I get caught doping I will be banned from competing for two years (the present standard sanction for first offenders), then I will be able to perform a cost-benefits analysis and decide what I want to do. If I instead confront a situation in which doping sanctions are differentiated, that is, decided on grounds of the cultural setting and the particular situation in which I made the decision to dope, then the eventual sanction is much more difficult to predict, which renders the cost-benefits calculation more inaccurate. Provided doping sanctions can be made to vary according to culturally and individually relative factors, prospective dopers will be in no position to discount the probable costs of their rule violations. I do not support the doping ban. But if I did, I would welcome a penalty policy that deprives doping offenders from the possibility of performing rational calculations about the eventual benefits of doping.

One might argue that maybe you are right in that potential dopers from developed open societies will probably be better deterred by differentiated sanctions. But the other side of that coin is that culture-sensitive sanctions, as the ones you are suggesting, will yield lesser deterrent effect for those athletes who come from disadvantaged countries. Therefore they will probably be more tempted to resort to doping than they are at present, with equally harsh sanctions for all.

My answer to that is a straightforward one: That's exactly the point of differentiated sanctions! As I argued above, fairness in competition will then be increased by the equalizing effect of doping. The iniquitous effect of sponsorship and State support of national sport might at least partly be neutralized by letting non-sponsored athletes from developing countries catch up with their more privileged competitors through the intake of substances presently proscribed. This policy will probably contribute to more exciting competitions by enlarging the circle of participating nations. Would it not be fascinating to experience a Cuban soccer team playing a World Cup final? Or see an Argentinean short-distance runner win the gold medal at the Olympic Games?

Conclusions

In this essay, I argued that, contrary to what is (in my view embarrassingly uncritically) accepted by most sport scientists and philosophers, doping is not only compatible with, but even expresses the true nature of, contemporary elite professional sport, according to the way the practice has evolved over the last few decades. Therefore, I argued, the doping ban should be lifted.

I also argued that current efforts by the IOC, WADA and other international sports bodies to enforce standardized sanctions for doping offences is unfair, in the sense that this implies judging and sanctioning dissimilar cases alike. Instead, if – contrary to my arguments – the ban is kept, then we should introduce differentiated, culture-sensitive sanctions for doping offences. Roughly, this differentiation means that the harder it is to abide by anti-doping regulations the more lenient the sanction. This policy, I argued, is not only fairer in the sense that it implies dissimilar cases are treated according to the relevant dissimilarities, but also in another sense of fairness, namely that disadvantaged athletes might get an opportunity to equalize the initial conditions of competition by doping. Finally, I argued that this fairer situation might even yield some desirable factual results, as it probably would contribute to the introduction of new actors in the sporting scene, thus adding to the excitement of sport competitions.

The conclusions advanced in this essay may appear provocative to some and to others as directly disgusting. However, I believe that social practices, among them sports, have a life of their own and often develop in ways we cannot always judge, at least on first sight, as desirable. However, I believe we, sport philosophers, should engage in trying to neutralize the worst aspects of that development primarily by accepting it as a fact and taking control of it, instead of trying to fight it with arguments related to a supposed sport ideal that seldom, if ever, exists in reality. This latter strategy does more harm than good, as it alienates the profession from the daily experiences of sport practitioners. What elite athlete in the twenty-first century would listen to the arguments of a sports theoretician speaking of amateur sport values from the nineteenth century?

Notes

[1] For more on the list of prohibited substances and corresponding sanctions, see WADA's anti-doping programme at http://www.wada-ama.org/rtecontent/document/list_2005.pdf.

[2] See, for instance, Tamburrini, 'What's Wrong with Doping?', 200–16. For another critical view of doping controls see Miah, *Genetically Modified Athletes*.

[3] Morgan, 'Fair is Fair, Or Is It?'.

[4] Exceptions to this include Tamburrini, 'What's Wrong with Doping?', 200–16 and Brown, 'Paternalism, Drugs and the Nature of Sport', 14–22.

[5] Butcher and Schneider, 'Fair Play as Respect for the Game', 21–48.

[6] Tamburrini, 'What's Wrong with Doping?', 202–4.

[7] See Morgan, 'Fair is Fair, Or Is It?'. USOC and USADA stand for United States Olympic Committee and United States Anti-Doping Agency, respectively.

[8] Ibid.

[9] Ibid., as cited in Sandel, 'The Case Against Perfection', 54.

[10] For a more comprehensive discussion on the arguments for and against modifying our natural predispositions in the world of sports, particularly in relation to gene technology, see Tamburrini and Tännsjö, *Gene Technology and Sport – Ethical Questions*.

[11] Morgan, 'Fair is Fair, Or Is It?', as cited in Simon, 'Good Competition and Drug Enhanced Sport', 126.

[12] According to the Journal Sentinel On Line, 'hundreds of athletes in sport after sport – baseball, golf, auto racing and even kickboxing – are turning to the surgery to boost their performance'. For instance, Atlanta Braves pitcher Greg Maddux had laser surgery to correct his vision in July 1999 as did Tiger Woods in October of the same year. The most popular type of eye surgery is called LASIK – laser-in-situ keratomileusis. See Journal Sentinel On Line. [cited 01 September 2005]. Available from http://www.jsonline.com/alive/ap/apr00/ap-athletes-eye-su040500.asp.

[13] Here it could be argued that anabolic steroids and EPO are still harmful for users, while there seems to be no known risks stemming from using creatine or oxygen tents. However, there is no reason to believe that currently banned doping substances might not be made relatively safe in the near future.

[14] Morgan, 'Fair is Fair, Or Is It?'

[15] Ibid.

[16] Ibid.

[17] Ibid.

[18] Ibid.

[19] Ibid.

[20] See, for instance, a survey conduced in Argentina among students at the Enrique Romero Brest Nr. 1 Institute of Physical Education. When consulted about the proposals to prevent doping, 73 per cent of the interviewed subjects favoured the policy of 'spreading the noxious effects of doping'. The option of 'augmenting sanctions' was selected by 36 per cent of the survey persons, 'increasing laboratory controls' by 29 per cent, and 'granting lesser importance to sporting results' by 23 per cent. (It was obviously possible to choose more than one option in the study.) For more on these results, see D'Angelo, Nápoli and Solís, *Percepción social sobre el doping y los sistemas de prevención en una población de estudiantes de Educación Física* or http://www.deportes.gov.ar/).

[21] For an account of the arguments for and against ethical relativism, see Harman and Thompson, *Moral Relativism and Moral Objectivity,* and The Bank of Sweden Tercentenary Foundation's *Relativism – A Research Project in Philosophy and History of Ideas, 2002–2005,* available at http://www.phil.gu.se/relativism/relativismENG.html.

[22] Ljungqvist, 'The International Anti-doping Policy and its Implementation', 13–18.

[23] For a more thorough account of this position, see Eriksson, *Heavy Duty – On the Demands of Consequentialism.*

References

Brown, W. M. "Paternalism, Drugs and the Nature of Sport". *Journal of the Philosophy of Sport* XI, (1984): 14–22.

Butcher, Robert and Angela Schneider. "Fair Play as Respect for the Game". In *Ethics in Sport,* edited by William Morgan, Klaus Meier, and Angela Schneider. Champaign, IL: Human Kinetics, 2001.

D'Angelo, Carlos, Mónica Nápoli, and Diana Solís. *Percepción social sobre el doping y los sistemas de prevención en una población de estudiantes de Educación Física.* (Social perceptions of doping and preventative systems in a population of Physical Education students) Argentina: Área de Prevención y Control Antidoping, Comisión Nacional Antidoping de la Secretaria de Deporte y Recreación de la Nación 2004.

Eriksson, Björn. *Heavy Duty – On the Demands of Consequentialism.* Stockholm: Almqvist och Wiksell International, 1994.

Harman, G. and J. J. Thompson eds. "Moral Relativism and Moral Objectivity". Cambridge, MA: Blackwell Publishers, 1996.

Ljungqvist, Arne. "The International Anti-doping Policy and its Implementation". In *Gene Technology and Sport – Ethical Questions,* edited by Claudio Tamburrini and Torbjörn Tännsjö. London and New York: Routledge, 2006.

Miah, Andy. *Genetically Modified Athletes – Biomedical Ethics, Gene Doping and Sport.* London and New York: Routledge, 2004.

Morgan, W. "Fair is Fair, Or is it?: A Moral Consideration of the Doping Wars in American Sport". *Sport in Society* 9, no. 2 (April 2006): 177–198.

Sandel, Michael. "The Case Against Perfection". *The Atlantic Monthly* 293, (April 2004): 54.

Simon, Robert. "Good Competition and Drug Enhanced Sport". In *Ethics in Sport,* edited by William Morgan, Klaus Meier, and Angela Schneider. Champaign, IL: Human Kinetics, 2001.

Tamburrini, Claudio. "What's Wrong with Doping?". In *Values in Sport – Elitism, Nationalism, Gender Equality and the Scientific Manufacture of Winners,* edited by Claudio Tamburrini and Torbjör Tännsjö. London and New York: E & FN Spon, 2000.

Tamburrini, Claudio and Tännsjö, Torbjörn, eds. *Gene Technology and Sport – Ethical Questions.* London and New York: Routledge, 2006.

Tännsjö, Torbjörn and Claudio, Tamburrini, eds. *Values in Sport – Elitism, Nationalism, Gender Equality and the Scientific Manufacture of Winners.* London and New York: E & FN Spon, 2000.

The Bank of Sweden Tercentenary Foundation. *Relativism – A Research Project in Philosophy and History of Ideas, 2002–2005.* Stockholm-Göteborg: Göteborg University and Stockholm University, 2005. Available from http://www.phil.gu.se/relativism/relativismENG.html.

Cultural Nuances: Doping, Cycling and the Tour de France

Angela J. Schneider

The Nature and Values of the Tour de France

On the nature and values of the Tour de France, only

> 'death' is the proof that one has fought to one's maximum – fascination of going beyond one's capacity, to test one's strength. In road cycling there are no limits to human effort: it represents the ultimate motivation to achieve. The road cyclist is the only true hero in the sports world – pure will power.[1]

The Tour de France is the ultimate endurance race. Riders cover well over 3,000 km in 20 stages. Each day riders are on their bikes for four or five hours at an average of 42 kph. The physical demands are enormous, and, what makes stage racing different from other endurance sports is that those daily demands are sustained over a period of three weeks. Many have expressed concern that the doping stigmatization and problems that cycling has is directly related to the fact that this kind of racing may well be the hardest sport competition that exists today. '10–25% don't finish the race, roundabouts are hard for riders and the people lining the road are hard.'[2] Generally speaking, a daily effort like this would require approximately 48 hours to recover but the maximum time that these riders can get is 16 hours. Although there are well-known, non-medically invasive, steps (for example, carbohydrates, protein and fluids) that can be taken, many believe that to make up for the missing 32 hours of recovery time, medical treatment is required.[3]

In research intended to identify the core values of road cycling the following values emerged as the key ones: endurance, perseverance, will power, competitiveness, survival instinct, loneliness, frustration capacity, overcoming struggles, sharing capacity and humility.[4] Some of those key values get further unpacked and explained as follows below. *Endurance* is defined as human effort beyond its limits – the human capacity of suffering without giving up. *Perseverance* is defined as the mental capacity to fight for an aim. The aim justifies the effort. *Survival instinct* is defined as a psychological battle without any compromise – only strength, effort and will power allow survival. *Overcoming struggles* is having the capacity to overcome all struggles, which may occur in connection with endurance.[5] On a symbolic and a psychological level, only 'death' is the proof that one has fought to one's maximum – the fascination of going beyond one's capacity, to test one's strength. In road cycling there are no limits to human effort: it represents the ultimate motivation to achieve. They believe that the road cyclist is the only true hero in the sports world – pure will power.[6]

Those values are, indeed, the key to understanding the Tour de France, its appeal and its connection to doping. Given the types of values that are honoured in long distance road cycling, it is of little surprise that a culture of doping has emerged. The history of the Tour makes it clear, for example, that public opinion about doping does not always conform to the prohibitionist line that is publicly embraced by many officials, and this in itself is a matter of real social significance. This tacit acceptance of certain kinds of doping by ordinary people would certainly help to account for the problem.

However, many see cycling as a transparent sport, where the effort and the will to win are made manifest. There is no room to hide during the event, and, generally, little room to cheat. Doping threatens that perception because it allows cheating to be hidden and to take place off the road and out of sight. Doping presents a real challenge to the otherwise transparent nature of the sport of cycling. Thus, when the Tour de France came under attack during the 1998 doping scandal, its organizers, team managers and athletes reacted to the political and media assault as a sport bent on defending its autonomy, its values and, not least, its survival.

The result of this scandal led to accusations that the sub-culture of professional cycling allowed semi-concealed consumption of banned performance-enhancing substances. The other values and shared experiences listed above make solidarity possible. There is an important question as to the nature of the solidarity among professional athletes. The 1998 drug scandal of the Tour de France and the following cycle of suspicion have clearly damaged the community. It was a community that seemed to have inspired loyalty and self-sacrifice, and then it became viewed by many as essentially an aggregation of individual entrepreneurs who have merely consented to maintain a mutually advantageous arrangement.[7]

Some former professional cyclists have tried to explain that they think doping is inherent in the psychology required for the sport and is seen by certain riders as a permissible strategy consistent with the practice of bluffing the opponent.[8] The history of the nature of the problem of doping in cycling is constructed in large part from the extensive media coverage of it.[9]

Castigating comments quoted from cyclists in the media may not have scandalized professional cyclists because there is a sub-culture that understands the allure of doping. These comments help to explain how doping, for some, assists in sustaining the spectacle the sponsors and public demand. The right to work (that is, worker-athletes) dominates the perspective in these comments, where doping keeps jobs. This, of course, makes sense when one acknowledges that the Tour de France was created for purely commercial reasons. What the creators of the Tour did not seem to realize was that they also created an event that generates much nationalism. Later in this paper, the issue of French nationalism is addressed for creating, at the very least, a perceived, if not real, bias against non-French riders.

Although some of the interviews quoted in this paper took place prior to 1998, those interviewed in 2002 came to similar conclusions about the pressures to dope.

> Losing is very difficult; there is much pressure to win. Everyone is always looking for reasons why the other one won. They are always suspicious of the one who wins. They are constantly looking for something to explain success – others are using it, so I need it. It becomes a self-fulfilling prophecy.[10]

Drugs of Choice

It seems that there was a shift away from stimulants as the drug of choice, towards erythropoietin (EPO), at least leading up to 1998. The dissonance of accusation, indignation and disappointment that followed the 1998 scandal struck at the heart of the idea that the cycling world constituted a coherent community built on shared ideals. The cycling community has been criticized that it is not a community based on cooperation, the shared acceptance of principles, and an ethos of restraint on behalf of shared goals. Rather, it has been claimed that it is essentially an arrangement that allows its members to pursue individual goals in a self-interested way and may well be compatible with community coherence in a functional sense, for example, the Tour de France as a profitable enterprise.[11]

The doping scandals of recent years have threatened a sense of honour that some riders, officials and physicians take very seriously, so seriously they have left the sport.[12] The majority of those interviewed at the 2002 Tour de France claimed that attitudes have changed in cycling over the past few years and that progress has been good in regard to doping.[13]

Code of Ethics

The sense of honour demonstrated by some does make it possible to see that the cycling community may be viewed as more than just an alliance of self-interested entrepreneurs. Some officials have tried invoking, and even imposing, this sense of honour. This has also been one of the few responses available to the cycling community when doping scandals cast the sport into disrepute. For example, before the 2001 Tour de France, the general director convened the riders at a mandatory meeting in Dunkirk and required them to sign a ten-point 'Code of Ethics' pertaining to doping.[14] However, this sort of disciplinary measure was criticized as amounting to nothing more than a public relations gesture.

If accusations about drugs were not enough to damage the community, at least one book came out, in June 2001, in which the author accused a rider of having sold a stage victory to another rider during the 1997 Tour. The author also alleged that another star had taken money to let other riders win races.[15] Critics argue that these accusations provoked responses that called attention to a code of conduct the cycling community was willing to defend in an open and coherent manner.

It is further claimed that one of the accused issued a categorical denial that also invoked the idea of an ethical code.[16] Another Team's press chief also claimed that the riders' conduct was governed by ethical standards.[17] It was further argued by another former rider that honouring such gentleman's agreements created a genuine community spirit:[18] these testimonies appear to support the existence of an ethical code.[19] They also explain in part why cycling has been accused of being a closed nature community that observes its own rules and why the sport has the reputation as a haven for drugs. (This point will be discussed further in another section that follows below.)

Similarly, some academics have argued, 'the moral rules that apply within the cycling world differ sharply from those that apply outside it. We are talking here about two cultures with radically different value systems.'[20] When the 1998 doping scandal hit cycling, the culture that the civil authorities represent, stepped in and over the sport authorities representing the culture of cycling. One of the ethical questions here is whether the special status of the sport world entitles its members to an exemption from the values and culture of outsiders, or even the countries in which the sport events take place. If the answer is 'no', then which set of values do we use for our ethical baseline as it were? Further, if this answer applies to the particular example of doping in cycling, it should also have universal application to all sports.

The Spectacle of the Tour de France

On the success of the Tour de France: 'The riders in the Tour de France go where people live, they go to them, down their street – what other sport does that?'[21] The Tour is an immense spectacle, a cultural celebration that winds its way right through France. Organizers estimate that now upwards of 18,000,000 spectators, of all ages, view the Tour from the side of the road, having picnics and camping out. Long distance stage races are unique in that they take the very best performers in the sport right to the doorsteps of the spectators. The corporate sponsors' caravan precedes the racers along the route. The caravan consists of decorated vehicles that distribute promotional items to the spectators that line almost every metre of the route. Spectators arrive early along the route to jostle for a position hours before the caravan or riders appear. In some of the mountain stages, spectators camp out for days beforehand to claim the best spots.

Success in the Face of Scandal

The Tour de France spectacle is extremely successful. Thus, it is not surprising, and important to understand, the defiant attitude of supporters. Take for example the resistant position taken by the director of the Tour during the Tour doping scandal of 1998, as he replied to the view that the race should be called off.[22] This position expresses a strong relationship with a largely supportive public audience, as a sport scholar pointed out after the Tour scandal:

> The opponents of doping simply could not grasp that the revelations and the scandalizing media coverage during the summer of 1998 did not cause the cycling public to turn its back on the event. Given that the whole thing was presented as cheating and fraud, the Tour route should have been wholly depopulated when the riders passed by. But it was not. On the contrary, the public was eager to demonstrate its sympathy and offer its support to the embattled field. It was obvious that these people did not feel cheated.[23]

This point will also be reviewed in more detail in this paper in a later section that follows below.

Outsiders and critics questioned the public support and officials.[24] Media reports of representatives for the accused team made things much worse.[25] However, the success of the Tour throughout all of this has been clear. Each day the Tour receives blanket media coverage. The heavyweight national dailies routinely run two or three pages of coverage, while the sports newspapers run five or six. There is full day coverage on the television with an estimated cumulative viewing audience of one billion people. Some critics believe that the professional cycling community – as the extraordinary social phenomenon it was throughout much of the twentieth century – is a celebrated subculture whose doping seemed to have been quietly tolerated, as political authorities and the general public chose not to address doping within this milieu.[26] Further, this resistance to public disapproval and prosecution occurred within a modern civilization whose drug use norms can seem both arbitrary and hypocritical, and the tolerated doping sub-culture of the Tour should be seen in this context.

There are important reasons why this is so. Despite the existence of anti-doping laws dating from 1965, French society did not prosecute cyclists who were French heroes, the 'giants of the road'. It appears to the critics that the authorities that might have prosecuted those doping had concluded that the social benefits of doping among cyclists, and their success in the Tour, outweighed the costs to society-at-large.[27]

Along a similar vein, it is interesting to note that in the 2002 Tour at least two people died as a result of the Tour (these kinds of deaths are not unusual). One was a 7-year-old girl who was struck by one of the vehicles in the caravan as she stepped out to reach one of the trinkets thrown in the road; the other was her grandmother who watched in horror. Despite the massive amounts of media coverage enjoyed by the Tour, this incident rated only a couple of column inches, and only a very few columns of editorial comment. Apparently, these deaths were not considered important news items during the coverage of the Tour.

The Culture of the Tour

The Tour is a French party and celebration. Each stage begins and ends in a different town, which will, effectively, be closed to traffic for the day. Everything stops for the Tour. The Tour is a nationalistic and a local celebration. French riders, and their victories are universally celebrated, and local riders are feted and honoured. It is almost impossible to imagine how popular Lance Armstrong would have been had he been French. One of the most popular places along the route is that of the feed zone, prepared by the teams and race organizers. Riders are careful now not to take drinks from others, and will only accept them from their team. In the mountains, they may take water from the spectators to put on their heads or backs, but they do not risk drinking it because of the culture of suspicion and distrust.

Riders are workers, but cycling is not merely a labour culture. Authors seem to favour more romantic interpretations of these 'giants of the road'. A well-known celebration of the Tour is Roland Barthes' 1957 essay 'The Tour de France as Epic'.[28] It emphasizes 'the great risk of the ordeal', the 'magnificent euphoria' it makes possible, and the mythical essences that animate its colourful cast of characters.[29] The myth of the Tour, the tension between its 'vestiges of a very old ethic, feudal or tragic' and 'the world of total competition', obscures its commercial core.

> It is in this ambiguity that the essential signification of the Tour consists: the masterly amalgam of the two alibis, idealist and realist, permits the legend to mask perfectly, with a veil at once honorable and exciting, the economic determinisms of our great epic... What is vitiated in the Tour is the basis, the economic motives, the ultimate profit of the ordeal, generator of ideological alibis.[30]

Identifying riders as workers would negatively affect their status as heroes of an epic ordeal. More challenging is Barthes' treatment of doping – 'to dope the racer is as criminal, as sacrilegious as trying to imitate God; it is stealing from God the privilege of the spark'.[31] Without this kind of Barthean perspective, many outsiders and critics could not understand the public support of the Tour.

The Structure of Professional Cycling

There is evidence that the riders love the sport and look out for each other. For example, when there is a serious accident, the pack slow down to allow help to access the injured athlete and, if possible, to let the injured rider catch up. Since the doping scandals however, riders are concerned with the guilt by association with regard to doping and cycling. The pressure for some athletes is much greater because they are less educated. Some quit school at 15 years old, become professionals, and are not paid well. Some make $15,000 US a year; they have families to feed and have to make hard choices to make ends meet. Members of cycling teams endure a very long season, most of which is spent away from home. The professional cycling season can last as along as ten months of the year and it is not uncommon for athletes to be separated from their families for weeks at a time. This means that the team culture is very tight and closed to the outside. In this environment, compounded by the fact that the athletes, even on the same team, have to compete with each other, there is also a culture of secrecy around the 'tricks' each athlete might use to help him prepare. In athletes' search for the key to better performance there is also a great deal of reliance on masseurs and personal trainers who are often seen as having the key to success. Some physicians are also confided in and others are not. In addition, the traditions are based on fairly rigid hierarchies and involve fairly strict discipline. When this is combined with an awareness of the connection between doping and cycling in the public imagination, the result is a system that is closed. This fact presents a great challenge for any intervention initiated from the outside. Professional cycling is a closed society for a variety of reasons that are not always associated with the use of doping. Cycling is a very hard way of life, both physically and mentally, and its hardships certainly create bonds of sympathy and respect between some riders that can exist independently of the doping practices that may also bind some of them together.

Critics of cycling argue that its community has an endemic disdain for doping rules and holds a special status as a quasi-tolerated doping subculture. The sport of cycling battles a great problem with suspicions of doping in this context. The pressure to dope comes from coaches and managers who used to dope when they rode. But for the riders who choose to stay clean, it is impossible to escape judgment. It is impossible to prove a negative (doping test) every day. This vicious cycle goes on. The positive tests are used to confirm the suspicions, the media emphasize the negative stories, and this is used as evidence that everyone is doping. Athletes don't find the list credible, they don't trust the testing system, and submitting to the tests violates their privacy. Some riders were quoted as claiming, it is not even voluntary: 'No one starts out wanting to dope … but you become a victim of the sport'.[32]

It is concluded that the problem with this sort of solidarity is that it is the product of a siege mentality, and that telling the truth is incompatible with maintaining good team spirit because the riders are required to subordinate their personal self-interest to the law of silence rather than to an ideal in which the riders can take pride.[33] There is some evidence that the solidarity of the professional cyclists resembles a labour union.

However, it was not until the spring of 1999 that the riders formed an association and elected a president, after the 1998 scandal. This fact would seem to indicate that the group did not feel they required a union before this time and perhaps did not view themselves as 'workers'. In this light it is possible to see the athlete-worker as vulnerable or exploited. Anti-doping campaigns designed to address a social plague that threatens the public health, fail to distinguish between elite athletes and a general public that does not need doping to make a living. This is another important point to note when planning any interventions to deal with the problem. This tension has put cycling officials in a difficult position. There can be a conflict between employment-related doping and official demands for doping-free sport. There is great pressure to adopt strict anti-doping penalties that would mean long periods of unemployment for riders who are caught doping. There has been scepticism and claims that UCI doping control has shown itself to be ineffective. On the other hand, the UCI views itself as doing its job and is concerned with the health of professional riders and has clearly articulated the economic interests and feelings of the athletes.

Riders as Heroes

Professional cyclists tend to be reluctant heroes who are not inclined to dramatize their athletic ordeals even though they willingly risk life and limb. Perspectives on the physical ordeal that generates the drama for the Tour de France can be seen to be based on this division of labour.

> The sporting public knows the riders' sufferings in all of their forms. They follow the ritual year after year and have found meaning in the sheer energy that is expended, and have learned to appreciate great sacrifices.[34]

Some careful and thoughtful researchers defend the autonomy of the professional cycling subculture and its right to practice self-medication (that is, doping) without interference from outsiders.[35] This perspective is viewed as an essential antidote to the standard anti-doping doctrine that generally ignores the sociological and economic dimensions of the doping phenomenon. It is argued that the right to practice doping is an inherent part of elite sport: 'In our culture . . . doping has become taboo. By violating this taboo – within certain limits – the athletes open a door onto the "sacred".'[36] The argument is that only the members of this subculture are qualified to judge the riders' internal code of behaviour. Professional cyclists are part of a community willing to engage in physically dangerous behaviour that serves the larger society as a cherished spectacle. The fact that both athletes and their public are drawn to, and fascinated by, the extreme and risky, leads the sport of cycling into a dilemma.

This position leads to the rejection of the claim that the riders are oppressed workers. In large part, this kind of analysis rejects the harm or health argument against doping as being a contradiction in terms, since it is argued that elite sport is, by its very nature, unhealthy. On this account, the paternalistic health concerns regarding doping are viewed as being misplaced and even absurd:

> We still do not understand ... why the athletes are willing to take on the role of the
> victim, even when this involves taking drugs that may damage their health and are,
> in the most literal sense, life-threatening.[37]

The inconsistency of voluntary, celebrated risk-taking by elite athletes (for example, hurtling down mountainsides at 100 kph) and doping control regulation to protect their health seems absurd. It is difficult to argue the medical case defending professional cycling to the public. The larger health conundrum still persists, causes logical inconsistency for the war against doping, and is postulated to explain why the medical care and doping of riders degenerated into a tacit conspiracy rather than becoming a health-maintenance operation that could bear the scrutiny of outsiders.[38]

Doping and Cycling in the Public Imagination

Doping and cycling are intimately linked in the public imagination. Obviously, the media has played some role in this linkage. Some claim that it is primarily the Tour de France media coverage to blame for this linkage and that other professional sports like soccer do not have this kind of pressure from the media coverage they receive. Occasionally spectators will dress-up in costume to celebrate the Tour. On a few occasions spectators were seen dressed as syringes at the 2002 Tour de France, as figures 1 and 2 demonstrate.

Since the 1998 scandal, there has been little, if any, evidence of a decline in public support. It is concluded by some critics that an essential element of the Tour riders' claim to their exclusive subculture is the populism that sustains it as a popular cult and commercial enterprise.[39]

Figure 1

Figure 2

The connection between doping and cycling has reached the masses outside of sport and the country of France as well. In Switzerland, the equivalent of the national milk marketing board (a group about as mainstream as one could find) recently ran a print ad which featured a cyclist milking a cow with the heading: ' *Le lait, doping naturel*' (figure 3).

Figure 3

Thus, doping in cycling is far from being viewed with universal disapprobation: the concept is used by marketers to sell milk. Not only riders, but also spectators, revere the fundamental values of cycling. The endurance, competitiveness, will power and perseverance that allow riders to push to the very limits of human performance are characteristics that can easily incorporate doping in their drive to perform. And spectators understand and value these characteristics.

The link between long-distance cycling and the effects of doping is also very direct. While all sports practiced at the elite level push participants' bodies to the limits, in some sports pushing to the limit is the entire point of the endeavour. In this way, cycling is like weight lifting. In weight lifting the point of the sport is to push the body to the limits of its strength. The effects of doping on strength are direct and obvious. This is similar for long-distance cycling. The point of long distance cycling is to push the body to the limits of its endurance. The appeal of doping for cyclists is thus apparent.

There is, therefore, ambivalence in athletes' and spectators' responses to doping. On the one hand doping is seen as something that tarnishes the sport and provides a negative image for cycling. On the other hand, long distance stage racing is all about pushing the human body to its limits – and beyond. The athletes who do this are heroes. Doping can thus be condoned by spectators and accepted by athletes as the price that those who wish to be great are prepared to pay.

The example of the extremely popular French rider Richard Virenque is used to demonstrate this point because after more than two years of denying his drug use following the 1998 scandal, he finally confessed at his trial in October 2000. It is claimed that Virenque's testimony emphasizes both the exclusivity that characterizes the brotherhood of riders and the rhetorical devices that are employed to preserve its privacy.[40] Other riders have given less favourable interpretations of the cycling community's kind of solidarity and its relationship with doping.[41] The result is community fragmentation and a climate of suspicion.

The Physiological Severity of the Tour de France

The deeper issue, which many have claimed is in fact the cause of doping, is the physiological severity of the Tour and other long-distance competitions. It is noted that it is possible to see the difference between the fraternity of riders and the traditional labour union because,

> the slow-downs and strikes mounted by cyclists over the past half-century have been directed, not against their extreme suffering and diminished life-spans, but against the regulation of the drugs they use to cope with stress. In fact, the idea of moderating or 'humanizing' these competitions has attracted little interest among riders and their physicians. [42]

There are some calls now for the reduction of the physiological severity of the Tour, but they do not seem to be coming from the current riders, promoters, organizers or officials. At least one female rider suggests 'competitions that are on a truly human scale'.[43] It is interesting to note that many team doctors see their athletes as patients requiring medical care but do not seem to be calling for change; some authors have pointed to the striking passivity of high-performance sports physicians for whom the problem of 'inhuman' stress during training and competition never seems to be the issue.[44]

The physicians' organizations worldwide have taken a stance against the sport of boxing because of its health risks, but there is no such stance taken for cycling at the Tour de France. Rather, there seems to be acceptance of a model of 'reduction of harm' to defend medical intervention rather that reduction of harm by reducing the physical stress requirements of the Tour.

Some critics claim that this reduction of harm argument remains the least publicized proposition in modern sports medicine precisely because it is applied at the point where intolerable stress appears to call for banned substances that can provide relief. They argue that the Tour subculture created its doping predicament many years ago by accepting intolerable stress as the price of staying in business with a consequence of a doping culture it could not defend on principle.[45]

Tour de France fans seem to defend doping as an accommodation to the stress of the sport, but rarely is this done publicly because the riders' visible suffering appears to be an essential part of the Tour spectacle. A doping culture that sustains performance while destroying the body and which operates through peer pressure and secrecy is inherently unsustainable. Can the current physiological demands of the Tour de France, the demands that give rise to the doping culture, be defended? Can the 'special medical requirements', be defended, on principle, against outside criticism? The logical inconsistency regarding health leads many to question whether professional cycling essentially abandons true medical or health interests by virtue of what it does – leaving riders to fend for themselves. For change to really occur the organizers and riders must come to really believe that if doping is the answer – we are asking the wrong question.

Notes

[1] Union Cycliste Internationale, *The Essence of Road Cycling*, 3–5.
[2] Personal communication with a cycling official interviewed at the 2002 Tour de France.
[3] The well-known, non-medically invasive, steps are as follows. Careful monitoring and control of the carbohydrate requirements is one step. Understanding the role of carbohydrates (CHO) in the human energy cycle, the use of nutritional supplements such as energy bars (e.g., Power Bar) and recovery drinks (e.g., Gatorade), that are used as means to refuel CHOs, is especially important for cyclists, who can burn over 7,000 calories in one day of competition. CHO nutritional goals for cyclists include fuel intake before an event (avoiding gastrointestinal distress), consuming CHOs during events lasting more than one hour, and promoting the replenishment of fuels after events. Heavy training and racing can deplete body CHO stores, therefore, it is essential that one consumes energy and CHOs in order to match usage. Many cyclists practice CHO intake so the body becomes accustomed to consuming CHOs at certain times of exercise and competition. There is no set pattern available since each individual reacts differently to energy exertion and energy replenishment. This means that individualized pre-event, event and post-event nutrition regimens must be developed through practice. CHO guidelines suggest that 1 to 4 g/kg of CHO should be eaten one to four hours before a race or

training session, 0.5 to 1 g/kg of CHO per hour during a race, 1 g/kg of CHO per hour for the first two hours post-exercise. For max rate of glycogen replenishment, 1.2 g/kg per hour is needed. Due to the extreme changes the body experiences during such a long competition, some athletes enter competition slightly over weight to compensate for the weight loss during the competition. Since protein plays such a small role towards energy production, cyclists do not have an increased need for protein. As the general public, cyclists should follow standard food guides to receive the dietary protein requirements. However, instead of consuming the lower recommended portions for a particular category in the standard food guides, cyclist should gear toward the upper end of consumption (e.g., 5 to 12 portions of grain products, eat 12 servings instead of 5). It is recommended that they consume 0.86 g/kg of protein per day, and if a good diet is followed, protein supplements are not needed. Fluids in the human body are lost through radiation, convection, evaporation and waste excretion. When exercise is added, 500 to 3,000 ml/hour can be lost compared to the average of 2,200 ml/day. Lack of fluids can affect reduction in blood volume, decreased blood flow, decreased sweat rate, decreased heat dissipation, increased core temperature and create premature fatigue. Therefore, it is key that fluids be replaced constantly to match output because becoming thirsty means that you are already dehydrated. The ideal drink should be palatable, not cause gastrointestinal distress, contain some CHO, contain sodium, be isotonic, be cool, and not be acidic or gassy. People should drink 150 per cent of fluid loss to retain fluid balance. Some believe that education regarding caffeine and creatine should be addressed in cycling. They argue that caffeine can be a performance enhancer with its affects peaking 30 to 90 minutes after consumption. Research suggests that more than 9 mg/kg may actually hinder performance. They further argue that caffeine does increase alertness, decreases sleepiness, may reduce the perception of fatigue and pain, increases power output of muscle for a given nerve input at low frequencies, decreases potassium, and may spare muscle glycogen at the onset of exercise. The effects of decreasing potassium can be advantageous because in exercise, potassium increases, which can block nerve impulses. Therefore, the reduction in potassium can enhance muscle contraction. Furthermore, some researchers claim that contrary to popular belief caffeine does not affect urine output. Practical tips for cyclists include: if you normally drink coffee do not stop before a race because you can experience withdrawal effects; consumption before exercise may cause diarrhoea and it may cause anxiety. Caffeine exits the system within three to five hours and high doses appear to have a negative effect. It is argued by some researchers that since caffeine is being taken off the banned list (they believe because of the inconsistent testing results between athletes due to absorption and excretion rates), athletes can consume caffeine as an ergogenic aid. It is also argued that creatine, which is well known in power sports, can increase muscle mass when combined with weight training. However, these researchers maintain that while creatine is advertised for promoting use in endurance sports, which includes cycling, creatine will not improve endurance performance. They believe that the major focus for doping in cycling should be around use of erythropoietin (EPO).

[4] UCI, *The Essence of Road Cycling*, 24.
[5] Ibid., 23.
[6] Ibid., 24.
[7] Hoberman "Pharmacy on Wheels", unpublished manuscript, 2002.
[8] 'I am convinced ... that the vice [of doping] is inherent in the practice of elite cycling. Why? Because much of a rider's behavior involves bluffing his opponent, getting him into difficulty, exposing him to the wind ... in a word, fooling him! By a kind of natural extension, certain riders are inclined to see doping as a permissible strategy.' Quénet, *Le procès du dopage*, 142.
[9] For example, interviews like a 1969 interview of a five-time Tour de France champion (who is viewed by many as one of the greatest of the modern professional cyclists) are used to explain it. The athlete reports: 'I dope myself. Everyone [who is a competitive cyclist] dopes himself.

Obviously, we can do without them in a race, but then we will pedal 15 miles an hour [instead of 25]. Since we are constantly asked to go faster and to make ever greater efforts, we are obliged to take stimulants.' Gilbert, 'Something on the Ball', 32. Similarly, in 1977 a rider claimed, 'People talk so much about doping ... But if you don't take anything these days, then you're not going to get anywhere', 'Intern Dynamit', *Der Spiegel* 27 (30 June 1980): 183.

[10] Personal communication with a participant at the Tour de France, 2002.

[11] Hoberman "Pharmacy on Wheels", unpublished manuscript, 2002.

[12] 'We were accused that all dope – tarred with the same brush after scandal from 1998. I quit because of that and the risk of harm of getting hit by a truck on the road. The clubs were strongly affected by the scandal too – all accused of doping.' Personal communication with a former rider who quit and was watching the 2002 Tour de France.

[13] 'In 1997 I stopped cycling because of pressure to dope. There is less of a problem now in cycling. The problem is the former dopers that are coaching and managers, old riders who did use doping.' Personal communication with a former rider at the 2002 Tour de France.

[14] 'Bei meiner Ehre' (By My Honour), *Süddeutsche Zeitung* (9 July 2001).

[15] 'Es gibt zwei Zeugen' (There are Two Traits), *Süddeutsche Zeitung* (22 June 2001) and 'En sport fyldt med rullende avtaler', *Politiken* (21 June 2001).

[16] 'Es gibt zwei Zeugen', *Süddeutsche Zeitung* (22 June 2001).

[17] 'It is a tradition in cycling that the rider wearing the yellow jersey gives the day's victory to those who have been riding with him. It's a gentleman's agreement, as when Pantani gave Ullrich the victory on the Col de la Madelaine in 1998, and when Armstrong gave Pantani the victory on Mont Ventoux. But there is no way that money changed hands. Selling victories is not an established practice in cycling.' 'Vorwurf der Bestechlichkeit gegen Ullrich' (The accusation has been confirmed against Ullrich), *Süddeutsche Zeitung* (21 June 2001).

[18] 'What happens is that the rider wearing the leader's jersey gives the stage victory to one of the rivals who have been sharing the work, and this is one of the unwritten rules of the sport. The race leader is in a good position and can allow himself to give something to others. And he does it, because he knows it creates a kind of sympathy.' 'Ære til den ene, penge til den anden', *Politiken* (21 June 2001).

[19] 'There are those who think that cycling is a corrupt sport ... We do not feel this way. We think it is a wonderful and fascinating sport that contains a very high degree of justice that has been built into it ... its unwritten rules and moral concepts can be difficult to understand for anyone who has not grown up in it or lived one's way into its world. Because there is, of course, a morality and an ethics in cycling, and there are limits one does not cross.' 'Du kan ikke købe dig til noget, du ikke er', *Politiken* (25 June 2001).

[20] Møller, *Dopingdjævlen*, 92.

[21] Personal communication with a spectator at the 2002 Tour de France.

[22] 'Ten days from now in the Pyrenees, there will be as many spectators as ever. The admirable and performances will prevail over everything else.' 'Ein Sprengsatz bedroht die ganze Tour', *Süddeutsche Zeitung* (13 July 1998). 'We want the Tour, the riders want the Tour, and the spectators to whom we are obligated want it to go on. Even if the intellectuals in Paris may not understand.' '"Ich fühle mich wie ein Idiot"' ("I felt like an idiot"), *Süddeutsche Zeitung* (3 Aug. 1998).

[23] Møller, *Dopingdjævlen*, 137–8.

[24] The general director of the Société du Tour de France offered a solemn statement of principle: 'It is a question of credibility and ethics', he said only days after the scandal broke. Most noteworthy was the statement that, 'The Tour must remain clean'. 'Ein Sprengsatz bedroht die ganze Tour', *Süddeutsche Zeitung* (13 July 1998).

[25] For example, it is claimed that one manager of the accused team claimed, 'Our success has nothing to do with doping'. '"Ich fühle mich wie ein Idiot"', *Süddeutsche Zeitung* (3 Aug. 1998). Additionally, the team's head physician said, 'I'm there to take care of the athletes and their health ... I am against doping. Let justice take its course.' Ibid.

[26] Hoberman, "Pharmacy on Wheels", unpublished manuscript, 2002.

[27] Ibid.

[28] Barthes, 'The Tour de France as Epic', 79–80, 87.

[29] Ibid.

[30] Ibid., 86–8.

[31] Ibid., 83.

[32] David Walsh, 'Saddled with Suspicion', *Sunday Times* [London] (8 July 2001).

[33] Hoberman, "Pharmacy on Wheels", unpublished manuscript, 2002.

[34] Møller, *Dopingdjævlen*, 111.

[35] Ibid.

[36] Ibid., 113.

[37] Ibid., 111.

[38] Hoberman, "Pharmacy on Wheels", unpublished manuscript, 2002.

[39] Ibid.

[40] 'You can't understand, you're not part of the scene; in cycling, you don't say "doping".' Quénet, *Le procès du dopage*, 30.

[41] 'There are a lot of stupid guys in cycling . . . You really have to question whether they have any ethics at all. Before 1998 Tour you could understand why people were taking drugs, but since then we've crossed the line. We've got to the point where we can say "OK, let's stop it". It's become a moral issue. Before it could be called professionalism, now it's just plain cheating and that's what gets me down.' Andrew Longmore, 'Cycling – Time to stop cheating, pleads Millar', *The Independent* (27 June 1999).

[42] Hoberman, "Pharmacy on Wheels", unpublished manuscript, 2002. This was also found to be the case during the 2002 Tour, when only one rider and one team physician suggested that this should be done.

[43] 'Nearing 43, Still at Top Speed', *New York Times* (28 Oct. 2001). However, Hoberman has pointed out that the athlete in question, Longo, has been accused of doping more than once over the course of her long career.

[44] 'One of the remarkable aspects of the physicians' self-image is their constant boasting about their moderating influence, at the same time that they claim to be helpless when confronted with the prevailing [societal] conditions.' Singler and Treutlein, *Doping – von der Analyse zur Prävention*, 40–1.

[45] 'It is this punishing schedule which largely sustains the tolerance of doping within cycling and, if we are seriously concerned about the health of professional cyclists, then reducing the physical demands made upon cyclists ought to be the first priority.' Waddington, *Sport, Health and Drugs*, 168.

References

Barthes, Roland. "The Tour de France as Epic." *Mythologies*. New York: Hill Wang, 1979.

Gilbert, B. "Something on the Ball." *Sports Illustrated* (30 June 1969): 32.

Hoberman, John.

Quénet, Jean-François. *Le procès du dopage: La vérité du jugement*. Paris: Solar, 2001.

Møller, Verner. *Dopingdjævlen – analyse af en hed debat*. Copenhagen: Gyldendal, 1999.

Singler, Andreas and Treutlein Gerhard. *Doping – von der Analyse zur Prävention*. Aachen: Meyer & Meyer Verlag, 2001.

Union Cycliste Internationale. *The Essence of Road Cycling*. Aigle, Switzerland: UCI, 2001.

Waddington, Ivan. *Sport, Health and Drugs: A Critical Sociological Perspective*. London: E & FN Spon, 2000.

On Transgendered Athletes, Fairness and Doping: An International Challenge

Sarah Teetzel

Transgendered athletes face many global and cultural challenges in attempting to participate in sport at the national and international levels. Some might count the fact that transgendered athletes are free to join their local golf and country clubs, tennis clubs or soccer leagues as proof that sport truly is open to the masses and that anyone, no matter their age, sex, race, nationality, sexual preference or socioeconomic status, is welcome to participate in sport. Is this attitude of acceptance and integration merely for recreational sport, or does it extend beyond the confines of recreational pursuits to the elite level of sport?

Anecdotal evidence and reports from the few transgendered athletes who have championed for their right to play and compete in elite sports competitions suggest that the answer might be no. Though the acceptance of transgendered individuals is progressing in the workplace, and in social and recreational settings in North America, until recently the realm of elite sport remained one of the few areas still off limits to transgendered individuals. The increasingly tolerant and accepting attitude held by the public at large toward transgendered individuals has been slow to catch on and flourish among policy makers and officials at the highest level of international athletics. Sport, when viewed in its best light, is an effective tool in teaching young athletes morals, values and life skills, as well as promoting such qualities as fair play, tolerance, discipline and team work. However, while sport, and particularly the Olympic movement, is often credited with bridging the gap between nations and promoting harmony among people of different nationalities, races, religious beliefs and so on, the acceptance of athletes who self-identify with a gender other than male, female or the one they were assigned at birth, is one area of discrimination that sport has yet to fully conquer.

Transgendered athletes experience a different type of exclusion than racial minorities, the working class and women experienced at different points in the history of modern sport. The icy introduction that transgendered athletes first experienced, and many continue to experience, in elite sport does not hinge entirely on people's prejudiced or discriminatory views, but instead rests on the notion of fairness. The typically warm reception transgendered athletes receive when playing in recreational leagues compared to the controversies that erupt when a transgendered athlete excels at a sport and gains a world ranking, qualifies to represent his or her country, or competes in international athletic competitions exemplifies this occurrence. The most pressing issue here is whether a transgendered athlete, who has surgically changed his or her sex from that with which he or she was born, retains any physiological advantages associated with his or her sex at birth. Particularly with male-to-female transgendered athletes, the question of whether the athlete maintains or gains any performance-enhancing advantages from going through puberty as a member of the opposite sex is a major point of contention. In this article, I hope to identify the relevant factors that one must address in working toward an answer of whether or not it is fair for transgendered athletes to be able to compete at the elite level.

Typically, those who argue that allowing transgendered athletes to compete in sport is inherently unfair to the athlete's competitors often appeal to hypothetical scenarios where male athletes with exceptional athletic talent annihilate women's competitions. They envision scenarios such as Michael Jordan playing at his peak in the WNBA or Maurice Greene running in the women's 100m final at the Olympic Games. However, these extreme examples fail to consider the effects that sex-reassignment surgery and years of hormone therapy would have on even the most celebrated male athletes of our time. A lack of information on transgender physiology and misguided fears that border on discrimination by some fellow participants, sports fans and sports-governing bodies, thus often make the transgendered athlete's experience in sport less than ideal and have up until recently prohibited transgendered athletes from competing at the highest level.

I argue here that the challenges to sport that transgendered athletes' participation at the elite level creates predominantly relate to, and are confused with, anti-doping issues. This stems from the perception that the transgendering process can provide an athlete with the same type of advantage that athletes gain from using substances and procedures banned under the World Anti-Doping Code. I note that while there are conceivable advantages that an elite transgendered athlete might possibly possess over his or her competitors, conclusive evidence based on long-term scientific studies has either not yet been done or fails to show any unfair advantages at the elite level with statistical significance. Arguments to support this view draw on the scientific literature of performance enhancement and the transgendering process; the testimonials of transgendered athletes published in scholarly journals, newspapers and magazines; the arguments of athletes, medical professionals, and sports officials published in similar sources; and, finally, recent developments in the policies established by international sports organizations, such as the International Olympic Committee (IOC) and the World Anti-Doping Agency (WADA). I contend that much of the controversy surrounding the participation of transgendered athletes in elite sport stems from considering the transgender process a form of doping, and the widely held view that it is not fair for female athletes to have to compete against individuals born male (no matter their current classification). As such, I explore the meanings of fairness, gender and sex categories, as they apply at the highest level of sport, in order to critically analyse the controversy surrounding transgendered athletes' participation in elite sport.

Transgendered Athletes: A Brief History

Discrimination, oppression, rejection, harassment and prejudice frequently affect transgendered individuals within North American society.[1] The term 'transgender' applies to all 'people who transcend the conventional boundaries of gender, irrespective of their physical status or sexual orientation', and includes people who identify themselves as pre- and post-operative transsexuals, transgenderists, bigenderists, transvestites, cross dressers, drag queens, drag kings, female impersonators and male impersonators.[2] In terms of athletic participation at the elite level, however, the term 'transgendered athletes' applies only to post-operative transsexuals, as they are the only subset within the group of all transgendered individuals who have the potential to gain eligibility to compete in the opposite sex category to which they were born. All other transgendered individuals fail the IOC and/or International Sports Federation (ISF)'s specific criteria one must meet for inclusion at the Olympic Games, which I will discuss in more detail below. For the remainder of this essay, then, when I mention transgendered athletes, I refer to those athletes who identify themselves as transgendered and have undergone sex-reassignment surgery to transition to the opposite sex.

An American doctor coined the term 'transsexual' in 1923[3] to describe the phenomenon of 'female souls in male bodies',[4] and encapsulate the notion of 'women (men) trapped in male (female) bodies'.[5] Transgendered individuals in general, and transsexuals in particular, have faced discrimination for several centuries as a result of the historical classification of transsexualism as first a mental disorder, and then a sexual identity disorder, before it gained credibility as na option a free and autonomous individual can choose to undergo.[6] Hence, it is not that surprising that the first transgendered athletes who attempted to compete at high levels of sport fought uphill battles for most of their careers.

The first transgendered athlete to publicize and advance the plight of transgendered athletes was Renee Richards. In light of the United States Tennis Association's unwavering dismissals of her requests to play in women's tennis tournaments after her sex-reassignment surgery, Richards took the organization to court to gain legal recognition of her right to enter tennis competitions. However, she was not the first athlete to face discrimination in sport over her transsexuality. The first transgendered athletes known to compete in international sports competitions were hermaphrodites, female impersonators coerced into entering women's events by their national sport systems, and the unfortunate women who were unaware they possessed male chromosomes until their disqualification from the women's events following sex verification tests. These competitors were deemed non-women, had their records and titles revoked, and were banned from subsequent competitions following visual inspections of their genitalia or the detection of Y chromosomes in their cheek cell swabs. Athletes such as Polish sprinters Stanislawa Walasiewicz (Stella Walsh) and Eva Klobukowska, Czech runner Zdenka Koubkowa, German high jumper Hermann (Dora) Ratjen, French sprinters Clair (Pierre) Bresolles and Lea (Leon) Caula, and Australian skier Erika (Eric) Shineggar, to name just a few, are all now remembered more so for 'failing' their sex tests, or competing disguised as women, than for their athletic talents and achievements.

Richards' success in ensuring the United States upheld her rights as a transgendered woman in the late 1970s paved the way for future transgendered athletes to fight to compete in their self-identified sex division rather than the category stated on their birth certificate.[7] Male-to-female golfers Mianne Bagger and Danielle Swope, along with mountain biker Michelle Dumaresq, have further campaigned for the elimination of policies that allow only competitors who were female at birth to participate in women's competitions. Similarly, female-to-male skier and cyclist Eric Shineggar is one athlete who paved the way for female-to-male transgendered athletes to compete in the men's divisions. Interestingly, transgendered female-to-male athletes have met much less resistance than transgendered male-to-female athletes in obtaining permission to compete from the appropriate ISF. This suggests that the controversy surrounding transgendered athlete participation in elite sport lies in the perceived performance-enhancing qualities associated with the male physique that male-to-female transgendered athletes might still possess, and is not based entirely on blatant discrimination against the athletes themselves or a desire to prevent transgendered athletes from participating in elite sport. Contributing to this view may be an underlying disbelief that an athlete who was born a female could compete alongside elite 'naturally superior' male athletes. Despite the birth sex of the athletes involved, the rationale behind many transgendered athletes' quest for elite sport participation is to ensure that they, and their peers, receive fair and equitable treatment; however, what fair and equitable treatment entails requires further examination and clarification.

Fairness in Sport

What counts as fair in sport? There is much ambiguity and uncertainty about what one means when one speaks of fairness in sport. Is a fair sport one where all of the participants follow the rules, or one where participants all have an equal chance of succeeding? Does fairness concern the way participants play the game via their actions, intentions and characters, or does it involve having an equal opportunity to compete and a level playing field? We must keep in mind that sport cannot be completely fair because, if this were the case, there would be no winners and losers. Everyone would be equal in terms of skill, talent, genetic potential, opportunity, funding and so on, and all competitors would cross the finish line together in a massive tie. Viewed this way, sport, as we know, it is a very unfair activity.

In this journal, William J. Morgan examines fairness in sport and draws on two descriptions of fairness: one stemming from Rawls' notion of fairness as the 'reciprocal regard for the interests of individual participants', and the other from Schneider and Butcher's notion of 'respect for the game'.[8] According to Morgan, when one competes fairly in sport,

> one values the perfectionist life sport is all about [and] one can be understood as, first, acknowledging that the primary, but again not only, reason one engages in it is to realize the goods internal to it, which are all bound up in one way or another with the kinds of bodily excellence on display there, and second, as committing oneself to the cooperative social relations that underlie and guide the competitive pursuit of such goods.[9]

Fairness in sport, then, does not come down to simply trying to ensure every athlete has an equal starting point, although this is certainly an important consideration. Fairness in sport, which includes justice, impartiality and equality, involves more than just following the rules.

To answer the question of whether it is *fair* for transgendered athletes to compete in the opposite sex division to which they were born, one must consider several factors. From the widely accepted point of view of fairness, we could most definitely describe a transgendered athlete as acting fairly if he or she follows the rules of the game, embodies the spirit of the game, and makes a commitment to cooperate with his or her competitors in the process of competing. People's apprehensions about transgendered Olympians are thus not about these athletes playing fairly. We must differentiate between playing unfairly and possessing unfair physiological advantages that influence the outcome of the competition to get at the root of the contention.

Uncertainty regarding which sex category transgendered athletes should rightly compete in and who should make that decision abounds. As Janice Raymond argues, transsexuality is neither a medical issue nor a legal issue and thus one should not treat it as though it were. She notes, in *The Transsexual Empire*, 'Doctors fixate on hormonal techniques and constructed genitalia – artificial vaginas, breast implants, and the like – therapists view transsexualism as a humane solution to the agony of "gender dysphoria".' Furthermore, she explains, 'These perspectives are fragmented and ultimately blur the issue. They focus on the *foreground* of the transsexual phenomenon rather than on the multi-dimensional *background*.'[10] Raymond's concerns with focusing on particular aspects of transsexualism can be applied to the participation of transgendered athletes in elite sport. Who decides which transgendered athletes are eligible for competing in international sporting events is problematic as there is no moral authority on transgender issues.

The IOC's 2004 statement on sex reassignment in sport, known as the 'Stockholm Consensus' due to its conception at a meeting in Stockholm, Sweden, of the IOC Medical Commission and leading researchers who study transsexuality, clarifies transgendered athletes' position in the Olympic Movement. The document, available on the IOC's official website, lists a set of three criteria transgendered athletes must fulfil in order to have their cases heard by the Medical Commission for possible inclusion in their desired sex category.

The document states that males who underwent sex-reassignment surgery prior to puberty are eligible to compete as females, and female-to-male transgendered athletes can compete as males, so long as they were sexually reassigned before entering puberty. For those athletes who transitioned from male-to-female or female-to-male after puberty, the following criteria must be met before the athlete can compete as a woman or man, respectively: 1) The athlete has completed genital sex-reassignment surgery, including the removal of either the ovaries or testes; 2) The athlete has undergone a minimum of two years of post-operative hormone therapy to eliminate any sex-related advantages that might render him or her a competitive edge in sport; and, 3) The athlete's sex is legally recognized.[11] The IOC adopted the above criteria after the experts consulted by the IOC Medical Commission concluded that post-operative hormone therapy alters testosterone levels and muscle mass to the extent that a male-to-female transsexual would not, on average, possess any advantages over female competitors, nor would a female-to-male transsexual garner advantages over his competitors who were born male. Patrick Schamasch, director of the IOC Medical Commission, is quoted as saying that the IOC's transgendered policy was designed 'more to protect the athlete who has not been sex reassigned than to help the person who is … We are almost sure the advantage of the previous gender will have completely disappeared.'[12] Canadian IOC member and former Olympic athlete Charmaine Crooks tells a slightly different tale in her observation that allowing a transgendered athlete to compete as his or her self-identified gender,

> clearly shows that we [the IOC] will always address issues of human rights. That's something that we find very important. It also shows that when there is an issue, we will study it and if it fits with our fundamental values and philosophies, then we will act on it and act quickly, but also act in the best interest of all athletes.[13]

Crooks' remarks show that the IOC will not tolerate the deliberate exclusion of a marginalized group of people without a convincing reason to do so.

The Stockholm Consensus came into effect three months prior to the opening of the 2004 Olympic Games in Athens, Greece, but no transgendered athletes competed at those Games, the first in which they were eligible. In large part, this is due to transgendered athletes not having enough time to prepare for, or qualify to represent one's country at, the Olympic Games. As transgendered athletes were previously excluded from elite sports competitions, and many countries had already determined their 2004 Olympic rosters before the IOC implemented the Stockholm Consensus, no known transgendered athletes took part in the Athens Games. With the elimination of sex testing at the turn of the century, it is possible that some transgendered athletes choose not to publicize the fact that they had changed sexes or genders. The April 2004 issue of *Outside* magazine reports that transgendered mountain-biker, Michelle Dumaresq, who battled to represent Canada in international events, is in correspondence with approximately 115 transgendered athletes worldwide who keep their transsexuality a secret for fear of the suspected backlash and implications. Among the purported 115 athletes are an NCAA women's basketball player and two elite level female athletes who compete in Olympic events.[14] Yet even without known transgendered competitors currently competing at the Olympic Games, the controversy over whether they *should* be permitted to compete in any major sporting event remains a topic of contention in elite sport circles.

Endocrinology and Advantages

The endocrinology literature on how hormone therapy affects transgendered individual's athletic performances is inconclusive.[15] Hence, whether transgendered athletes truly possess unfair advantages when they compete at the elite level of sport in their self-identified gender categories remains vastly unknown. Due to a complete lack of studies conducted using subjects who were transgendered and trained intensively both before and after their sex-reassignment surgeries, the effects of hormone therapy, particularly the effects of oestrogen and testosterone, on athletic performance in elite athletes are often only purported, and not supported by reputable scientific research studies. Additionally, as senior medical director of the Australian Olympic team, Brian Sando, points out, 'A lot depends on whether a [male-to-female] transgender had trained heavily between his adolescent growth stage and the sex change operation'.[16] Since this is a query unique to elite sport participation, it is not surprising that the literature on the topic is sparse.

What researchers know about hormone therapies in transgendered subjects comes from research done on transgendered individuals who live normal, average lives, not from transgendered athletes who train intensively in order to compete at the international level. Thus generalizing that hormone therapy and sex-reassignment surgery eliminate any advantages an athlete born male has over her competitors once she completes her transition from male to female is often not convincing to those opposed to transgendered athletes competing at high levels of sport. For example, a study on transsexuality and testosterone in rats showed that one large injection of testosterone in the hypothalamus of a female rat will cause it to function like a male for the remainder of its life, which has been cited to support the claim that going through puberty as a male might produce long-lasting effects on a male-to-female transsexual's athletic abilities.[17] However, generalizing the results of a study involving rats to shed any light on the effects of hormone therapy in elite transgendered athletes is questionable at best.

Similarly, studies examining testosterone levels in elite athletes only involve male athletes who produce testosterone naturally. A study involving male varsity-level tennis players showed that testosterone levels in the body rise just prior to matches, and players with the greatest increases in their mean testosterone levels demonstrate more positive improvements in mood than those with smaller increases. Players with higher testosterone levels were found to be more successful in winning matches and those who won their matches demonstrated further increases in their testosterone than those who lost.[18] These results have since been substantiated in other contexts involving competition, leading researchers to postulate that winning raises testosterone levels in men and influences mood.[19] Further research showed male varsity-level rowers experience no significant changes in hormone levels during intensive exercise but their performances are positively related to the amount of total and free testosterone in their bodies at rest. Hence, the authors concluded, having more testosterone corresponded to better results in maximum exertion tasks.[20] However, it is unclear if the testosterone must be produced naturally in the body or if testosterone contained in hormone therapy produces the same results in female-to-male transgendered athletes. As such, the hormone levels of transgendered athletes remain a point of contention among those opposed to the Stockholm Consensus.

Testosterone studies are on going and prevalent, and conflicting reports of testosterone's uses and effects are common.[21] What researchers know with certainty is the role testosterone plays in the development of secondary sex characteristics in males, and the promotion of protein biosynthesis that aids in building muscle mass, promoting healing and burning fat, which contribute to the muscular, lean physique associated with male athletes. Rises in testosterone levels in male athletes prior to competition have been hypothesized by some researchers throughout the history of studying testosterone to cause such widespread advantages as improved psychomotor function and coordination, increased mental activity, and increased likelihood of employing strategies with higher risk.[22] While noting the relationship between testosterone and these skills requires further exploration, the authors of the study found pre-competition increases in testosterone level were much weaker or not present in female athletes as well as much weaker in novice athletes compared to their elite counterparts.[23] Testosterone therapy has also been shown to have an enhancing effect on spatial ability performance following three months of hormone therapy in transgendered individuals, whereas combined oestrogen and anti-androgen therapy in female-to-male transgendered individuals was not found to diminish spatial ability, as one might predict.[24] Clearly, these characteristics, not to mention the increased muscle mass, strength and power most commonly associated with testosterone, are desirable for an elite athlete to possess.

Similarly, the dominant female sex hormones oestrogen and progesterone are thought to affect athletic performance, but in a negative manner. Changes in the concentrations of hormones throughout the menstrual cycle can theoretically cause both performance enhancing and inhibiting effects. Inter- and intra-individual variability in hormone responses has traditionally precluded understanding exactly how oestrogen and progesterone affect athletic performance. Oestrogen produced in the muscle and fat is the main sources of endogenous oestrogen for post-menopausal women, women without ovaries, and females following sex-reassignment surgery. Consequently, hormone therapy that includes oestrogen is an essential part of the transgendering process for male-to-female transgendered athletes. Male-to-female transgendered athletes may have strength and speed advantages from their exposure to testosterone in utero and in puberty despite the effects of hormone therapy. Results from a study of 19 male-to-female and 17 female-to-male transgendered individuals undergoing hormone therapy showed that individuals taking oestrogens and anti-androgens for a year had increased levels of subcutaneous fat and larger fat cell sizes. Conversely, a year of testosterone administration resulted in decreased amounts of subcutaneous fat and diminished fat cell size in the subjects.[25] These findings help demonstrate that hormone therapy helps transgendered athletes attain a physique similar to their competitors.

While science supports the performance-enhancing benefits of testosterone, and rationalizes the inclusion of the hormone and its derivatives on the WADA's banned list, the opposite is also true; denying an individual testosterone via androgen deprivation reverses the performance-enhancing changes male athletes gain during puberty. These changes include an additional height increase of 12–15 centimetres, larger bones and muscle than females, and the ability to produce more strength than females.[26] The effects of prior androgen exposure in male-to-female transgendered athletes following sex-reassignment surgery are suspected to carry over for an unknown period, but will diminish following the combined regimen of androgen deprivation and oestrogen therapy. However, the effects of testosterone on height and dimensions of the body, for example, the size of feet and hands, are irreversible and may be capable of conferring performance-enhancing benefits to transgendered female athletes.[27] Once again, it is important to note the lack of research involving long term, carefully controlled, double-blind studies using elite transgendered athletes as subjects to verify these changes. As a result of the intricacies involved in sport and the vast number of factors, including genetics, hormones, response to training, diet and training regimen, that contribute to one highly trained and skilled athlete triumphing over another, what the miniscule differences crucial for winning and losing are exactly is extremely difficult to pinpoint and identify. As such, the authors of the study surmise:

Our analysis is not refined enough to detect these small differences, allowing only an approximation. As far as our data allow conclusions, the answer for female-to-male transsexuals is probably yes [they can compete fairly], provided the administration of testosterone has not generated and does not generate supraphysiological testosterone levels, as these levels and exercise induce a surplus in muscle mass over exercise alone. For male-to-female transsexuals there is an element of arbitrariness. There is no evidence pro or con that the prenatal/perinatal testosterone exposure of men has an impact on future physical traits.[28]

A division is drawn between conceivable advantages a male-to-female transgendered athlete might possess over female competitors and those that a female-to-male transgendered athlete could hold over the male competition. One must consider both forms of advantage when examining if it is fair for transgendered athletes to compete at the elite level, and if the purported advantages are similar to those gained by doping.

The rules stipulated in the World Anti-Doping Code prohibit athletes from consuming exogenous sources of testosterone, oestrogen, and the majority of their derivatives due to the perceived performance-enhancing properties associated with these compounds. By definition then, athletes who consume testosterone and oestrogen are breaking the rules that elite athletes agree to adhere to and are consequently considered cheaters. However, exceptions based on medical need, in the form of a therapeutic-use exemption (TUE), were incorporated into the World Anti-Doping Code for a reason, and granting a TUE to a transgendered athlete seems like a reasonable and appropriate action to take. While doing so may be reasonable and appropriate, one must question whether it is *fair* that some athletes can use banned substances whilst others commit doping infractions for performing what seem to be, intent aside, analogous actions.

Following sex-reassignment surgery, transgendered individuals become 'medically managed individuals',[29] due to their dependence on hormone therapy to induce and maintain desired physical changes. Cross gender hormone therapy, involving either testosterone or a combination of oestrogen and testosterone-blocking agents, is thus a necessity for the post-operative transsexual as it both develops the secondary sex characteristics of the desired gender and suppresses the unwanted functional reminders of the renounced gender.[30] These drugs are requirements for transgendered athletes, but, at the same time, anti-requisites for elite sport competitors.

Transgendering as a Form of Doping?

The World Anti-Doping Code's 2005 Prohibited List International Standard clearly prohibits the use of exogenous testosterone, oestrogen, and anti-estrogenic compounds without the prior granting of a TUE. The majority of health care providers involved in transgendered individuals' transitions follow guidelines established by the Harry Benjamin International Gender Dysphoria Association for performing sex-reassignment surgery, prescribing hormone replacement therapy, and caring for transsexual patients.[31] Despite their reputation as a leader in caring for transsexuals, the Association has yet to comment on sport or health risks for transsexual athletes. Privacy issues might also arise for transgendered athletes granted TUEs for testosterone or other banned substances, which is an issue that currently remains unexplored. Not granting transgendered athletes TUEs would send a clear message that these athletes were not welcome at the Olympic Games because a criterion for transgendered athletes to compete directly conflicts with substances on the banned list. The same exogenous compounds transgendered athletes need to take therapeutically to approach the endogenous levels present in the bodies of male and female athletes would result in expulsion from sport for a minimum of two years if non-transgendered athletes partook in the same course of action.

Many medical professionals who treat transsexuals believe that sex-reassignment surgery and hormone therapy negate any advantages the athlete might have had over the opposite sex prior to the transgendering surgery. As one doctor who treats transgendered patients explains:

> Transsexuals' bodies change sufficiently to justify allowing them to compete. Most changes are the result of hormone therapy, which primarily affects muscle mass. Men who become women lose much of their muscle mass, while women who become men tend to develop muscles more easily than they used to. In either case, skeletal structure doesn't change much. To say that a genetic man or woman is different than a transgender man or woman is impossible, because then you're saying that taller women are at an advantage so they shouldn't compete.[32]

Male-to-female transsexuals are often prescribed oestrogen and progestin as part of their hormone therapy regimens, usually in the form of 80–100 μg of 17β-estradiol for 6–12 months, in combination with anti-testosterone drugs, which together suppress testosterone to the desired level of less than 50μg/dL and decrease male sexual characteristics.[33] The amount of oestrogen a transgendered female consumes is approximately two to three times greater than the amount taken by a postmenopausal woman undergoing hormone replacement therapy.[34] Progesterones are often also prescribed to enhance breast growth and decrease breast irritability and sensitivity.[35]

Female-to-male transsexuals undergo a similar hormone therapy in order to increase their blood testosterone levels to 500 μg/dL by ingesting 150–400 mg of injectable or oral testosterone every two weeks, in a regiment tantamount to that performed by hypogonadal men.[36] Contrasted with the amount of testosterone consumed by male athletes using anabolic steroids, which is speculated to be in the range of at least 250–1000 mg per week, a transsexual's hormone therapy is considerably less. For that reason, testosterone prescribed as part of a transsexual's hormone therapy is not thought to have a marked influence on athletic performance, such as that typically demonstrated by an athlete abusing steroids. Normal free testosterone levels vary between 300–1000 μg/dL in men and are typically 100 μg/dL or lower in women,[37] so raising a female-to-male transgendered athlete's blood testosterone up to 500 μg/dL using hormone therapy puts him in the lower normal range for men and would seemingly not produce any performance-enhancing advantages relative to his competitors who produce testosterone naturally. The level of testosterone present in non-athletic female-to-male transsexuals following two years of supplementing with testosterone is in the upper normal range for males, whereas their oestradiol levels drop to levels found in postmenopausal women.[38] One might wonder if the female-to-male athlete on hormone therapy would then easily pass a doping-detection test for the many varieties of steroids since his testosterone level would likely fall within the acceptable limits for males. However, one must keep in mind that the small amount of testosterone produced naturally in the body differs structurally from the exogenous sources consumed as part of the hormone therapy, so the athlete would demonstrate signs of exogenous testosterone use.

The World-Anti Doping Code will ban a substance or method and prohibit athletes from using it if it meets two of the following three criteria: 1) It enhances performance, 2) It causes harm, and 3) It violates the spirit of sport.[39] A brief examination of transgendered athletes' use of hormone therapies relative to these three criteria follows and offers support for the TUE transgendered athletes must obtain to pass a doping-detection test.

Hormone therapy in transgendered athletes has not been shown to provide a transgendered athlete with a competitive advantage beyond what his or her competition is provided with naturally, although it may in fact enhance the performance of the athlete compared to his or her past competing as the opposite sex. Hormone therapy does not seem to provide an enhanced performance relative to the rest of the field. The additional muscle mass and resulting strength a female-to-male transgendered athlete will gain from hormone therapy would provide him with a competitive advantage over the women he competed against before sex-reassignment surgery. However, the same hormone therapy does not appear to provide a competitive advantage relative to his male competitors who produce testosterone naturally. While 'enhanced performance' is not synonymous with 'competitive advantage', in considering fairness and equity, one must determine if the transgendering process provides athletes with competitive advantages relative to their male or female competitors rather than focusing on the performance changes that occur as one transitions from female to male.

Further, there is no convincing evidence to support that either the transgendering process or training and competing at the highest level of sport is harmful to a transgendered athlete, or at least any more harmful than it is to any other athlete. A study involving 816 male-to-female transsexuals and 293 female-to-male transsexuals to examine the mortality and morbidity associated with cross-sex hormone treatment showed that neither male-to-female nor female-to-male transsexuals experience higher mortality than the general population. This finding led the authors of the study to conclude that the use of hormone therapy by transgendered individuals is acceptably safe.[40] In fact, transgendered individuals' biggest health risks come from avoiding regular screenings for breast and prostate cancers, not having regular pelvic and testicular exams, and from sharing 'dirty' needles to inject hormones, not from taking hormones. Mental health issues, particularly depression, are more prevalent in transgendered individuals than in the total population,[41] but competing in sport following the transgendering process has not been shown to be harmful.

Finally, the spirit of sport is a difficult and elusive concept to try to elucidate, as it is open to the individual attempting to define its interpretation. Adhering to the spirit of sport involves more than just following the rules of a particular sport and even more than appealing to a sport's ethos. The spirit of sport is more than just the spirit or ethos of basketball, cycling or cross-country skiing, for example, as it encompasses sport as a whole, not just one particular sport. For that reason, it seems that barring any obvious instances of unfairness or advantages possessed by transgendered athletes, following the spirit of sport would amount to welcoming transgendered athletes into the highest levels of sport rather than shunning them and prohibiting them from participating. However, holding this view without critically analysing the resulting possible scenarios it may create fails to consider the performance-enhancing benefits an athlete might gain through the transgendering process from factors other than sex hormones, in addition to failing to ensure the principles fairness involves are upheld.

With the likelihood of transgendered athletes gaining a competitive advantage from hormone therapy seemingly negated by the endocrinology literature, and testosterone and oestrogen therapy following sex-reassignment surgery being condoned by both medical authorities and the IOC, on what basis then might adversaries of transgendered athletes participating in elite sport base their rationales? A transgendered female athlete, who went through puberty as a male, may experience an unfair advantage over her competitors stemming from physiological adaptations she went through during puberty. To the best of our knowledge, none of the conceivable advantages based on physiology have been evaluated, reported or refuted with statistical significance in the context of sport. Perhaps this is to do with their dismissal as mere non-plausible attempts to bar or hinder the participation of transgendered athletes by utilitarian researchers who embrace equity for all and want to see transgendered athletes welcomed at the highest levels of sport. Alternatively, perhaps the literature on the physiological adaptations and changes that transpire in athletes following sex-reassignment surgery is so sparse that it is currently impossible to pass judgment. In any case, I put forth several possible advantages transgendered athletes could conceivably boast in sport with the hope that science will one day find them groundless. Nevertheless, in the interest of fairness, I feel they must be explored, considered and subsequently dismissed before anyone can say with conviction that it is fair for a transgendered athlete's competitors to face transgendered athletes as their legitimate rivals in the hunt for world records and Olympic gold medals.

Athletes, fans and sports administrators who oppose the integration of transgendered individuals in elite sport seem to base their argument on the belief that it is unfair for a 'formerly male' athlete to compete against females and to a lesser degree for a 'formerly female' athlete to compete against males. These critics generally maintain that the physiological adaptations and advantages sustained by male-to-female transgendered athletes give them competitive advantages over women in terms of their size, strength, motor skills, heart and lung capacities, higher muscle concentration, lower body fat percentage and the previous training they did as a member of the male sex prior to sex-reassignment surgery. Could these physiological advantages manifest themselves as competitive advantages or does sex-reassignment surgery and post-operative hormone therapy negate each one? Moreover, can we ever determine this with 100 per cent certainty? There seem to be several possible advantages that a male-to-female transgendered athlete may have over her competition when permitted to compete in women's events, which sex-reassignment surgery or post-op hormone therapy do not eradicate. Consider, for example, the size of an average man's hands compared to the average woman's hand size. While there is certainly variability among women in the size of their hands and some women have hands significantly bigger than some men, on average most would agree that men have larger hands than women. Does this affect performance in ball sports that require extraordinary control and manipulation of the ball at the elite level? Having larger hands might correspond to a greater ability to grip, retain and move the ball in sports such as basketball and water polo. Rules WP 3.3 and WP 3.4 in the Federation Internationale de Natation (FINA)'s official rules and regulations, which governs international swimming, diving and water polo competitions, state that water polo games played by men must use a ball with a circumference of between 0.68–0.72 metres with a pressure of 90–97 kPa whereas women's matches must be played using a ball that measures 0.65–0.67 metres in circumference and 83–90 kPa.[42] The smaller women's ball might be easier to catch, throw, handle and manipulate with larger hands and individuals with large hands might have a competitive advantage over those with small hands.

Similar to a possible larger hand benefit, transgendered female competitors might also gain an advantage from having larger feet. Particularly in swimming, where the feet and legs act as an important source of propulsion, one might benefit from having flipper-sized feet. Anecdotal evidence, such as the worldwide press's fascination with, and hoopla over, Australian swimming hero Ian Thorpe's size 17 feet at the 2000 Olympic Games in Sydney demonstrate the purported advantage a swimmer may gain from his or her foot size. However, there are highly-trained swimmers with smaller than average feet that win medals and swimmers with large feet who finish at the back of the pack. Furthermore, that Thorpe's feet caused so much interest due to their astonishing size demonstrates that not many men, or women for that matter, have feet that large and we would not expect the average transgendered male to have the propulsion potential of Thorpe.

Feet aside, Ian Thorpe's stature and physique also are likely to contribute to his swimming success, as does his hard work, training and perseverance. In many other sports, having a height advantage also renders an advantage over one's competition; particularly in sports such as volleyball and basketball the advantage of height cannot be ignored. One might expect that a team of transgendered women athletes might have a considerable height advantage over a team of non-transgendered women. However, looking at the current roster of the Canadian national women's basketball team shows a range of height from 1.65m to 2.00m with an average height of approximately

1.84m,[43] which is well above the average height of males in most countries. This leads to an important consideration in determining the fairness of transgendered athletes competing in elite sport: Olympic medallists and sports stars are so much superior to the average human being in terms of fitness, physiology and genetics that an average male would not be able to go through the complete transgendering process and have a hope of becoming a world-class female athlete without years of serious and intensive training. How an above average or elite male athlete will perform as a transgendered woman remains to be determined, though.

How other physiological differences in men and women affect athletic performance are more difficult to quantify. Pondering the effects of having a larger heart and a bigger set of lungs than one's competitors that together affect cardiovascular functioning seems futile when one does not understand the intricate details of these systems and how they affect an athlete's level of fitness. It is easier, though, to question if an athlete retains greater jumping and agility capabilities after transitioning from male to female. While increased muscle mass from hormone therapy is shown with statistical significance in female-to-male transgendered individuals, the amount of muscle wasting male-to-female athletes experience is less studied.[44] Testimony by male-to-female transgendered athletes suggests the decreases in muscle size and strength are quite substantial, and as transgendered female golfer Mianne Bagger notes from personal experience, 'estrogen is a performance-diminishing drug'[45] that decreases muscle mass. However, to squelch the speculation surrounding muscle size and strength in post-operative transsexuals competing in elite sport, measurements of jumping height, strength, power and so on both before and after transitioning need to be documented. Until then, female transgendered athletes will have to deal with the speculation that they have advantageous jumping skills in events like the long jump, triple jump, high jump, as well as in volleyball, basketball and any other sports that list jumping as a skill requirement.

One might speculate that male athletes who were born female would face similar inquiries about the fairness of them competing against their male competitors. These arguments, however, are often overshadowed by the more pressing unfair advantage that some interpret to arise when a formerly male athlete competes against a field of women. That the ideal woman was traditionally perceived as weaker, slower and less aggressive than the ideal male surely influences the perception that a former male competing in women's events creates a more 'unfair' situation than a former woman competing in men's events does. Just as there are events in which a male-to-female transgendered athlete might have a speculated physiological advantage over her competitors, there are also events where a female-to-male transgendered athlete could conceivably hold a performance-enhancing physiological edge. In events like diving and figure skating where competitors must exhibit fluidity and grace, a smaller, less lean stature might be of assistance. Additionally, women tend to have greater endurance and the ability to use fat as a fuel source in order to conserve carbohydrates in ultra-long distance races such as ultra-marathons and lake swims. Whether these characteristics show up in transgendered women remains unknown.

It must be emphasized that the conceivable advantages mentioned above that a transgendered athlete might enjoy are also found within men's and women's sex categories in sport due to the inter-variability naturally present within each category. If, and to what extent, these possible performance-enhancing advantages exist requires further scientific study and analysis before one can claim that the hypothesized advantages turn out to be anything more than hypothetical. Several scientists currently studying the affects of sex-reassignment surgery have found no evidence, pro or con, to suggest male-to-female or female-to-male athletes have a significant competitive advantage over their competitors based on their sex at birth.

If it were the case that these hypothesized situations corresponded to real competitive advantages, then one must consider the possibility that frustrated, glory-seeking, non-transgendered athletes might turn to the transgendering process as a means of increasing their chances of success, and attaining the fame and monetary rewards that go along with athletic achievement. In this sense, one could liken the transgendering process to an innovative form of doping. Some might immediately scoff at the mere thought of this occurring in sport, but it is worthy of our consideration to at least ponder the implications this might entail.

In a profession that is so competitive that some athletes are willing to risk their lives to gain the slightest edge over their competitors by experimenting with untested and unregulated gene therapies and using substances they know have contributed to the deaths of their colleagues, would it be unfathomable that an athlete would change his or her sex if he or she felt success would be more easily attained in the opposite sex division? Although individuals who have transitioned from one sex to another may dismiss the idea of someone undergoing the same procedures if he or she did not truly feel it was necessary, once again, it is important to consider this question in the context of elite sport. Indeed, transgendered tennis player and leader in male-to-female transsexuals' quest to participate in sport, Renee Richards, famously rejected the notion that male-to-female transsexuals undergo surgery to win medals and achieve athletic success with her statement, 'How hungry for tennis success must you be to have your penis chopped off in pursuit of it?'[46] However, Richards also disagrees with the IOC Medical Commission's finding that male-to-female transsexuals do not possess competitive advantages based on their physiology as she argues, 'hormone therapy is not much different from steroids, and no amount of therapy can change the basic physiological heart and lung differences'.[47]

Nevertheless, some athletes claim they will do anything to win and might include sex-reassignment surgery as an option. Many women's sports still carry the stigma of being less prestigious than the men's equivalent, particularly those that receive less media coverage, less funding and have smaller fan bases. As such, one might find it preposterous that a male athlete would change genders to increase his likelihood of qualifying for a women's Olympic team when he could experiment with genetic manipulations, or other banned performance-enhancing methods, to help qualify for the men's team. Transgendered athletes who suffer from gender identity disorders as members of their sex at birth clearly benefit from the transgendering process.

However, it seems possible that, like the potential misuse of genetic therapies and TUEs, some athletes will attempt to compete as the opposite sex if they feel doing so will get them closer to competing at the Olympic Games. To dismiss this idea as simply ridiculous may be a hasty mistake. It is important to remember that the transgender literature and the sport literature tend not to intersect very often, which means that arguments traditionally used to justify or explain transgendered athletes' choices are often not made with the context of sport in mind. There are additional considerations that one must include when studying transgendered athletes' participation in elite sport because, unlike most workplace and social circumstances, sport can be affected by having an advantageous physiology because the body is the primary means used to achieve success in sport.

Fairness Revisited

The key concerns involved in transgendered athletes' participation at the highest levels of sport can all be traced back to issues of fairness – fairness and non-discrimination to transgendered athletes, and fairness to their competitors. The challenge is to find a solution that treats all involved in sport fairly and discriminates against no one. To do so, one must decide if the possible advantages suggested in the previous section would constitute advantages or *unfair* advantages. In every sport at the elite level there are certain athletes that have advantages over their competitors, whether it be from their height, their ease in adding muscle mass, their fast reflexes and so forth. But, we often think of these individuals as having won the genetic lottery, not as athletes competing with unfair advantages. Similarly, there are always some athletes who have top of the line equipment, the best coaching money can buy, and enough financial support that they can train fulltime while others make do with used equipment and have to work to support themselves. When a favourable physiological characteristic or a wealthy background counts as an advantage and when it does not is neither clear nor apparent.

One could gain insight on how the transgendering process affects athletic performance by talking to those with the most intimate knowledge of the changes that transpire; that is, those who have competed in both the male and female sex categories at a competitive level of sport. These talented athletes know first hand how good they were relative to their male and female competitors before and after their transitions from one sex to the other. Athletes who have lived through the transition from one sex to the other can thus offer insight into the physiological changes that happen to their bodies. Michelle Dumaresq reportedly went from being a 1.83 m tall man weighing 95 kg to a 1.75 m tall woman weighing between 77–81 kg after sex-reassignment surgery and hormone therapy.[48] She reports a decreased ability to build and retain muscle mass and agrees that transgendered athletes should have to wait the IOC's recommended two years before competing as she notes, 'I know personally how long my body took to change, and two years is plenty'.[49] She also denies that the advantage her critics claim she has exists.[50] Male-to-female golfer Mianne Bagger offers the observation that changes occur gradually and are difficult to measure, similar to the changes an adolescent goes through at puberty. She notes, 'One day you realize that you maybe can't lift something that you once could. For me, I know I don't hit the ball as far as I used to.'[51] Female-to-male collegiate figure skater Alyn Libman approaches the changes he underwent from a different perspective. He reports that the IOC's transgender policy 'validates the fact that I exist, that transgender athletes exist, and we're people. And we should have the right to compete in the Olympics if we're good enough as athletes.' He also notes that hormone therapy has made him stronger, increased his endurance, allowed him to add muscle mass easily, and made his jumps higher and more explosive, which helps him compete against other male figure skaters.[52]

Aside from possible competitive advantages, several other contentious issues at play do not seem particularly fair. One is the criteria the IOC requires a transgendered athlete to meet before being considered for admission onto the playing field. The IOC's policy is only relevant for post-operative transsexuals as it 'excludes physical or chromosomal intersexuality and gender identity disorder secondary to another mental disorder, such as schizophrenia'.[53] Thus, the Stockholm Consensus is a document dealing solely with male-to-female and female-to-male transsexuals. Other individuals identifying themselves as transgendered, such as bigenderists, transvestites, cross dressers, drag kings and queens, female impersonators and male impersonators are not permitted to compete in their desired sex category unless they meet the IOC's requirements for transsexual athletes.[54] The policy discriminates against both transgendered athletes who opt not to undergo sex-reassignment surgery and those who choose not to undergo hormone therapy for an extended length of time. However, in the interest of fairness for all, not just fairness for transgendered athletes, the IOC must impose these limitations because they preclude individuals competing with true, verifiable competitive advantages. Taking a stance that renders sport as fair as possible for the greatest number of participants may not make sport open and welcoming to all, but it does ensure that it will be fair for the majority.

The IOC's third requirement, that the appropriate legal authority must recognize an athlete's sex is problematic due to the vagueness of who counts as an 'appropriate' authority to make this decision. Considering the wide range of attitudes held toward transgendered individuals worldwide, it is not that surprising that not all nations will recognize a sex-reassignment operation, issue a revised birth certificate, or recognize gender or sex categories other than the one listed on the athlete's original birth certificate. Despite the fact that 'sexual identity is a legal status that depends on public policy and self identification',[55] a post-operative transsexual's new sexual identify may not be recognized by all governments in the world and may thus disqualify him or her from competing at the Olympic Games. Requiring 'proof' that one has completed the transgendering process evokes memories of the forced exclusion of female athletes who failed their sex tests at the Olympic Games between the late 1960s and the late 1990s. Placing the onus on the transgendered athlete to demonstrate his or her legal sex, via governmental recognition, seems like a step backward rather than a progressive step ahead.

Sport historian and former Canadian track star, Bruce Kidd, puts forth a strong response to criticism over allowing transgendered athletes to compete in elite sport:

> The minute the law of the land says that a person has made the sex change, they should be eligible for athletic competition as a person of that sex. When a person has gone through the legal and medical procedures and has established himself or herself as a member of the opposite sex – has changed sex for legal purposes – that should be accepted by athletic organizations ... there are simply so many other inner qualities in sports, let's not single out this one.[56]

Kidd makes a valid point and captures what the fairness debate hinges on. Pragmatically speaking, what constitutes fairness in sport is what we decide we want fairness to include.

We allow athletes to improve their vision to 20/15 or better using laser eye surgery and to use any performance-enhancing supplement not explicitly banned by the World Anti-Doping Code, yet we prohibit them from transfusing their own blood and topping up their natural testosterone levels with exogenous sources.[57] Clearly then, what is permitted and prohibited in sport, and thus what is fair for an athlete to do to his or her body for the sake of sport, is not differentiated based on the naturalness or artificialness of the enhancement in question. It has been argued that transgendered athletes 'represent a challenge to a central tenet of organized sport: that artificial enhancement of the body destroys the level playing field essential to fair competition'.[58] Could one justifiably credit the decline of the level playing field to the few transgendered athletes who might someday compete in the Olympic Games? When the worldwide estimate is that only 1 in 11,900 people is a male-to-female transsexual and 1 in 30,400 people is a female-to-male transsexual,[59] attributing the unfairness present in sport to the inclusion of transgendered athletes is itself *unfair*. This does not, however, rule out a possible contribution to the overall unfairness. Jean Wilson, editor of *Harrison's Principles of Internal Medicine*, drives this point home with her statement:

> People are not equal in athletic prowess in regard to height, weight, coordination, or any other parameter, and it follows that this [transgender] is just another way in which athletes would not be equal. It is important that all society, including sport organizations, recognize that gender development is not always clear cut. The only appropriate way to assign these people to one or the other sex is to allow them to choose for themselves.[60]

IOC Medical Commission consultant and medical professor at Yale University, Myron Genel, agrees and goes on the record as saying that two years of post-operative hormone therapy is sufficient to eliminate physical and strength advantages. He points out that some characteristics, such as size, are not often reversible, and he maintains, 'if you're going to discriminate against transgendered athletes on the basis of their height or their wingspan, then we ought to set clear limits for women who compete, since there are six-foot-six women who compete in sports such as basketball and volleyball'.[61]

I do not claim that athletes with superior athletic skills stemming from their genetic frameworks should not compete because they hold unfair advantages over their peers. Rather, their appeal and the subsequent admiration and respect they receive often stems from the extraordinary physical characteristics they possess. For example, most do not think that former Romanian national basketball team member and Washington Bullets player Gheorghe Muresan should have been banned from playing in the NBA or international tournaments simply because at 2.31 meters tall he possessed a considerable height advantage over his competitors, which gave him an edge in performing some of basketball's skills. When Muresan stopped playing basketball, it was because his injuries forced him to retire, not because he had an unfair advantage. The playing field in sport is unequal, and arguably unfair, simply based on the variance in genetic endowment among participants. Coupled with the corrupting commercial forces of sport that provide some athletes with enormous sums of money to enable full-time training and athletic participation while others struggle to afford even the necessary gear to participate, the playing field in sport is far from level.

I cannot decisively comment on whether or not anyone truly gains an unfair advantage at the elite level of sport when transgendered and non-transgendered athletes compete together. There are convincing arguments from both those who oppose and those who favour the inclusion of transgendered athletes at the highest level of sports competitions. Variance within male and female sex categories is so vast that it is difficult to tell if a new member of a sex category has an unfair advantage or not relative to the rest of the field. Generalizing is complicated because hormone levels and athletic talent differ dramatically between individuals.[62] Turning to the medical experts, the athletes, and those who study sport helps shed light on potential fairness issues associated with transgender sport.

While many medical experts appear satisfied that transgendered athletes do not possess any unfair competitive advantages over their competitors from their previous training or physique, former Olympic pentathlete, Pat Connolly, from the United States raises the issue of fairness once again when she points out:

> [The IOC transgendered athlete policy is] the biggest insult to women and everything we've gone through. Gradually over the years, (the Olympics) started adding events for women. Why? To give women an opportunity to compete... Because there's an essential difference between men and women. Any dummy on the street knows the difference.[63]

Connolly's style of argument style leaves a lot to be desired, but one cannot deny the passion and conviction behind her words. Her comments raise important issues and are somewhat substantiated by comments made in the endocrinology literature:

> The question of whether reassigned male-to-female transsexuals can fairly compete with women depends on what degree of arbitrariness one wishes to accept, keeping in mind, for instance, that similar blood testosterone levels in men have profoundly different biological effects on muscle properties, rendering competition in sports intrinsically a matter of how nature endows individuals for this competition.[64]

Connolly, it seems, prefers a strict division of men and women based on their sex at birth. The difficulty inherent in defining what constitutes women and men is an additional thorn in an already thorny issue.

By promoting acceptance, tolerance and inclusion in sport, rather than highlighting differences in physiology that endocrinologist have so far deemed inconsequential or inconclusive regarding their ability to create an unfair advantages in sport, the sporting environment should be welcoming and non-discriminatory to transgendered athletes. While significant steps have been made to include transgendered athletes in golf and tennis, due to protests, legislation and lobbying by transgendered athletes interested in participating in those sports, it is more difficult to establish fair and equitable policies in sports that depend primarily on speed and jumping ability.

Conclusion

The IOC's transgender policy mandates that ISFs cannot prohibit transgendered athletes from competing in their desired sex category at the Olympic Games if the athlete fulfils the IOC's three requirements. However, permitting transgendered athletes to compete does not ensure that they will not face violence and discrimination in sport from their competitors, sport fans and officials. Education is needed to make sport more inclusive for transgendered athletes and more research on the effects of the transgendering process on athletic performance will help convince doubtful critics that transgendered athletes do not garner any unfair advantages in elite sport. Until conflicting evidence emerges, a transgendered athlete, who has undergone hormone therapy for at least two years following sex-reassignment surgery, is a legitimate contender for the medal podium at all levels of sport.

Throughout this essay, I have argued that it is inappropriate to liken transgendered athletes, who meet the IOC's requirements to compete at the Olympic Games, to athletes who use banned substances and methods, intentionally break rules and abuse TUEs to excel at sport. While many of the most pressing issues involved in transgendered athletes' participation in elite sport are similar to doping issues, there is a marked difference between using performance-enhancing drugs to increase athleticism and using the same drugs as part of a prescribed hormone therapy. However, doubts still linger over how fair it is for transgendered athletes to compete in their desired sex category and much of this controversy comes down to what counts as fair and unfair in sport. Therefore, despite the assurance from endocrinologists that transgendered athletes likely do not possess any identifiable competitive advantages over their competitors, allegations of unfairness will continue to surface periodically until irrefutable studies are complete.

Acknowledgements

The author is grateful to both Angela Schneider and Charlene Weaving for their constructive feedback and suggestions on an earlier version of this essay.

Notes

[1] Harper and Schneider, 'Oppression and Discrimination among Lesbian, Gay, Bisexuals, and Transgendered People and Communities', 243.

[2] Feldman and Bockting, 'Transgender Health', 25.

[3] From 1869–1923, North American physicians used the term 'sexualempfindung', which was coined by German physician Dr Westphal, to describe individuals who sought to live their lives as members of the opposite sex.

[4] Bullough, 'A Nineteenth Century Transsexual', 81.

[5] Raymond, *The Transsexual Empire*, xiii.

[6] Michel, Mormont and Legros, 'A Psycho-endocrinological Overview of Transsexualism', 365.

[7] Hood-Williams, 'Sexing the Athletes'.

[8] Morgan, 'Fair is Fair, Or Is It?'

[9] Ibid.

[10] Raymond, *The Transsexual Empire*, xiv.

[11] IOC, 'Press Release 18 May 2004 IOC approves consensus with regard to athletes who have changed sex', 1 [cited 02 July 2005]. Available from http://www.olympic.org/uk/news/media_centre/press_release_uk.asp?id = 855.

[12] Rona Marech, 'Olympics' transgender quandary: Debate rages on the fairness of new inclusion rule'. *San Francisco Chronicle* (14 June 2004), A1.

[13] Hui, 'An Olympic Victory for Transsexuals'.

[14] Billman, 'Michelle Raises Hell', 53. Interested readers can also access this article online at http://outside.away.com/outside/toc/200404.html

[15] Though several studies involving testosterone and oestrogen are described, these only represent the tip of the iceberg. Research on how testosterone and oestrogen function and what each actually does in the body has been on going since the identification of hormones and the emergence of endocrinology as a field of medicine. The studies mentioned shed light on the possible hormone-based advantages and disadvantages transgendered athletes may possess. However, the author does not claim to have exhausted all possible resources on the effects of oestrogen and testosterone on athletic performance.

[16] Simms, 'Transgender in Sport', 1.

[17] Roth, 'Transsexualism and the Sex-Change Operation', 7.

[18] Booth *et al.*, 'Testosterone, and Winning and Losing in Human Competition', 556.

[19] McCaul, Gladue and Joppa, 'Winning, Losing, Mood and Testosterone', 486.

[20] Jurimae and Jurimae, 'Responses of Blood Hormones to the Maximal Rowing Ergometer Test in College Rowers', 73.

[21] Rothman and Rothman, *The Pursuit of Perfection*, 131–67.

[22] Kivlighan, Granger and Booth, 'Gender Differences in Testosterone and Cortisol Response to Competition', 59.

[23] Ibid., 60.

[24] Slabbekoorn *et al.*, 'Activating Effects of Cross-sex Hormones on Cognitive Functioning', 423.

[25] Elbers *et al.*, 'Changes in Fat Cell Size', 1371.

[26] Gooren and Bunck, 'Transsexuals and Competitive Sports', 425.

[27] Ibid., 426.

[28] Ibid., 429.

[29] Raymond, *The Transsexual Empire*, 33.

[30] Meyer-Bahlburg, 'Hormones and Pyschosexual Differentiation', 696.

[31] Moore, Wisniewski and Dobbs, 'Endocrine Treatment of Transsexual People', 3469.

[32] Dr Lori Kohler as quoted in Marech, 'Olympics' Transgender Quandary', A1.

[33] Moore, Wisniewski and Dobbs, 'Endocrine Treatment of Transsexual People', 3468.

[34] Ibid., 3467.

[35] Ibid., 3469.

[36] Ibid., 3470.

[37] Values taken from WebMD Inc. articles on Oestrogen and Testosterone, available online at http://www.webmd.com.

[38] Turner *et al.*, 'Testosterone Increases Bone Mineral Density in Female-to-male Transsexuals', 560.

[39] World Anti-Doping Agency, *World Anti-Doping Code*, 16.

[40] van Kesteren *et al.*, 'Mortality and Morbidity in Transsexual Subjects treated with Cross-sex Hormones', 337.

[41] Feldman and Bockting, 'Transgender Health', 25–7.

[42] FINA, 'Rules and Regulations', available online at http://www.fina.org.

[43] Roster information, including current players' heights is available on the Canadian national basketball team's website, available online at http://www.basketball.ca.

[44] Moore, Wisniewski and Dobbs, 'Endocrine Treatment of Transsexual People', 3469.

[45] As quoted in Tuller, 'Pro Golfer goes Professional'.

[46] Sez, 'Transgender Olympians'.

[47] Ibid.

[48] Billman, 'Michelle Raises Hell', 53.

[49] Hui, 'An Olympic Victory for Transsexuals'.

[50] Baker, 'Cyclist lauds IOC Transgender Plan'.

[51] Marech, 'Olympics' Transgender Quandary', A1.

[52] Ibid.

[53] Meyer-Bahlburg, 'Hormones and Pyschosexual Differentiation', 693.

[54] Ibid.

[55] Reed, 'Transsexuals and European Human Rights Law', 50.

[56] Addelman, 'All-Inclusive Athens'.

[57] Tuller, 'Pro Golfer goes Professional'.

[58] Ibid.

[59] Feldman and Bockting, 'Transgender Health', 25.

[60] Kraus, 'Sports: Transgender Issues'. In www.glbtq.com 2002. [cited 20 June 2005]. Available from http://www.glbtq.com/arts/sports_transgender_issues.html.

[61] Hui, 'An Olympic Victory for Transsexuals'.

[62] Zeigler, quoting Pauline Park from New York Association for Gender Rights Advocacy, in Cyd Zeigler, 'USGA Welcomes Trans Golfers'. In *outsports.com*. [cited 03 June 2005]. Available from http://www.outsports.com/moresports/050325transgolf.htm.

[63] As cited by Marech, 'Olympics' Transgender Quandary', A1.

[64] Gooren and Bunck, 'Transsexuals and Competitive Sports', 425.

References

Addelman, Rebecca. "All-inclusive Athens." *The Varsity* (22 March 2004) [cited 25 June 2005]. Available from http://www.thevarsity.ca/media/paper285/news/ 2004/03/22/Feature/AllInclusive.Athens-637880.shtml?page=1.

Baker, Geoff. "Cyclist lauds IOC Transgender Plan." *Reuters* (28 Feb. 2004)

Billman, Jon. "Michelle Raises Hell: The hottest transgender talent in professional sports is making competition see pink." *Outside Magazine* (April 2004): 53.

Booth, A., G. Shelley, A. Mazur, G. Tharp, and R. Kittok. "Testosterone, and Winning and Losing in Human Competition." *Hormones and Behavior* 23, no. 4 (1989): 556–71.

Bullough, Vern L. "A Nineteenth Century Transsexual." *Archives of Sexual Behavior* 16, no. 1 (1987): 81–4.

Butcher, R.B. and A.J. Schneider. "Fair Play as Respect for the Game." *Journal of the Philosophy of Sport* 25 (1998): 1–20.

Elbers, J.M., S. de Jong, T. Teerlink, H. Asscheman, J.C. Seidell, and L.J. Gooren. "Changes in fat cell size and in vitro lipolytic activity of abdominal and gluteal adipocytes after a one-year cross-sex hormone administration in transsexuals." *Metabolism* 48, no. 11 (1999): 1371–7.

Feldman, Jamie and Walter Bockting. "Transgender Health." *Minnesota Medicine* 86, no. 7 (2003): 25–32.

Gooren, Louis J.G.C. and Mathijs C.M. Bunck. "Transsexuals and Competitive Sports." *European Journal of Endocrinology* 151, no. 4 (2004): 425–9.

Harper, G.W. and M. Schneider. "Oppression and Discrimination among Lesbian, Gay, Bisexuals, and Transgendered People and Communities: A Challenge for Community Psychology." *American Journal of Community Psychology* 31, no. 3–4 (2003): 243–52.

Hood-Williams, John. "Sexing the Athletes." *Sociology of Sport Journal* 12, no. 3 (1995): 290–305.

Hui, Stephen. "An Olympic Victory for Transsexuals." *Seven Oaks Magazine*, (10 Aug. 2004) [cited 03 July 2005]. Available from http://sevenoaksmag.com/features/25_olympic.html.

Jurimae, J. and T. Jurimae. "Responses of Blood Hormones to the Maximal Rowing Ergometer Test in College Rowers." *Journal of Sports Medicine and Physical Fitness* 41, no. 1 (2001): 73–7.

Kivlighan, Katie T., Douglas A. Granger, and Booth Alan. "Gender Differences in Testosterone and Cortisol Response to Competition." *Psychoneuroendocrinology*, 30, no. 1 (2005): 58–71.

McCaul, K.D., B.A. Gladue, and M. Joppa. "Winning, Losing, Mood and Testosterone." *Hormones and Behavior* 26, no. 4 (1992): 486–504.

Meyer-Bahlburg, Heino F. L. "Hormones and Pyschosexual Differentiation: Implications for the management of Intersexuality, Homosexuality and Transsexuality." *Clinics in Endocrinology and Metabolism* 11, no. 3 (1982): 681–702.

Michel, A., C. Mormont, and J.J. Legros. "A Psycho-endocrinological Overview of Transsexualism." *European Journal of Endocrinology* 145, no. 4 (2001): 365–76.

Moore, Eva, Amy Wisniewski, and Adrian Dobbs. "Endocrine Treatment of Transsexual People: A Review of Treatment Regimens, Outcomes, and Adverse Effects." *The Journal of Clinical Endocrinology and Metabolism* 88, 8 (2003): 3467–73.

Morgan, William J. "Fair is Fair, Or Is It?: A Moral Consideration of the Doping Wars in American Sport." *Sport in Society* 9, no. 2 (2006): 177–198.

Raymond, Janice G. *The Transsexual Empire*. Boston: Beacon Press, 1979.

Reed, Robert. "Transsexuals and European Human Rights Law." *The Journal of Homosexuality* 48, no. 3 (2004): 49–90.

Roth, Martin. "Transsexualism and the Sex-Change Operation: A Contemporary Medicolegal and Social Problem." *Medicolegal Journal* 49, no. 1 (1981): 5–19.

Rothman Sheila M. and David J. Rothman. *The Pursuit of Perfection: The Promises and Perils of Medical Enhancement*. New York: Random House, 2003.

Schneider, A.J. and R.B. Butcher. *The Ethical Rationale for Drug-Free Sport*. Ottawa: Canadian Centre for Drug-Free Sport, 1993.

Sez, G. "Transgender Olympians." In *Eros Guide San Francisco* [cited 06 June 2005]. Available from http://www.eros-guide.com/articles/2004-06-01/transolympics/.

Simms, Debbie. "Transgender in Sport." In *Australian Sports Commission Reports*. [cited 20 June 2005]. Available from http://www.activeaustralia.org/women/transgender.htm.

Slabbekoorn, D., S.H. van Goozen, J. Megens, L.J. Gooren, and P.T. Cohen-Kettenis. "Activating Effects of Cross-sex Hormones on Cognitive Functioning: A Study of Short-term and Long-term Hormone Effects in Transsexuals." *Pyschoneuroendocrinology* 24, no. 4 (1999): 423–7.

Tuller, David. "Pro Golfer goes Professional." In *Slate Medical Examiner* (20 Sept. 2005). [cited 28 September 2005]. Available from http://slate.msn.com/id/2126602/?nav=ais.

Turner, A., T.C. Chen, T.W. Barber, A.O. Malabanan, M.F. Holick, and V. Tangpricha. "Testosterone Increases Bone Mineral Density in Female-to-male Transsexuals: A Case Series of 15 Subjects." *Clinical Endocrinology* 61, no. 5 (2004): 560–6.

van Kesteren, P.J., H. Asscheman, J.A. Megens, and L. Gooren. "Mortality and Morbidity in Transsexual Subjects Treated with Cross-sex Hormones." *Clinical Endocrinology* 47, no. 3 (1997): 337–42.

World Anti-Doping Agency. *World Anti-Doping Code*. Montréal: World Anti-Doping Agency, 2003.

Creating a Corporate Anti-doping Culture: The Role of Bulgarian Sports Governing Bodies

Vassil Girginov

Introduction

'Doping is a battle which can never be won', stated Jacques Rogge, President of the International Olympic Committee (IOC), in 2003 on a visit to Sofia marking the 80th anniversary of the Bulgarian Olympic Committee (BOC). The IOC president did not just make a gloomy prediction; rather, he addressed the amount of outstanding work that still needs to be done by sport organizations, educational establishments, researchers and anti-doping enforcement agencies in this regard. This would allow the development of a corporate anti-doping culture that would align the efforts of international agencies with those of national sport governing bodies and athletes themselves.

The fight against doping in modern sport encompasses a number of practices and institutions that have evolved over the past 40 years. These practices are enshrined in various codes and symbols, which constitute an inseparable part of the culture of sport organizations. Studies on the culture of sport organizations are still rare. This holds particularly true for studies dealing with the role of the sport governing body (SGB) in creating a corporate anti-doping culture. Consistent efforts of the international and national sporting and political communities and ongoing media campaigns have transformed the drug issue, from the early concerns with testing, to a matter of social and legal responsibility. It has become a norm for SGBs to have an anti-doping policy. This, however, does not mean that an organization and its members have internalized the values of the anti-doping code and have started to live up to its expectations.

This essay addresses the largely unexplored issue of national sports governing bodies' role in interpreting and promoting an anti-doping culture that would ensure the success of the policies and various measures aimed at eliminating the use of prohibited performance-enhancing practices in sport. It draws on Garrett Morgan's notion of enactment of culture.[1] Borrowing from Karl Weick, Morgan proposed that organizations enact their environments as people assign patterns of meaning and significance to the world in which they live. He argued that, 'we must attempt to understand culture as an ongoing, proactive process of reality construction'.[2] This view of culture, according to Morgan, 'has enormous implications for how we understand organizations as cultural phenomena, for it emphasizes that we must root our understanding of organizations in the processes that produce systems of shared meaning'.[3]

A similar view of sport organizations as an enactment of shared reality urges us to redefine the role of sport managers and officials and presents them as reality constructors. Thus, they are seen as agents exercising important influences on an organization's culture. It follows that sport organizations' structures, rules, policies and symbols perform an interpretative function, because they act as primary points of reference for the way people think about, and make sense of, the context in which they work.

Morgan proposed eight such images or metaphors of organization, including: organizations as machines, organisms, brains, cultures, political systems, psychic prisons, flux and transformation and as instruments of domination.[4] While remaining conscious about the interplay between those eight metaphors, this essay employs the metaphor of sport organizations as cultures to develop an understanding of the challenges faced by the international sport movement in endorsing a global anti-doping policy. More specifically, it explores the interpretations of the World Anti-Doping Code (WADC) using, as a case in point, the Bulgarian Weightlifting Federation (BWF), one of the leading schools in this sport in the world.

In the words of Morgan, 'modern organizations are sustained by belief systems that emphasize the importance of rationality, and their legitimacy in the public eye usually depends on their ability to demonstrate rationality and objectivity in action'.[5] This is what SGBs try to demonstrate when they sign on to the WADC, which they do for two main reasons: first, because they are genuinely concerned about the integrity of sport, and second, because failing to do so would result in public disapproval, withdrawal of funding and eventual suspension from national or international sport movements. As this essay demonstrates, the practices of SGBs vary according to their belief systems, history and traditions in certain sports. The culture metaphor offers four major strengths as it: (i) directs attention to the symbolic significance of almost every aspect of organizational life; (ii) shows how organization ultimately rests in shared systems of meaning, hence in the actions and interpretative schemes that create and recreate meaning; (iii) encourages us to recognize that the relations between an organization and its environment are also socially constructed; and (iv) makes a contribution to our understanding of organizational change.[6] Employing a culture metaphor to study SGBs' interpretations of anti-doping policy helps us better understand some of the major challenges in implementing the WADC. These four metaphors will be examined in turn, but before we do that it is important first to go beyond the moral debate about the WADC and to consider it in an organizational context and as an instrument of cultural change.

The Organizational Context of Doping and its Enactment by Sport Governing Bodies

Modern sports are highly organized, specialized, bureaucratic, competitive and record-oriented enterprises.[7] There is no such thing as an independent, versatile all-powerful athlete. The process of becoming an elite athlete involves skilful coordination of the work of various organizations including: clubs; sport governing bodies at national and international levels; multi-disciplinary research; and technical agencies. This is an organizational process that, in most instances, requires full-time professional management. Crucial in this process is the role of SGBs at the national level. They are responsible for administrating all aspects of different sports in various countries, for representing them internationally, but even more importantly, for promoting sound practices that represent the sites where anti-doping dispositions could be created. A number of high-profile enquiries into the use of doping in sport such as those conducted by Dubin (Canada), Black (Australia), Coni and Jacobs (Britain) have criticized SGBs precisely for failing to create those dispositions. In a response to the attack on the IOC in the Dubin Report, Michelle Verdier, the press spokeswoman for the IOC, echoed clearly this view: 'without the IOC the Ben Johnson affair in Seoul would never have come to light. It was the first body to take the problem of drugs in sport, and remember the IOC only runs the Games for a fortnight every four years. Who has the control of the competitors for the rest of the time?'[8]

The above situation, however, presents the IOC and the World Anti-Doping Agency (WADA) with a problem in regard to universality and particularity. The general organizational difficulty in both cases is how they are to operate at a global (universal) level whilst such apparently intractable differences exist at the particular (local) level. Borrowing from Tayeb's insightful distinction between *etics* (universals as viewed from afar) and *emics* (locally meaningful elements) aspects of organizations,[9] it could be suggested that the World Anti Doping Code would be the *etics,* whereas the way these are interpreted by SGBs would be the *emics* of anti-doping culture. Sports on the Olympic programme can be seen as universal in that they enjoy worldwide popularity and all participants play them according to the same rules. But the cultural meaning of each sport and the interpretation of its rules vary between countries. When taken out of their cultural context even legal matters pale into insignificance. Like Olympism, the World Anti Doping Code seeks to be universal in promoting the values of respect, solidarity, fair play, multiculturalism, et cetera in sport. This is a quite specific set of values, which, as Parry argued, also requires differential interpretation in different cultures,[10] that is, stated in general terms whilst interpreted in the particular. In his view there are different conceptions of Olympism that will interpret the general concept in such a way as to bring it to real life in a particular context. Since the WADC represents a set of universal Olympic values, it follows that different cultures will approach it and prioritise its implementation differently. William Morgan's critical remarks in this volume, that the current anti-doping strategy (*emics*) of the US Anti-Doping Agency undermines the moral principles of fair play (*etics*), illustrate the point.

Therefore, our understanding of the nature of doping in sport will inform our interpretations of the rules that govern its policies of deterrence and prevention. As Garrett Morgan maintained, 'the point is that the norms operating in different situations have to be invoked and defined in the light of our understanding of the context. We implicitly make many decisions and assumptions about a situation before any norm or rule is applied.'[11]

Houlihan documented the evolution of the anti-doping policy and the role of the Council of Europe, the IOC and international sport organizations.[12] He identified five policy focuses pertinent to the 1950s, 1960s, 1970s, 1980s and the 1990s, respectively. Two important interrelated strands of the policy focus that emerged only recently concern 'the steady shift from the athlete to the athlete's entourage and the increasingly common debate as to whether the athlete was best seen as the villain, victim or co-conspirator' and 'the degree to which the domestic governing body should be held responsible for the drug abuse of its member'.[13]

The shift in the focus of the world anti-doping policy from athletes to organizations marks an important cultural orientation, which recognizes the mutually constructive relation between the individual and the group, and further reinforces the organizational context of the issue. This is because a similar concern about the role of the collective begs the question of what SGBs (the collective) have done do help their individual members (the athletes and officials) develop the appropriate attitudes needed to nurture an anti-doping culture. The role of SGBs is not confined to establishing rules but also to promoting education that helps athletes acquire the right dispositions. As Girginov and Parry observe, 'it is by participating in a practice (and by practising its skills and procedures) that one begins to understand its standards and excellences, and the virtues required for successful participation'.[14]

The individual-group dichotomy reflects a fundamental cultural value tension that underpins the behaviours of members of different cultures. Hampden-Turner and Trompenaars' Dilemma theory[15] provides a stimulating account of the nature of this management dilemma and a strategy for its resolution. For example, if we believe that the resourceful individual comes before society, then our thinking and behaviours are likely to run like this: 'concentrate on your own interest and you will automatically serve your members and society better, which in turn will let you concentrate on your interests', and the circle is complete. Conversely, if we put society first, our thinking and behaviour are likely to follow the opposite logic: 'serve your members and society to the best of your ability and you will automatically achieve your own personal goals, which in turn will let you serve the society',[16] and the circle again is complete. Either way of approaching management will have a profound effect on how an organization is run, its time horizon, how its performance is measured or how its people are rewarded. Hence, the individual will try to use the collective to achieve greater personal success. In contrast, the group will try to promote a social discourse that nurtures a collective spirit shared by its members. This circular type of thinking about culture is different from Hofstede's linear view, which sees it as opposites on a bipolar axe.[17] Hickson and Pugh,[18] Morden[19] and Hampden-Turner and Trompenaars[20] have discussed the role of cultural values in making management decisions In a rare study Girginov, Papadimitriou and D'Amico demonstrated the link between culture and sport managers' behaviours.[21] Considering the WADC not only as a set of rules to be followed by those concerned, but also as an instrument for shaping the organizational context of SGBs, allows one to better understand the mutually constructive relations between athletes, managers and organizations.

The World Anti-Doping Code as an Instrument of Cultural Change

From an organizational point of view the World Anti-Doping Code (WADC) can be seen as an attempt to influence the thinking and behaviours of sport governing bodies. Its two main purposes '(i) to protect the Athletes' right to participate in doping-free sport and thus promote health, fairness and equality for Athletes worldwide, and (ii) to ensure harmonized, coordinated and effective anti-doping programmes at the international and national level with regard to detection, deterrence and prevention of doping'[22] are akin to an organization's mission statement as they set out the WADC's main purpose, vision of the future and the outcomes it is striving to achieve. SGBs' mission statements provide a frame within which various organizational activities can happen. These are often referred to in organizational literature as the organization's 'philosophy' or 'set of values'. As such, the WADC, developed in 2003, is not qualitatively different from a number of fashionable managerial initiatives currently in operation in different countries (for example, public-voluntary-private partnerships in sports development, benchmarking, Quest, or market orientation) aiming at improving the performance of SGBs. Its implicit aims are to create a kind of 'cultural revolution', to use Morgan's expression, which would replace the old way of organizational thinking about doping and put the well being of the athlete and the integrity of sport as its top priorities. It is not a coincidence that the word 'Athlete' appears in capital letter in WADC's declared purposes.

It took the international sporting and political community nearly 40 years to arrive at this understanding of a doping policy, which in Europe has undergone a qualitative transformation from a charter to a governmental convention.[23] The emphasis of the WADC is on policy implementation, which places managers and SGBs at the heart of the enterprise. The WADC's aspirations to create a new moral order in elite sport, or new forms of organization and management, amount to creating a new corporate culture. Conceptually it builds on the notion of Olympism as a universal philosophy, while empirically on the findings of a number of inquiries into doping in various countries, which suggests the existence of a widespread drug culture. The figures speak for themselves – 25 per cent of the 1988 Australian Olympic track and field squad had taken, or were taking performance enhancing drugs;[24] 83,000 Canadian children between the ages of 11 and 18 have used anabolic steroids, and anabolic steroids are now the third most popular drug offered to children in the UK.[25]

The WADC's aspirations also represent a challenge to the organizational culture of SGBs and governments alike around the world because they involve the creation of shared systems of meaning that are accepted, internalised and acted on at every level of an organization. It is worth reminding ourselves that 70 per cent of the firms that set off on this new path of cultural change were unsuccessful, largely because they failed to replace the bureaucratic logic governing the old mode of operation.[26] Earlier, Morgan warned that 'mission statements may be important', but certainly are not sufficient to 'get people on the same wavelength', and that 'it is one thing for top management to develop a sense of vision. It is quite another to communicate that vision in an accountable manner so that the vision becomes a reality.'[27] A number of studies provide support for this view: Smith demonstrated for various sectors in North America that only 19 per cent of the culture efforts were rated as breakthrough;[28] Troy found a 32 per cent change in a group of 166 North American and European companies;[29] Carr *et al.* noted a 10 per cent success rate in managing the change process,[30] while Collins observed similar incremental change in the field of leisure services in England.[31]

It should be noted that while the members of a particular group or SGB share similar cultural values, it would appear that a manager's position in an organization has an impact on how they approach and interpret particular policies. Moreover, organizational culture is a pluralistic concept, which, as Martin argued, involves the three competing perspectives of integration, differentiation and fragmentation that are always simultaneously present in organizations.[32] Each represents a particular managerial horizon, where the integrative perspective concentrates on organization-wide consistency, the differentiation perspective focuses on dichotomous sub-cultural conflicts, and the fragmentation perspective views organizations as fluid and characterized by ambiguity, complexity and a multiplicity of interpretations. In Martin's view, the key point is that these three perspectives are not just an intellectual position. Rather, they have political implications because, for example, a concentration on the integration perspective means ignoring the ambiguities and complexity of real life as experienced by managers at lower levels of an organizational hierarchy. Harris and Ogbonna provided empirical evidence for Martin's claim that the nature of hierarchical position shapes and conditions organizational members' perspectives on culture.[33]

It would be possible, therefore, to expect that similar issues would emerge in the formulation and implementation of the WADC. While the WADA is interested in achieving harmonization of its policy across all SGBs (that is, integrative perspective), SGBs would be concerned with the interpretation of the code in a particular cultural context (that is, differentiation perspective), and coaches and athletes would emphasize the importance of reality in dealing with doping on a daily basis (a fragmented perspective). This perspective is consistent with the construction of the roles and responsibilities of international and national SGBs, where both the IOC and the IWF (International Weightlifting Federation) have the right to withhold funding to, and sanction membership of, national SGBs who are not in compliance with the WADC. Yet the ultimate responsibility for drug violations, or the so-called strict liability principle, stipulates that athletes have to be solely and legally responsible for what they consume. The next four sections deal with four strengths of the culture metaphor identified earlier using the Bulgarian Weightlifting Federation (BWF) as a case in point.

The Symbolic Significance of Organizational Life

This aspect of culture metaphor focuses on the human side of the organization. It may include elements of a SGB's life, such as its structure, hierarchy, organizational routines and rules. The BWF was established in 1963 and soon after laid down the foundations of what would become a world-leading model of excellence. At the heart of this model of elite athletes' development was the idea of a systematic programme of high intensity and volume including three training sessions a day. A typical working day for a weightlifter started at 8.00a.m. and finished after midnight with an average amount of weights lifted between 30–40 tones. Pivotal to this model was a national team, and those who were selected would follow this routine for 11 months a year with only four weeks off training and competition. The success of the national team, therefore, became crucial for the well-being of the BWF. This necessitated putting in place a whole structure of talent identification and nurturing, organizationally underpinned by the tenets of the systems approach, with its preoccupation with the well-being of the system.[34]

As a result, between 1956 and 1988, weightlifting established itself as the most successful Bulgarian sport, with 24 Olympic medals earned including 10 titles and 561 world records.[35] However, the BWF also set an unenviable record of being the only SGB whose athletes were stripped of their Olympic titles four times: in 1976, 1988 and 2000. They also set a precedent at the World championships in 2003 in Vancouver when three athletes were banned from participation before the tournament started, allegedly for manipulating their earlier drug tests.

Structurally, the management of the BWF has not changed substantially over the years, despite recent political and economic turmoil in Bulgaria. A 1999 decision of the BWF's General Assembly stipulated that the EB (Executive Board) should include only experts, which makes it an exclusive SGB where 'outsiders' are not welcome. The voluntary base of the BWF has always been very limited, numbering less than 100 volunteers. A similar organizational make-up ensures a great deal of consistency in views and practices and contributes to the usual reluctance to change. For example, the current leadership of the BWF includes former athletes turned national coaches and top administrators. The BWF is heavily dependent on government subsidies. It is the most funded SGB in Bulgaria with shares ranging from 9 per cent to 14 per cent of the total state subsidy for all Olympic sports. Dunning and Waddington offered an interesting figuration for understanding the relationship between the 'established' and the 'outsiders' in drug taking in sport. In their analysis, 'outsiders', labelled as 'drug-users', constitute a threat to the 'moral order of the established', that is, the clean.[36] If the same logic is applied to the operations of the BWF, those with no weightlifting background should be labelled 'outsiders', and dealing with them would always be problematic.

As the first aspect of culture metaphor demonstrates, the BWF is an exclusive and self-recruiting organization with a well-defined hierarchy where the key positions appear to be those of the national coach and the two top managers, the president and the secretary general. Top managers inevitably come to represent their organizations, thus what they say and do have far-reaching implications in terms of symbolic and practical value. It follows that outside views as to how the BWF should conduct its business are not seen as credible, as they come from non-experts, and are thus not taken seriously or followed up. In this type of organization, innovations are difficult to introduce if the top management does not support them even if the initiative comes from the WADA, the ultimate authority in doping matters.

Sport Organizations as Systems of Shared Meaning

The second aspect of culture metaphor shows how the organization of SGBs rests in shared systems of meaning. This emphasizes the actions and interpretative schemes that create and recreate meaning. It sensitizes us to the importance of various means of shaping organizational activity by influencing its ideologies, beliefs, norms and other practice-guiding organized actions. As Morgan argues, 'since the 1980s there has been growing realization that the fundamental task facing the leaders and managers rests in creating appropriate systems of shared meaning that can mobilize the efforts of people in pursuit of desired aims and objectives. The two key words here are *"appropriate"* and *"shared"'* (our emphasis).[37]

The conceptual orientation of the BWF subscribes to the ideology of 'narrow elitism', characterized by its preoccupation with the national team instead of the whole process of sports development. Key features of this ideology are its infallible drive to produce the best results and its close relations with the state's official political line. Most elite sports systems in the world are heavily subsidised by the state, but this funding, as for the BWF, is contingent upon the delivery of medals.[38] The constant supply of positive doping tests has inevitably undermined the credibility of the BWF. However, it is determined to demonstrate that it is the best weightlifting school in the world, as a publication marking the over 50 years of organized weightlifting in Bulgaria maintains.[39]

The apparent contradiction between the BWF's image of the best school in the world and its unenviable doping record could be explained with the logic of the same ideology of elitism. It was eloquently articulated by the former Secretary General of the BWF (1994–2004), national coach (1992–94) and two-time Olympic champion (1972, 1976), Norair Nurikian. We asked him what he would say to an audience of parents who would like their children to take up weightlifting but have concerns over the BWF's doping record, to which he replied: 'I've been asked this question many times and the only possible answer I've always given is this: the Belgians and the Swiss don't get caught with drugs because they don't have weightlifters. Those who get caught are the Russians, the Chinese, us and all other great in this sport.' We persisted and asked him to elaborate further why that was the case. His answer was:

> Well ... it is all down to the strive to be the best ... I don't like the word doping. Many people tend to think that 'they lift because they take drugs'. This is not true. Athletes take some stimulants, but because we are lagging well behind the advances in medicine ... well, there are many cutting edge drugs that are very clean but those cost hundred times more. So, because we are falling behind we use some dated things while the technologies are highly advanced and keep advancing. With all due respect, but as we also happen to know a few things, take the American athletes for example. How would they be able to run so incredibly – with scotch and lemonade? No way![40]

It would not be an unsubstantiated assumption to claim that everybody in the BWF shares this view. But it is a well-established belief that taking stimulants is an inseparable part of elite sport. It is seen as a game everybody plays, in which getting caught is an acceptable outcome though unsought and undesirable as it might be. Hence, the belief becomes 'appropriate' and is 'shared' by organizational members. Compare this logic to the one promoted in the WADC. The peculiarity of this aspect of culture metaphor is that beliefs, norms and social practices are self-organizing and have the capacity to reproduce themselves, and over time become not only points of reference, but valuable resources as well. The BWF's most precious resource has always been the 'know-how' or the methods of selection and training. This explains why the national head coach was spared after the damning 1988 Olympics drug scandal (we return to this informative incident below), although it was common knowledge that he was the main culprit. Since he took over the national team in 1968, he has been responsible for introducing a highly centralized and uniform system of training for all age groups.

His system epitomizes a range of values, norms and practices, which were supposed to be shared and followed by everybody. No detours were allowed and those who dared to question the rules were quickly dealt with. It is a self-perpetuated system, as it was responsible for producing a myriad of world and Olympic champions. Those people now represent a valuable symbolic and tangible capital. What is more, they appear as bearers of a specific organizational culture as they work as coaches with the national teams of over 20 countries around the world. Several of those coaches have already produced Olympic and world champions for various countries. This, of course, does not automatically make them 'drug-ambassadors'. However, if we assume that they are a product of the kinds of culture described above and have been schooled in these methods, the suspicion that they would employ questionable means to achieve results will always linger.

Sport Organizations and their Environment

This aspect of the culture metaphor recognizes that the relationship between a SGB and its environment are socially constructed and that they are extensions of those involved. As Morgan put it: 'organizations are always attempting to achieve a form of self-referential closure in relation to their environments, enacting their environments as extensions of their own identity'.[41] A similar understanding will have profound implications for SGBs' strategic management, which is also a product of cultural interpretations. Higgins and Mcallister argue that 'one of the real keys to achieving the sought after strategic performance is the management of the cultural artefacts that relate to the values and norms pertinent to the strategic change'.[42] Failing to achieve this management of artefacts (myths, sagas, heroes, language and rituals about an organization) creates barriers in an organization's interaction with its environment.

Of particular relevance for this analysis are the relations between the BWF and the state on one hand, and the BWF, the IOC and the International Weightlifting Federation (IWF), on the other. While the BWF is ideologically and financially dependent on the state, it is the interplay between the latter three organizations that determines, to a large extent, the standing of the sport nationally and internationally. Three related incidents illustrate this relationship. First, at the 1976 Montreal Olympics, one Bulgarian weightlifter tested positive for performance-enhancing drug use and was stripped of his title. Neither the state nor the media showed any interest in this case. There were no hearings, investigations or punishments. The lack of reaction, according to the former BWF President (1985–88, vice-president 1975–85, and IWF vice-president 1984–92), was due to two main factors related to organizational environment. Firstly, Bulgaria was a world champion in 1974 and it would have been inappropriate to use an isolated case to question the practices of this SGB. Secondly, at the time there was no agreement about the list of prohibited substances between the IOC and the IWF, which created confusion for many SGBs.[43] If an organization's practices are not externally scrutinized and internally reviewed there would be no correction to its own image.

Second, at the 1988 Seoul Olympic Games, two Bulgarian weightlifters tested positive for drugs (with spuriously high dosage of phurosemid – a class D prohibited substance – in their urine samples) and lost their medals. This urged the management to withdraw the team from participation half way through the competition. This time, the media got heavily involved and kept the story on the top of the public agenda for several weeks. As a result, the entire BWF's Executive Board resigned. Interestingly, as mentioned above, the head coach, who is widely regarded as 'the architect of weightlifting', was spared. A similar interpretation of the responsibilities of a SGB and its members appears to be at odds with any organizational standard. However, it supports Morgan's assertion that many of the problems organizations encounter in dealing with their environments are intimately connected to the kind of identity they are trying to maintain.[44] This identity reflects also the BWF's relations with the IWF and the IOC. It is widely known that before the 1988 Games the Bulgarian team set a goal of seven Olympic titles plus a win in the team competition.

The IWF did not perceive that as a 'healthy' development for the sport of weightlifting and tried to pressure the BWF to reconsider and reduce its target to two titles. The BWF refused to back down and, after a hugely damaging scandal that affected the whole sport, the Bulgarian weightlifters finished the competition with only two titles. Allegedly, after the tournament, a highly ranked IWF official told the national team representatives, 'why didn't you listen to what we offered you, so we had to have all these circuses'.[45] We should not forget that behind the scandal there is the personal drama of those involved. The incident ruined the life of one of the banned athletes who ended up in prison for rape and assault. Denham's study on the enactment of drug policy in Major League Baseball[46] provides a similar example of the relations between a SGB, the state and the media in an American context. He demonstrated how the media actively promoted a culture of no-tolerance to the lack of out-of-competition testing, which MLB eventually adopted.

Third, the case of the 2003 World championships in Vancouver, where quotas for the 2004 Athens Olympics were to be contested, set a precedent in the world of weightlifting. A few days before the championships, without consulting the EB and without any evidence, the president of the IWF single-handedly suspended three Bulgarian athletes from participating, not on the ground of positive test results, but for allegedly manipulating their doping samples. The decision triggered a spiral of mutual accusations, threats and even a physical assault on the IWF president by his BWF counterpart. The Bulgarian Sports Ministry stood firmly behind the team and threatened to sue the IWF for violating its own code of conduct. Shortly after that, however, the BWF made a u-turn and offered a number of privileges to the athletes concerned if they would drop their charges against the IWF. This kind of behaviour is indicative of the complexity involved in the relationship between a SGB and its environment, and that these relations are constantly being constructed and negotiated. In regard to the case, the former BWF's president (1985–88) remarked: 'this is number one sport in the country. The Ministry of Sport either feel involved in what has happened or they feel they've been right and should fight till the end.'[47]

Historically the IWF-BWF nexus has always been of particular importance. This nexus provided three key benefits: domestic and international legitimacy, support and influence in the world weightlifting community. After 1988, however, those links began to strain due to concerns over athletes' doping records. Bulgarian weightlifters are no longer seen as a model to be emulated, but are instead considered a liability to the IWF as at the past eight Olympic Games seven Bulgarian weightlifters, including four Olympic champions, have been stripped of their medals for using banned substances. By extension, high profile doping scandals like these made international weightlifting a liability for the image of the Olympics, as the Seoul incident led the then IOC vice-president, Dick Pound, to publicly call for dropping weightlifting from the Olympic programme.

The IWF had to appear to be doing something to fix the problem, and after the 2000 Sydney Games the federation threatened to suspend the Bulgarian national team from participating in international competitions for five years. In an attempt to appease the situation in 2003, the IWF president was invited to Bulgaria and was met by the Prime Minister and top sport officials who awarded him an honorary Doctorate from the National Sports Academy. The IOC Programme Commission Report at the 117th Session of the organization provided a thorough audit of the standing of all sports and their contributions to the Games. The ultimate purpose of this exercise was to identify 'vulnerable' sports that could become candidates for deletion from the Olympic programme. According to the report, weightlifting's doping profile of 27 (out of 5,347 tests for a total of 0.5 per cent) positive drug tests in 2003 compares well with the other major drug violators, such as swimming with 19 (out of 9,270 or 0.2 per cent), athletics with 120 (out of 18,876 or 0.64 per cent) and cycling with 61(out of 12,352 or 0.49 per cent) violations.[48]

Those results by no means reflect the true picture of the drug problem in sport, but at least offer some comfort to the leaders of national and international weightlifting federations. They serve also as a warning to other SGBs that their doping image has to be carefully managed or they too may face expulsion from the Olympic Games programme. In this process, SGBs have to both promote their own identities and accommodate other parties' views. By doing that they assert an important facet of organizational culture that links an organization's beliefs and ideas about who they are and what they are trying to do with the environment in which they operate. The problem remains that nobody ever explained what actually happened in the three cases discussed above and who should take responsibility for what in each incident. The way the Vancouver case was framed by the media, state officials and the BWF itself promoted a discourse of 'a world conspiracy against the best in the world'. For example, several statements by the former sport minister, Vassil Ivanov, made the headlines: 'we are going to sue the International Weightlifting Federation for US$10 million', and 'I trust unreservedly our athletes'.[49] This kind of discourse diverts attention away from the efforts required to create a corporate culture, which is based on the idea of cooperation and shared meanings.

Culture and Organizational Change

The final culture metaphor contributes to our understanding of organizational change. This issue is central to an analysis of doping culture as it directs attention to the values and images that are to guide SGBs' actions. As Morgan maintains: 'since organization ultimately resides in the heads of the people involved, effective organizational change always implies cultural change'.[50] Changing a SGB's policy, rules and procedures is not enough to appreciate how patterns of culture shape day-to-day action. SGBs also have to find ways of managing the new anti-doping culture.

Different approaches addressing the need to change the doping culture have been proposed, and some of them directly challenge WADA's mission. Dawson saw harm minimization and education as the way forward,[51] while Savulescu, Foddy and Clayton, amongst others, advocate legalizing performance-enhancing drugs.[52] Houlihan's examination of compliance in international anti-doping policy criticized WADC's over-reliance on sanctions and proposed an alternative strategy of system design. As he argued, 'within this perspective a central focus is on the capacity – administrative, economic, legal and political – of governments to ensure the compliance of public and private actors'.[53] This management approach offers some useful insights into SGBs' behaviour, but it tends to consider capacity as a system (legal, administrative and financial) and not as a cultural issue. A more comprehensive view is taken by Donovan *et al.*, who employed a behavioural science perspective to develop a conceptual framework for achieving performance-enhancing drug compliance in sport.[54] Despite its merits, however, the emphasis of this approach is on the behaviour of the athlete and largely fails to address the role of SGBs as custodians of the key values that form athletes' behaviour.

It should be noted that the first three aspects of the culture metaphor are closely related to the notion of organizational change. We have seen that organizations develop and maintain an image of themselves, which they try to extend to the environment in which they operate. A change in doping culture implies re-evaluation of some of those fundamental values and beliefs on which the image is based. A series of organizational events following the poor performance of Bulgarian weightlifters at the 2004 Athens Olympic Games could be seen as a confirmation of the assertion made above that the main problem of the BWF is connected to the identity of the best weightlifting school in the world which it is trying to maintain. Conscious of that, the former president of the BWF (2000–2004), world champion (1979, 1981, 1982) and a failed top contestant for a new term in office, Anton Kodjabashev, publicly stated after the 2004 Games that 'the architect of Bulgarian weightlifting has achieved successes but those were entirely due to doping and the chemistry'.[55] The words appear consistent with actions as two years earlier he fired the head coach. It is not clear if this statement reflects what a SGB leader really thinks or if it was used as a pre-election gimmick to silence the opposition supporting the former head coach. This situation was used by a group of 26 clubs who got behind one of the victims of Vancouver 2003 and put forward his candidature for president. He promoted the idea of an athlete centred SGB, but failed to win. None of the contenders for the leadership position, however, clearly articulated what should be done to change the tarnished image of this sport or how to improve its reputation. The election results suggest that the BWF is going to follow a policy pretty much in line with what it has been doing best in the past.

The challenge of changing the doping culture is growing significantly with the rising number of governments and sport organizations who have signed the WADC. In 2003, 93 governments signed the Copenhagen Declaration on doping that served as a blueprint for the WADC. In May 2005, 166 governments had endorsed the Code and by mid-August that number had increased to 173. The WADC of the WADA promotes a kind of corporate culture that rests in distinctive capacities or incapacities built into the attitudes and behaviours of the SGBs worldwide. The four culture metaphors employed by this analysis help shed new light on this mutually constructive relationship. They emphasize the symbolic significance of organizational life, how organizations create systems of shared meaning, the construction of the relations between an organization and its environment, and how change occurs in organizations. As the case of the BWF demonstrates, in order to understand the nature of the anti-doping environment in which it is supposed to operate, it has to try to understand itself as an organization. Morgan calls organizations that see themselves as discrete entities fighting for survival in a hostile world 'egocentric'. They have a relatively fixed notion of who they are and are determined to sustain that identity at all costs. A similar view motivates a SGB to overemphasize its importance while neglecting the significance of the wider system of anti-doping relations in which it exists. This system includes sports organizations, national governments, educational establishments, research institutions, individuals, and of course, international cooperation. While an acceptable level of agreement at the level of the *etics* of doping (universal approval of WADC) has been achieved, the real challenge to corporate anti-doping culture remains getting the *emics* (SGBs' practices) in line with the *etics*.

Notes

[1] Morgan, *Images of Organization*.
[2] Ibid., 141.
[3] Ibid.
[4] Ibid.
[5] Ibid., 146.
[6] Ibid., 146–50.
[7] Guttman, *From Record to Ritual*.

[8]   As cited in Goodbody, 'Drugs Enquiry Criticises Governing Bodies', 5.

[9]   Tayeb, 'Organisations and National Culture', 429–46.

[10] Parry, 'Sport, Universals and Multiculturalism'.

[11] Morgan, *Images of Organization*, 140.

[12] Houlihan, *Dying to Win*.

[13] Ibid., 171.

[14] Girginov and Parry, *The Olympic Games Explained*, 13.

[15] Hampden-Turner and Trompenaars, *The Seven Cultures of Capitalism*.

[16] Ibid.

[17] Hofstede, *Culture Consequences*.

[18] Hickson, and Pugh, *Management Worldwide*.

[19] Morden, 'Models of National Cultures – A Management Review', 19–44.

[20] Hampden-Turner and Trompenaars, *Building Cross-cultural Competence*.

[21] Girginov, Papadimitriou and D'Amico, *Cultural Orientations of Sport Managers*.

[22] World Anti-Doping Agency, *World Anti-Doping Code*, 1.

[23] Council of Europe, *European Anti-Doping Convention*.

[24] Data from Dawson, 'The War on Drugs', 1–3.

[25] Data from Dawson, 'Drugs in Sport – the Role of the Physician', 55–61.

[26] Data from Morgan, *Images of Organization*, 142.

[27] Morgan, *Riding the Waves of Change*, 49.

[28] Smith, 'Changing an Organisation's Culture', 249–61.

[29] Troy, *Change Management*.

[30] Carr, Hard and Trahant, *Managing the Change Process*.

[31] Collins, 'Does a new Philosophy Change the Structure?', 204–16.

[32] Martin, *Cultures in Organisations: ThreePperspectives*.

[33] Harris and Ogbonna, 'A Three-perspective Approach to Understanding Culture in Retail Organisations', 104–23.

[34] For an account of the system approach to the management of sport organizations see Bobev *et al.*, *Organization and management of physical culture* (in Bulgarian), and P. Chelladurai, *Managing Organizations for Sport and Physical Activity: A Systems Perspective* (in English).

[35] Dimitrov, *Vdiganeto na tezesti v Bulgaria: Ocertchi po istoria* (Weightlifting in Bulgaria: Sketches on History), part 2.

[36] Dunning and Waddington, 'Sport as Drug and Drugs in Sport', 352.

[37] Morgan, *Images of Organization*, 147.

[38] See, for example, Oakley and Green, 'The Production of Olympic Champions: International Perspectives on Elite Sport Development System', 83–106; *Guidelines for Subsidizing Sport Clubs from the State Fund for the Support of Physical Education and Sport*; and Sport England, *A Sporting Future for All*.

[39] Dimitrov, *Vdiganeto na tezesti v Bulgaria: Ocertchi po istoria* (Weightlifting in Bulgaria: Sketches on History), parts 1 and 2.

[40] Personal communication with BWF Secretary General (Sofia, 16 Feb. 2004).

[41] Morgan, *Images of Organization*, 256.

[42] Higgins and Mcallister, 'If you want strategic change, don't forget to change your cultural artefacts', 65.

[43] Personal communication with BWF former President (Sofia, 16 Feb. 2004).

[44] Morgan, *Images of Organization*, 256.

[45] Personal communications with BWF former Secretary General (Sofia, 1994)

[46] Denham, 'Sport Illustrated, the Mainstream Press and the Enactment of Drug Policy in Major League Baseball', 51–68.

[47] Personal communication with BWF former President (Sofia, 16 Feb. 2004).

[48] International Olympic Committee, *Programme Commission Report to the 117 IOC Session.*

[49] *7 Days Sport*,_3438 (16 Nov. 2003).

[50] Morgan, *Images of Organization*, 150.

[51] Dawson, "The War on Drugs", 19.

[52] Savulescu, Foddy and Clayton, 'Why we should allow Performance Enhancing Drugs in Sport'.

[53] Houlihan, 'Managing Compliance in International Anti-Doping Policy: The World Anti-Doping Code', 199.

[54] Donovan, Egger, Kapernik and Mendoza, 'A Conceptual Framework for Achieving Performance Enhancing Drug Compliance in Sport', 269–84.

[55] Personal communication with A. Kodjabashev.

References

Bobev, S., Petrova, N., Kalakinov, J. and Bankov, P. *Organization and Management of Physical Culture.* Sofia: Medicina & Fizkultura, 1985.

Carr, D., K. Hard, and W. Trahant. *Managing the Change Process: A Field Book for Change Agents, Consultants, Team Leaders and Reengineering Managers.* New York: McGraw Hill, 1996.

Chelladurai, P. *Managing Organizations for Sport and Physical Activity: A Systems Perspective.* Scottsdale, AZ: Holcomb Hathaway Publishers, 2001.

Collins, M. "Does a New Philosophy Change the Structure? Compulsory Competitive Tendering and Local Authority Leisure Services in Midland England." *Managing Leisure* 2 (1997): 204–16.

Council of Europe. *The Council of Europe's Work on Sport 1967–91*, Vol. 1, Strasbourg, Council of Europe, 1992.

Dawson, R. "Drugs in Ssport – the Role of the Physician." *Journal of Endocrinology* 170 (2001): 55–61.

———. "The War on Drugs." *BMC News and News* (Oct. 2000): 1–3.

Denham, B. "Sport Illustrated, the Mainstream Press and the Enactment of Drug Policy in Major League Baseball." *Journalism* 5, no. 1 (2004): 51–68.

Dimitrov, D. *Vdiganeto na tezesti v Bulgaria: Ocertchi po istoria* (Weightlifting in Bulgaria: Sketches on History) St Zagora: Shibilev, 2004.

Donovan, R., G. Egger, V. Kapernik, and J. Mendoza. "A Conceptual Framework for Achieving Performance Enhancing Drug Compliance in Sport." *Sports Medicine* 32, no. 4 (2002): 269–84.

Dunning, E. and I. Waddington. "Sport as Drug and Drugs in Sport: Some Explanatory Comments." *International Review for the Sociology of Sport* 38, no. 3 (2003): 351–68.

Girginov, V., D. Papadimitriou, and R. D'Amico. *Cultural Orientations of Sport Managers.* Forthcoming 2005.

———.J. Parry. *The Olympic Games Explained.* London: Routledge, 2005.

Goodbody, J. "Drugs Enquiry Criticises Governing Bodies." In *Times Online* (28 June 1990). [cited 18 Aug. 2005]. Available from http://www.timesonline.co.uk/article/0,9081-821798,00.html.

Guidelines for Subsidizing Sport Clubs from the State Fund for the Support of Physical Education and Sport. Sofia: Tip-Top Press, 1998.

Guttman, A. *From Record to Ritual: The Nature of Modern Sport.* New York: Columbia University Press, 1978.

Hampden-Turner, C. and F. Trompenaars. *Building Cross-cultural Competence.* London: Yale University Press, 2000.

———. *The Seven Cultures of Capitalism.* London: Piatkus, 1993.

Harris, L. and E. Ogbonna. "A Three-perspective Approach to Understanding Culture in Retail Organisations." *Personnel Review* 27, no. 2 (1998): 104–23.

Hickson, D. and Pugh, D., eds. *Management Worldwide: The Impact of Societal Culture on Organisations around the Globe.* London: Walter de Gruyter, 1995.

Higgins, J. and C. Mcallister. "If you want strategic change, don't forget to change your cultural artefacts." *Journal of Change Management* 4, no. 1 (2004): 63–73.

Hofstede, G. *Culture Consequences.* London: Sage, 1980.

Houlihan, B. "Managing Compliance in International Anti-Doping Policy: The World Anti-Doping Code." *European Sport Management Quarterly* 2, no. 3 (2002): 188–208.

——. *Dying to Win: Doping in Sport and the Development of Anti-doping Policy.* Strasbourg: Council of Europe Publishing, 1999.

International Olympic Committee. *Programme Commission Report to the 117 IOC Session.* Lausanne: IOC, 2005.

Martin, J. *Cultures in Organisations: Three Perspectives.* Oxford: Oxford University Press, 1992.

Morden, T. "Models of National Cultures – A Management Review." *Cross Cultural Management* 5, no. 1 (1999): 19–44.

Morgan, G. *Images of Organization.* London: Sage, 1997.

——. *Riding the Waves of Change.* London: Jossey-Bass Publishers, 1988.

Oakley, B. and M. Green. "The Production of Olympic Champions: International Perspectives on Elite Sport Development System." *European Journal for Sport Management* 8 (2001): 83–106.

Parry, J. "Sport, Universals and Multiculturalism." Paper presented at the main session of the International Olympic Academy, Olympia, Greece, 2003.

Savulescu, J., B. Foddy, and M. Clayton. "Why we should allow Performance Enhancing Drugs in Sport." *British Journal of Sports Medicine* 38 (2004): 666–70.

Smith, M. "Changing an Organisation's Culture: Correlates of Success and Failure." *Leadership and Organisation Development Journal* 24, no. 5 (2003): 249–61.

Sport England. *A Sporting Future for All.* London: Sport England, 2000.

Tayeb, M. "Organisations and National Culture: Methodology Considered." *Organisation Studies* 15, no. 3 (1994): 429–46.

Troy, K. *Change Management: An Overview of Current Initiatives.* New York: The Conference Board, 1994.

World Anti-Doping Agency. *World Anti-Doping Code.* Montreal: WADA, 2003.

Doping in the UK: Alain and Dwain, Rio and Greg – Not Guilty?

Jim Parry

Athletes are not quite like ordinary citizens. 'Ordinary' laws and moral principles apply to athletes as much (or as little) as anyone else – but athletes are subject to another set of considerations *just because* they seek to enter the cooperative enterprise of competing with and against others in sporting contests. As 'contractors to contest', they must accept certain constraints in ord er to count as acceptable opponents.

One such putative constraint is that against doping in sport. Much has been written on the theory, facts and morality of doping, and on the justification for banning it. In Britain, the chief sources of study and comment seem to have been Grayson 1999, Waddington 2000, Houlihan 2002, and articles from the *Journal of Philosophy of Sport*, including those collected in Morgan and Meier 1988, and from collections edited by Tamburrini and Tännsjö, 2000 and 2005.

This essay is an attempt to explore the issue of doping in sport via applied ethics, showing how complicated and messy individual cases can be, and how our judgements about them are coloured by a range of moral possibilities and intersecting contextual features. Sometimes the sheer weight of competing considerations, together with the uncertainty of empirical determinations, overwhelms our ability to arrive at conclusions acceptable even to ourselves – sometimes there just aren't any clear-cut answers.

The essay, then, will address issues of the relation between theory, empirical evidence, background scientific assumptions, the ethics of sports and sports rules, and the context-dependence of our judgements. It will do so via an examination of four recent cases involving British athletes, Alain Baxter (skiing), Dwain Chambers (athletics), Rio Ferdinand (football) and Greg Rusedski (tennis). These cases present us with very different though overlapping features, which open up a wide range of issues for consideration. It will explore the adequacy and morality of the actions of the athletes and their support teams, and of certain rules, procedures, decisions and judgements surrounding these cases. The outcome will be assessments of the relative innocence and guilt of each athlete in respect of a variety of factors.

In order to set the scene for our four cases, let me very briefly address some of the central questions.

Why do Athletes take Drugs?

There are many reasons given for taking drugs, which refer to the supposed benefits of doping:

- Enhanced performance (direct and indirect)
- Decreased recovery period, allowing more intensive training
- Masking the presence of other drugs
- Making the weight
- Staying the course (simple endurance – e.g. long-distance cycling)
- Psychological edge (promoting the athlete's confidence)
- Keeping up with the competition (coercion – pressure to follow suit)

Why do we Think it is Wrong to take Drugs?

1.   Pre-competition Agreements

The primary wrong lies in simple rule breaking. The rules function as a kind of pre-competition agreement that specifies an athlete's eligibility to compete and his rights, duties and responsibilities under the agreed rules. What's wrong with doping is the secretive attempt to evade or subvert such a 'contract to contest', an explicit example of which is the Olympic Oath, by which athletes swear that they have prepared themselves ethically, and will keep to the rules. To subvert the contract to contest threatens the moral basis of sport, jeopardizes the integrity of the sporting community and erodes public support and trust.

However, the rules themselves require a basis of justification, since the anti-doping rules must appeal to some issue of principle in addition to rule adherence. Considerations advanced include the following:

2. Unfair Advantage

Arguments against performance enhancement through doping are not simply arguments against performance enhancement, since that is what athletes constantly seek to achieve by training, coaching, nutrition, the application of sports science, et cetera. Neither is the argument simply against performance enhancement by means that confer an unfair advantage, since many legal means are beyond the resources of most countries. Rather, the argument is specifically against unfair advantage conferred by illegal means.

3. Harm

Many argue that doping may be harmful, because the substances are inherently harmful, or because they have been administered without medical supervision, or because they have been inadequately tested. Further, it is argued that harm to other athletes is caused by the coercion they feel to follow suit in order to maintain competitiveness.

4. Social Harm

With the huge expansion in the market for drugs in gyms and fitness clubs, there is now an emerging claim for a further wrong: that, by modelling dope as a lifestyle, athletes contribute to the social problem of thousands of sport, fitness and bodybuilding fans consuming substances whose long-term effects are unknown. Athletes, it is said, should be more aware of their social responsibility.

Why do we Ban Doping?

It is one thing to say that doping is wrong, and quite another to ban it, which requires the apparatus of testing, judicial procedure and enforcement. So alongside such principles we see various rationales for testing and enforcement, including:

- Fairness Preservation (against unfair advantage)
- Athlete Protection (against harm to health and reputation)
- Retribution and punishment
- Deterrence via detection
- Lifestyle prescription
- The 'role model' requirement

But there are also two kinds of arguments against a ban. The first is 'empirical', suggesting that we cannot test effectively and fairly, because:

- there is inadequate coverage (not enough resources for testing and testers, or not enough support from civil authorities)

- the tests not good enough (one test for EPO had only 92 per cent accuracy, and the cycling federations were afraid to have their decisions tested in court, since they could have been ruined by one court action)
- athletes with the best knowledge and resources know how to avoid detection, which is why the testing procedures catch so few (there is a suspicion that, out of the relatively few cases of detection, there is a large proportion of cases where the athlete was convicted of some very minor infraction, or on a technicality, or for a non-performance enhancing substance, or where there is a reasonable doubt that the athlete did anything wrong at all)
- there are many cases which seem to be simple mistakes

The second kind of argument is 'moral', suggesting that we should not ban on grounds of infringement of liberty and should not test on grounds of invasion of privacy. This kind of argument would also point to the many cases of injustice in the history of testing and enforcement, and to the tyranny of value and lifestyle prescription.

Why isn't it just down to Individual Choice?

Some argue that a ban is simply parentalist – that we cannot justify interference in the individual athlete's decision-making processes. Tamburrini, for example, says, 'the ban on performance-enhancing methods constrains the professional activities of athletes, and ... the reasons often advanced to support that constraint do not stand criticism'[1].

However, Schneider argues that the 'individualistic' view fails to give adequate recognition to the private/public distinction. It seems to suppose that any individual's 'private' views and decisions (such as to engage in doping, or to seek performance-enhancing genetic technology) are privileged, and should be taken into account by any existing institutions (such as sports practices). Schneider objects that such private views should not be allowed to 'trump' the values expressed in and through the practice – that there is a 'public' view here that should take precedence.[2]

In this she is surely right – there has to be, as a minimum, a debate between the representatives of the practice and intending reformers. Individual reformers cannot simply expect that those who defend the cherished values of an established practice will (or should have to) accede to individuals' private views as to what will benefit the practice. Why should people who want 'clean' sport have to accept dopers?

The history of sports development is littered with examples of reformers, dissenters and break-away factions who founded new versions of a sport, or even new sports, which seems to suggest that some established practices were successful in 'defending' themselves against incursion. Some have suggested that this is the way forward for dopers: they should announce themselves as dopers, and set up their own versions of various sports. But this won't solve our problem, because there is no guarantee that some dopers won't refuse to identify themselves as such, since they presently only succeed in their plans if they're secretive. Just as at present, there is no guarantee that any individual would deny himself the advantage of pretending to be clean whilst secretly doping. If he doesn't respect the anti-doping rules now, why should he respect the clean/doped distinction later?

So I accept, with Schneider, that sports practices are not 'private', and need not be constrained to take account of everyone's private preferences. They are communal practices, and encapsulate certain shared views, adherence to which is a prerequisite of entry and participation. Of course, rules change – sometimes as a result of pressure from within the practice, and sometimes from without – but only (in some sense) *with the consent of* the practice.

However, to call them 'public' practices overstates the case, since it suggests that the sports practices themselves are (or should be) sovereign, against private interests. This ignores the fact that they exist within and cannot (or on occasion should not be allowed to) remain isolated from wider society, which may legitimately take a view on the desirability of allowing a certain sports practice, or a certain activity within a sports practice. For example, in the UK, duelling and bare-fist boxing are illegal; and within rugby certain bodily assaults have become actionable.

So, instead of simply the public and the private realms, we must draw a distinction between the private realm, the practice realm and the public realm, which permits us to recognize that there may be issues that highlight the relationship between the practice realm and the public realm. There may need to be a conversation between views arising within and representing the sports practice, and views reflecting changing and developing attitudes in wider society – for example on such matters as the use of drugs and body technologies. Public attitudes have changed dramatically in recent years, and this can be expected to have some impact on sports practices.

The Ethical Basis of the Idea of Sport

Let me comment upon a positive feature of the debate about performance-enhancing drugs. The drugs debate has forced everyone to think in ethical terms, and to appeal to ethical principles. But if we take these appeals seriously, and follow them through, there are some interesting consequences. Assume that drug-taking in sport is wrong, and ask the question: '*why* is it wrong?' The answers we have given above were all stated in terms of some ethical principle that is claimed to be central to our idea of sport, which drug-taking allegedly violates. Let us revisit two of those arguments and see where the underlying principles lead us:

1. *Unfair Advantage or Inequality of Opportunity*

Some say that what is wrong with drug-taking is that it confers an unfair advantage. Notice that no-one can (sincerely) make this objection to drug-taking unless he is sincere in his commitment to sport as embodying fairness, and as disallowing unfair advantages as being against the idea of sport.

However, many of those who hold this objection against drug-taking seem perfectly prepared to allow various kinds of very obviously unfair advantages. For example, only certain countries are able to generate and enjoy the fruits of developments in sports science; and only certain countries are able to take advantage of the knowledge and technology required for the production of specialized technical equipment. Is this fair? The company that produced the so-called 'moon-bikes' for the US cycling team in the 1984 Olympic Games later shamelessly marketed them under the slogan: '*The Unfair Advantage*'.

Let's widen the issue: it seems to me a fact that international competition is grossly unfair, because some countries have the resources to enhance the performance of their athletes, and some don't. Those nurtured within advanced systems might take time to consider the extent to which their performances are a function not just of their abilities as individual sportspeople but also of the social context within which they have been nurtured. Have not their performances been enhanced? Are not their advantages unfair?

Consistency requires that we revisit the whole idea of disadvantage, and also inequality. For example, why not include more 'ethnic' sports in the Olympic programme, rather than continuing the present Western hegemonic domination? Kabbadi, a sport popular on the Indian sub-continent, is a sport based on the game form of 'tag', which is known in most societies in the world. It requires minimal facilities and no equipment. Why should we westerners not have to learn such sports and compete on those terms, rather than collude in the disappearance of indigenous sport forms in favour of our own curriculum?

Anyone who relies on 'unfair advantage' arguments in the case of doping must also revisit and reconsider such arguments in other contexts.

2.   Rule-Breaking or Cheating

Others say that drug-taking is wrong simply because it is against the rules of competition. But pace-making is against the rules of the IAAF, although it is allowed so as to facilitate record-breaking attempts in the commercial promotion of media spectacle, and no-one is disqualified. In fact, runners can earn large fees for performing this 'service'. If officials so readily flout their own rules, they are poorly placed when athletes do the same, or when critics demand better justification for the rules that presently exist.

In a world where the values of sport are sometimes forgotten under the pressures of medal-winning and the marketplace, it ill behoves those responsible to turn a moralistic eye on athletes. Why should athletes take any notice of the moral exhortation of those who have profited from the commercialization of sport, when they see the true values lived and expressed by those around them?

The drugs debate has made everyone stand on ethical principle. But think how sport might develop (what it might become) if those principles were not merely used opportunistically over the drugs issue, but rather were acted upon consistently in the interests of truly fair competition and equality of opportunity. I think that there is an opportunity here to open up debate again about the ethical basis of sport, so that our sports practice (and the sports science and training theory that support it) becomes rooted in firm principles that encapsulate what we think sport *should be*.

A Thought Experiment

1. The Harmless Enhancer

Imagine that, along with my colleague Leo Hsu, I have succeeded in producing a pill whose entirely natural ingredients are derived from herbs to be found only in a remote part of Taiwan, and so far unknown to Western medical science. The ingredients have been used in traditional medicine for 3,000 years without harmful effects, but our new (and secret) applications have revealed hitherto unsuspected (and remarkable) performance-enhancing effects. Are there any reasons why we should not use it?

This imaginary scenario 'takes out' a certain kind of medical critic, whose complaints are mainly related to harms – actual or supposed, demonstrable or alleged. This scenario *ex hypothesi* requires us to imagine a substance which is (a) proven to have *no* harmful effects and which is (b) a *proven* performance-enhancer: and it asks us to consider the question, 'What, if anything, could be wrong with taking a harmless enhancer?'

2. The Undetectable Enhancer

Imagine further that such a pill is completely undetectable in use. This imaginary scenario 'takes out' the intrusive and (let's not forget it) enriched pharmacologists – for their role has been both to develop performance-enhancing drugs and also to develop ways of detecting them! This scenario *ex hypothesi* requires us to imagine a substance which is (a) *in principle* undetectable in use and which is (b) a proven performance-enhancer: and it asks us to consider the question 'What, if anything, could be wrong with taking an undetectable enhancer?'

Responses

My main answer is that, despite the fact that they were harmless and undetectable, it would be wrong to take these enhancers if they were banned, because it is simple rule-breaking. If anyone seeks to evade any rule for advantage, especially when they do it knowingly and secretively, then that is the clearest possible case of cheating. True, there may well be arguments outstanding regarding the justice, relevance or importance of the rule itself; but so long as the rule is the rule we ought all to obey it, on pain of sanction.

To get into the Ritz, men must wear ties. Whether or not this is a stupid or trivial requirement is irrelevant to whether I get into the Ritz. There are plenty of places to eat, but if I want to eat at the Ritz, I had better wear a tie.

Sports competitors prepare and compete on certain more or less precise understandings described by the rules. Any attempt to evade these rules for advantage is cheating. It is an attempt to subvert the very basis upon which alone the activity is possible; it is to pervert the logical and moral basis of the whole social practice of sport. *This* is the greatest harm perpetrated by doping cheats: not the alleged medical harm to self or the coercion of others, but the harm to self and others caused by behaviour, which threatens the social practice of sport itself.

Now we must turn to a detailed consideration of our cases, where we shall see some of these features, reasons, principles and arguments in application. We shall also be able to assess each case against the notion of secretive evasion of rules for advantage, and to ask whether the behaviour exhibited threatened the social practice of sport.

ALAIN BAXTER

The Case

Before his slalom competition on the last day of the Winter Olympic Games in Salt Lake City, the Scottish skier Alain Baxter took the American version of a Vicks nasal spray decongestant that, unlike the British version, contained lev-methamphetamine. As a result of his positive test he was denied the only skiing medal ever won by a Briton in the history of the Olympic Games. He appealed to the International Olympic Committee's (IOC) Court of Arbitration for Sport (CAS), which heard the case at the Winter Olympic Games in Salt Lake City in October 2002 and which cleared him of intending to cheat. However, his result was not reinstated, nor his bronze medal.

Principles

1. Strict liability

Strict liability is the legal principle that identifies fault and assigns liability regardless of circumstances. A landlord must not allow his premises to be used for drug trafficking. If his tenants traffic, he is liable, regardless of whether he colluded in it or profited by it, or whether he was even aware of it. Claiming ignorance or stupidity is no excuse.

Another example from sport is that of Romanian gymnast Andrea Raducan, who had a gold medal withheld at the Sydney 2000 Olympics after testing positive for pseudo-ephedrine, having taken two Neurofen tablets for a headache under the supervision of team doctor Oana Ioachim, and having entered this on the requisite declaration form.

We can see why we need such a principle as strict liability. It denies an excuse to those who should have taken more of an interest, or who should have taken more care. Its justification must be that, without it, many guilty defendants would escape serious charges, for example, of corporate negligence or drug smuggling. Without it, almost anyone could offer an excuse – to allow people to claim lack of intent, ignorance or stupidity would open the floodgates.

In sport, the argument is that even if an athlete unknowingly took a doping substance, or took it without any intent to gain an advantage, other athletes should still be protected from any advantage he might have gained (see the comments of Flint *et al.*, 2003, on the CAS adjudication).

But strict liability can sometimes produce what seem to be very harsh and unjust outcomes for some individuals in particular cases. Many unwitting drug mules languish in jails as a result of having drugs planted on them by people they thought were friends – because ignorance or lack of intent are no excuse.

The same applies to Baxter. The facts are not altogether clear, but some versions say that he failed to take medical advice, presumably because he was confident of the contents of the spray, the British version of which he used frequently without concern. He said that he had been bought an inhaler that was not his usual brand by his brother, which he did declare to doctors. But then,

> I saw the inhaler I wanted to buy in the first place because I have been using it since I was a kid. At the time it never crossed my mind it was different to the British one. In my mind I had no reason to get it checked.[3]

However, it seems that the American version of the Vicks spray is 'clearly marked on the American anti-doping website's list as one to avoid',[4] so that if Baxter had thought to check, the information was available. Thus it could be said that Baxter's fault (if any) lay in his failure to take steps that were open to him in order to protect himself, such as submitting all of his medications to medical authority, and double-checking substances for himself – but this in itself shows the lengths to which athletes must now go to avoid prosecution.

Craig Reedie, British Olympic Association chairman and IOC member, commented: 'The BOA is very disappointed with the decision reached by the IOC. We take the view that Alain has suffered a dreadful penalty. No way can Alain be described as a "drugs cheat".'[5]

The main rationale for testing is commonly supposed to be fairness preservation (against unfair advantage). However, Baxter and Raducan are both considered to have gained no advantage at all, and yet they have been punished by the denial of their just reward. How can this be justified? Only if we assert the primacy and overwhelming importance of the principle of strict liability in fairness preservation, and the instrumental use of these athletes in the service of deterrence.

2. Restorative Medication

This raises the issue of whether (and, if so, when and how) we can distinguish the performance-enhancing and the 'restorative' (or 'compensatory') usage of drugs – the issue of dope *versus* medication.

In one sense, all restorative/compensatory usage is also performance-enhancing. It enables me to perform to the best of my ability on the day, despite the fact that I have, say, a headache or a cold. But let us distinguish this sense (as 'restoring' my performance to its optimal) from that of an 'additional' enhancement.

The problem is that it is difficult to determine the threshold according to which am I restored, and above which my restoration in fact tipples over into a possible additional advantage. If a decongestant 'opens my pipes' when I have a congesting cold, won't it also open them a little more than usual when I'm perfectly healthy, thus conferring an advantage?

One example of the effect of this difficulty is that of Rex Williams, then President of the World Snooker and Billiards Association, who was banned in 1977 for using beta-blockers, which he was using on medical prescription for a heart condition. That is to say, he needed the beta-blockers in order to be 'normal'. In effect, the doping regulations made it impossible for him to compete on equal terms with others, presumably because an additional benefit could not be ruled out.

Such cases have led to the development by WADA of an International Standard for Therapeutic Use Exemptions (TUE), which sets out the criteria for the granting of a TUE, which must be applied for no less than 21 days in advance of an event, and must involve no additional enhancement of performance, the absence of a reasonable therapeutic alternative and evidence of significant need.[6]

3.   The Science of the Substances

Often, the science of the particular substances involved goes unchallenged or unexplored, when the whole case rests upon dubious science. In Baxter's case, for example, we should note that there are two varieties of methamphetamine. The 'lev-methamphetamine' variety found in Baxter's sample (and used in some nasal decongestants) is commonly thought to have no performance-enhancing properties, and the manufacturer, Proctor and Gamble, sent a statement to this effect to the CAS. However, the International Olympic Committee (IOC) does not distinguish that from the 'dextro-methamphetamine' variety, a stimulant known also as 'speed', which may enhance performance by improving reaction times. The IOC bans both, and Baxter's test would not have distinguished between them.[7]

In the case of Raducan, IOC President Jacques Rogge publicly conceded that her use of the drug was not performance enhancing, but nevertheless supported the punishment, saying 'the rules are the rules'. And it is clear that the IOC does not have to prove the performance-enhancing qualities of a particular drug in a particular case.[8] All that the CAS has to do is to apply the IOC rules that ban certain substances.

But the cases of Baxter and Raducan make it clear that there is a huge responsibility on the shoulders of those who compile the list of banned substances, for there is a massive gap between the propositions:

- substance X has performance-enhancing qualities

- substance X was found in Y's body
- Y's performance was enhanced

4.   *The Science of Minute Quantities*

Many athletes have been detected with the tiniest quantities of banned substances, where the tiniest quantities are enough to convict. Is this fair? One view says that testers can't know that tiny traces come from tiny doses – for they might be tiny traces of larger doses taken much earlier. Since there is no way of estimating the size of dose from the size of trace, unless there is supplementary information available, the strict liability approach is the only way to catch offenders.

A similar problem arises in the case of comparisons of minute quantities with similarly minute quantities that are within the range of the naturally occurring. A study at Aberdeen University suggested that a combination of food supplements and strenuous exercise could produce levels of nandrolone above the acceptable, even up to 20 nanograms per millilitre, whilst 5 nanograms per millilitre would indicate a positive test.

When margins are so small, and the consequences of a positive test so significant, we ought to be *very* careful before announcing guilt. Remember, we are relying absolutely on the accuracy and reliability of the testers, the tests themselves and of the procedures used.

5.   *The Substance in the Event – Blanket Testing*

In addition to the science of the substances in general, we might also investigate the actual performance-enhancing capacity of a particular drug in a particular event. Graham Bell, the performance director for British skiing said,

> A drug like methamphetamine would not help an alpine skier. At the end of the day it's about skill and staying on your feet, and there's not a pill that's been invented that could make you ski better.[9]

Now, Bell might be right or wrong about this – but it does raise the question of 'blanket testing' (testing everyone for everything). If a substance is considered not to be performance-enhancing in a particular event, to insist on tests and sanctions in that event suggests that another rationale for testing is in fact operative, and not the principle of fairness preservation. I can think of three possibilities:

(i) that the testing procedures are such as they are in order to fit the convenience of the testers (it's presumably easier for them to apply one set of rules for everyone)
(ii) that such a practice is considered in some sense fair to all athletes
(iii) that there is some moral rationale operating, in addition to fairness preservation – for example the assertion of the social responsibility of the athlete as role model.

But these are never the overt rationale used by testing authorities, who rely for their legitimacy on anti-performance enhancement, based on the fairness preservation rationale.

Outcome

No one thinks that Alain Baxter tried to cheat, nor that he knowingly took a banned substance, nor that he gained any advantage on the day (apart from the restorative benefit of the medicine). Although he was not guilty of those things he still lost his bronze medal, but he was banned from competition for only three months by the skiing federation (the FIS), presumably in view of the many mitigating factors in the case.[10] The psychological effect of the accusations and procedures on the athlete, however, is impossible to calculate.[11]

DWAIN CHAMBERS

The Case

Dwain Chambers, a British track athlete and European 100 metres champion, tested positive for Tetrahydrogestrinone (THG), a form of anabolic steroid banned under the IAAF doping regulations, during an out-of-competition test at his German training base on 1 August 2003. Chambers did not deny that the drug was present in his urine sample, but denied knowingly taking a banned substance. Instead, he blamed his Georgian coach Remi Korchemny and his nutritionist Victor Conte of BALCO Laboratories, Los Angeles, who he says were responsible for his nutritional and supplemental regimes.[12]

Principles

1.   Strict Liability Again

Chambers protests his innocence – but then he would do so whether innocent or guilty, for he has his family, his friends and the outside world to face. However, protestations of innocence are useless against the strict liability provision. Sebastian Coe writes:

> Chambers' mitigating plea is likely to be one of ignorance. It will not cut much ice. The genesis of his difficulties may well lie in the hands of a Georgian émigré, now a resident of the United States, but the responsibility for what he has consumed, even unwittingly, I am afraid, lies fairly and squarely with the sprinter.

For the International Association of Athletics Federations or UK Athletics to depart one millimetre from the legal concept of strict liability is to drive a coach and horses through the last few years of hard pounding in the war against drugs.[13]

2.   Secrecy and Intent

Don Catlin, a molecular pharmacologist and director of the Olympic Analytical Laboratory at the University of California at Los Angeles, who led the effort to isolate and analyse THG, says that scientists familiar with androgenic steroids and their illicit use in athletics were not at all surprised by the discovery of THG. He says,

> We've known about designer steroids for many years, but up to now we've never been able to prove that someone is actually making them . . .
>
> The fact that we finally characterized one is certainly no reason to celebrate. I'm much more worried about the next THG out there that we haven't found yet.[14]

The idea of the 'designer steroid' clearly indicates that there do exist people at a high level in the supply chain whose whole intent is to provide substances for performance-enhancement which will evade the current regulations or the means of enforcing them. Such secretive evasion of a rule may be thought to compound an offence, for it indicates a level of forethought and planning. If the athlete fully understands that he is consuming such a substance, then he shares fully in the intent to deceive which forms the basis of his cheating.

Richard Pound, President of the World Anti-Doping Agency (WADA), speaking after the announcement by UK Athletics of Chambers' punishment, said:

> We are pleased that the process has produced this result of a two-year ban, which is in compliance with the World Anti-Doping Code for a first offence for the use of steroids. This is a particularly important decision because a disciplinary committee has now confirmed that THG is, in fact, a banned substance related to a steroid named on the Prohibited List. THG is a steroid created specifically to enhance sports performance and allow competitors to cheat. A two-year sanction for its use is completely appropriate.[15]

3. The Role of the Coach (and other support staff)

David Moorcroft said that UK Athletics had included £300,000 in its annual budget since 1999 to fight doping cases, and he wanted to see the fight against drugs to be taken beyond the athlete. He said,

> The rule of strict liability means the athlete is responsible for what is in their body but I would like to work with the IAAF and the World Anti-Doping Agency to try and unravel why these things happen.
>
> I've felt for a long time that behind every positive case are people around the athlete. The sport needs to figure a way that we could either investigate the coaches and agents or make strict liability apply to the support team around an athlete.[16]

This raises questions of responsibility in two senses. Firstly, if coaches, doctors or managers are actually responsible for suggesting, supplying or prescribing dope or supplements to their athletes, then surely they, too, should be held responsible for any offences against the rules of the sport. Secondly, if they are to be seen in a supervisory or management relation with their athletes, then they should take some responsibility for advising and protecting the athlete.

Chambers was managed by John Regis, the former European 200m champion, who heads the athletics division of the Stellar Agency. Regis admitted that, despite his role in looking after Chambers' career, the athlete had been 'largely unprotected'.[17] However, there are small signs of change. Istvan Gyulai, the IAAF general secretary said:

> There is a clear intention within the IAAF to look behind the scenes and there is a growing conviction that it is not just the athlete who carries the blame. We already have a rule which empowers the ruling council to take action against any person – a coach, agent, doctor or manager – who helps with doping. It's never happened before but it can be at the discretion of the council and involve a ban for a year, two years or for life.[18]

4.   Safety

Some substances have been developed so rapidly and recently that there cannot have been time for the usual trials conducted on substances intended for use on humans. Dr Olivier Rabin, the science director of the World Anti-Doping Agency, is reported as warning that Chambers could suffer effects beyond the two-year ban imposed, since taking THG has possibly put his long-term health at risk.

> A new drug can cause toxic damage to the liver, kidneys, brain and blood. That's why drugs go through extensive tests and have to be approved by an ethical committee.[19]

> To me it's insane. This went from the test tube to the athlete. There is a huge risk. Who knows what will happen in the future? It is extremely scary that this substance never had any testing on animals before being given to elite athletes, who have in effect acted as guinea pigs.[20]

5.   Retrospective Testing

With the invention of a new test for THG, some authorities have been keen to re-test athletes whose collected test samples have been retained by the testing authority. For example, in the United States re-tested samples from the national athletics championships in June 2003 revealed four THG 'positives'.

It has been suggested that this is unfair, on three grounds: firstly, simply that it is retrospective, secondly that it puts the athlete in 'double jeopardy', and thirdly that there is no precedent.

The first argument goes as follows: retrospective legislation is widely regarded as unsatisfactory, since citizens cannot be expected to act in accordance with law that has yet to be written. We act on the law as it is, and we should be judged accordingly. Applying new law retrospectively is unfair. So, similarly, it is unfair to re-test retrospectively, hunting for new substances only recently discovered.

This argument does not hold, even in the case of legislation in general. Murder is against the law, now and in the past. The invention of DNA profiling permits us to identify past murderers with new methods, and there is no unfairness in that.

Similarly, steroid doping is against the rules, now and in the past. The invention of testing for the steroid THG permits us to identify past dopers with new methods, and there is no unfairness in that. Retrospective testing is not retrospective legislation.

The second argument notes that the principle of double jeopardy states that a person cannot be tried twice for the same offence, nor be convicted of different crimes arising from the same conduct. Because of this, some have seen re-testing as problematic, since it puts the athlete twice in jeopardy:

> At the heart of the legal debate is whether samples that have been previously given the all-clear can then be subjected to a second analysis, a process that would go against the principle of 'double jeopardy' that is enshrined in British law.

> 'The issue with retrospective testing is whether we have got the right to test a negative sample a second time', said a UK Sport spokesman.[21]

However re-testing is not re-trying. Re-testing is about detection, so as to bring someone to 'trial' for the first time. Double testing is not double jeopardy.

An important side-issue to note here is that one of the chief exceptions to the principle of double jeopardy is in respect of the professions. If a member of a profession (such as athletics) commits a crime and in so doing also infringes the disciplinary code of his profession, he may be liable to be dealt with under that code as well as by the law. So an athlete considering using a Class A drug does indeed face double trouble.

The third argument notes the lack of precedent and lack of an agreed policy across sports and across countries. Knight says:

> The legal debate is further complicated by the fact that UK Sport carry out drug tests across 41 sports, each of which has its own set of rules. They are consulting with administrators from all the affected sports to establish a common policy, though the fact that there is currently no provision for re-testing samples in any of the sports' regulations has only added to the headache.[22]

In addition, there is confusion at the international level. Some governing bodies have ordered the immediate re-testing of stored urine samples (for example in athletics and swimming, where samples collected at the sports' respective world championships in Paris and Barcelona were sent for a second analysis). However, FIFA, the world governing body of football, decided not to re-test samples on legal advice. So it does seem as though we stand in need of adequate codification of the rules, and their consistent application.

6.   Individual and Team Guilt

It is one thing to face the consequence of one's own folly or misfortune, and quite another to visit it upon others. Where a guilty individual takes part in a team sport, the effect on other competitors has to be considered.

A ban for Chambers will mean he and his team-mates, Darren Campbell, Marlon Devonish and Christian Malcolm, being stripped of their silver medal from the World Championships 4 × 100m.[23]

This was indeed the outcome, but our immediate response is to ask why they should suffer, too, when they are guilty of nothing, not even of knowledge of Chambers' doping. Presumably, one argument is that, even though they were innocent, they cannot be allowed to benefit from his cheating.

Some people think that this principle extends from 1 in 4, to 1 in 11. When Rio Ferdinand was still playing for Manchester United, whilst waiting for the hearing of his case regarding his missed dope test, Sepp Blatter (President of FIFA, the world federation of football) suggested that Ferdinand should not be playing club football. He said: 'I thought he was suspended. You would have to nullify all the matches he has played.'[24] On precisely this point, however, UEFA (the European governing body) did not act. Recently, Wales lost to Russia in a two-leg play-off for a place in the Euro 2004 finals in Portugal, but the Russian Yegor Titov failed a drug test after the first leg in Moscow, and the Welsh FA submitted a written complaint to UEFA, asking for the result to be overturned so that Wales could take Russia's place at the finals. UEFA declined to nullify the result, and Russia went to Portugal, minus Titov.

So we seem to be left with no clear directive here, although I will return to this theme in the next section. Meanwhile, let us conclude by noting that at least one member of the Welsh team, Robbie Savage, thought that UEFA's decision was fair enough. He said, 'Over the two legs they beat us fair and square and they deserved to go through to the finals ... it's the biggest disappointment I have ever had in my career'.[25]

Outcome

Chambers received a two-year ban, and it is doubtful whether he will return to athletics. His case, however, raises issues that sports authorities have not yet been able to resolve satisfactorily.

RIO FERDINAND

The Case

Rio Ferdinand was found guilty by a Football Association tribunal of failing or refusing to provide a sample for UK Sport anti-doping officials on 29 September 2003 at Manchester United FC's Carrington training ground. After being informed that he was to be tested, he says that he forgot, left the ground and went shopping. The testing period was two hours, according to the officials, and Ferdinand rang after an hour and a half to say that he had forgotten about the test, but was now available. The testers decided that there was insufficient time for him to attend, and he was deemed to have missed the test. On 19 December he was banned for eight months from all competitions, including England's Euro 2004 campaign, and fined £50,000.[26]

Principles

1. Failure to Attend

As with breathalyser or blood testing for alcohol in the motoring context, a dope test refusal in sport carries a presumption of guilt. In addition, a failure to attend or to make oneself available for testing is often counted as a refusal.

In principle, it might seem harsh to punish Ferdinand when no doping offence has been proven, and when there is good reason to suppose either that he committed no offence or that his offence did not confer a performance advantage (and I shall discuss both possibilities in due course). However, we can see the reason why a refusal should be treated so seriously, for it denies the authorities a legitimate opportunity to secure evidence of the offence. Similarly, we can see the reason why test evasion should be treated as seriously as refusal, especially when conditions of testing are laid out in advance, and why a failure to attend should be treated as an evasion unless exceptional and attested reasons are provided.

In Rio's case there seem to be a number of possibilities:

(i) He forgot. It just slipped his mind. This was Rio's defence, but it simply beggars belief. If true, it would have been an astounding lapse in player responsibility. How could a senior professional footballer have failed to notice the importance and seriousness of the occasion, to the extent of leaving the ground with his driver, and going shopping?

In any case, it is surely an astounding lapse in supervision of the player. Presumably, this is the responsibility of UK Sport's anti-doping officials (although there is an issue here of whether or not Manchester United's own officials permitted the UK Sport people adequate access to the ground and to players). But Manchester United's officials were also responsible for an astounding lapse in protection of their player, of their investment of £30 million in Rio, and of their club's season, which nose-dived when Rio was suspended.

If (i), then both he and the club deserve his fate, for their incompetence and unprofessionalism in not realizing the seriousness of the situation, the requirements upon them to act, and the probable outcome of non-compliance.

(ii) He deliberately avoided the test because he did not appreciate the importance of the requirement to be tested. It is the responsibility of Football Association, the Professional Footballers' Association (which is the players' trade union), UK Sport and MUFC both to educate players as to the requirements and the likely punishments, and to conduct the testing in an idiot-proof fashion. It seems that they all failed in some respect.

Professional players also need to adopt professional attitudes, though. There is a possibility here that a high-ranking player behaved in a casual or even arrogant manner, believing either that he was so important as to be above the law, or that the punishments were unlikely to be severe.

In mitigation, however, there was no consistent FA policy to rely on (see examples later), there was evidence of leniency in prior cases, and apparently no player support facility available anywhere – at the FA, the PFA or MUFC.

(iii) He deliberately avoided the test because he believed that the test would reveal something in his system that he wanted to conceal. To test this suggestion, we must consider the nature of the hypothetical 'something' ...

(a) A banned substance? Here we are reliant on the science of the situation. Rio apparently tried to be tested that day, but the testers had left, so he was tested two days later, when he tested negative. Is there a substance such that a 48-hour delay would make a difference in detection? If not, it looks as though Rio was innocent of taking a performance-enhancing substance. However, not all banned substances are performance-enhancing.

(b) A recreational drug? Again: is there a substance such that 48 hours would make a difference? If so, a suspicion might arise that the reason for test avoidance could have been to conceal use of a recreational drug. Now we have to raise the question: what should drug tests test for? Of course, UK Sport will test for everything on the banned list, but this undermines the primary rationale that testing is for fairness preservation, and the denial of unfair advantage.

On this occasion, we had a 'blanket' test, and MUFC seem to have had the right to see the results, which immediately introduces other rationales, such as the social responsibility ('role model') rationale and the 'lifestyle' rationale.

If a recreational drug were involved, and the player sought to avoid detection by postponing the test until 48 hours later, this seems a small enough offence. If it had been possible to see this as simply an internal disciplinary matter, it could have been settled between player and club. As it is, a lack of clarity, combined with the intrusiveness of anti-doping rules, might have been factors in the more serious procedural offence having been committed (failure to take the test).

(c) The presence of a medical condition or a prescribed medicine? Medical matters immediately raise issues of privacy, and Rio reportedly rang his medical centre from his mobile phone before going shopping. There might have been many reasons for this, but one possibility, presumably, is for medical advice on what might be revealed by the test. After having been reassured, it would then be possible for him to offer to take the test after all.

Alternatively, it would have been useful if he could have negotiated, on a basis similar to medical confidentiality, that any non-relevant substance should not be revealed to MUFC or anyone else. But it is very unclear how a player might go about such a negotiation, and it is not clear that anyone advises or reassures players on matters such as these. We might ask whether there is a code of practice, a hotline, or a support service available for players, or someone to turn to.

If Rio was seeking to preserve privacy on a medical matter, I think most people would feel sympathy on at least privacy grounds. It is unfortunate that there was no clear and agreed prior procedure for dealing with such issues, which had been adequately communicated to players.

2.   *Performance-enhancing and 'Recreational' Drugs*

Discussion of drugs in sport takes place in a context of social concern regarding the use of 'recreational drugs' in the general population, but the source of concern is different in each case. We must distinguish the fairness preservation rationale against drugs in sport from the various rationales put forward against recreational drugs, and we must not confuse performance-enhancement and recreational uses of drugs by sportspeople.

But this is just what UK Sport did, in testing for all substances. It is almost as if they were acting as agent for the club management's overseeing of the player's lifestyle. This seems to me to over-aggrandize the anti-doping agency's role and remit. It certainly extends it well beyond the performance-enhancement rationale that gives it unquestioned authority and such wide-ranging powers. Such unwarranted intrusion into players' private lives prejudices its fragile legitimacy, which is based on an acceptance of its independent pursuit of fairness preservation.

This point was not widely recognized in the discussion until the Mutu case. Adrian Mutu, the Romanian striker playing for Chelsea, tested positive for cocaine in October 2004 and was sacked by his club. Although there seems to be some unfairness here, since drug testing in the workplace is generally seen as contrary to human rights provisions unless health and safety is an issue, the sports doping regulations permit little opportunity for sports employers to make the distinction between performance-enhancing and recreational drugs, since both are on the banned list.[27]

Thompson says: 'We would not tolerate urinalysis . . . as a condition of employment in a bank or a factory'.[28] So why do we tolerate it in sport? It must be justified in sport only because of the contract to contest – the pre-contest agreement between athletes to compete without performance-enhancement by drugs.

However, there is a different rationale under which highly paid professional athletes might reasonably consent to operate. Although such close attention by employers to one's private life would not be tolerated in most spheres of life, there is something different about a very highly rewarded public figure who has signed a particular form of contract. Some contracts even include prescriptions against alcohol and late nights, and most players believe that the reward is worth the discipline.

Finally, there is the 'role model' argument – that players should set a good example, and the 'practice preservation' argument – that players should not bring the game into disrepute. However, both of these would be more persuasive

if clubs and regulators took a similarly firm stance over the regular abuse of alcohol, on-field aggression, open disrespect for authority, and allegations of sexual aggression, that have become a feature of the game.[29]

3. Suspension Pending Enquiry or Appeal

After his failure to attend for testing, Rio continued to play for his team. However, in other professions, the accused is not allowed to continue activity whilst under enquiry relating to conduct, or appeal. There are two competing principles at work here: one says that the individual is innocent until proven guilty; the other says that he should be suspended pending the outcome.

The first protects the rights of the individual, whilst the second protects the integrity of the practice, in this case, football. We should ask what happens if Rio is guilty, and Manchester United have won games with him playing? It seems excessive to render all the results null and void – but it seems weak to allow them all to stand.

One suggestion is that we should assess the extent to which the player contributed to the result. He might be thought to have been just one of eleven, playing the kind of role in the victory that one of the substitutes might well have done – in which case there does not seem to be much of a case for overturning the result. On the other hand, if the player had scored the winning goal, or had scored three, he might be thought to have been the deciding factor. (The discussion of individual and team guilt in the Dwain Chambers case refers here.) In Rio's case, he seems to have been an important factor in his team's defensive performance, and so we must ask what has been his likely effect on the teams he played against whilst under enquiry and appeal. What if, for example, he contributed significantly to the defeat of a team that was subsequently relegated, or knocked out of a competition?

It is difficult to see how we can deal with such matters on a case-by-case basis, because such a procedure presents enormous difficulties of calculation and comparison and raises the spectre of injustice across cases. A clearer resolution, and one that respects football, would be to insist upon suspension after a failed or missed drugs test, followed if necessary by a swift enquiry or appeal.

That is to say, Rio should not have been playing in those games at all.

4. Clarity and Consistency of Testing Procedures, Protocols and Penalties

The Football Association admitted that they had been caught out by Rio Ferdinand's drugs case. David Davies, the FA's executive director, said of their testing procedure: 'It is apparent to some of us it was not introduced with people who wouldn't turn up in mind. We didn't envisage someone failing to take a test.'[30] Neither had the FA paid sufficient attention to the timescale and efficiency of their procedures (for one thing, the appeal procedure was long and cumbersome), to rule clarity, transparency of process, and awareness of their rules, protocols and penalties.

We can ask questions, too, about the management of the actual testing event itself. Ferdinand was deemed to have missed the test, even though he called the testers within 90 minutes of his appointed time. Who was it who decided that two hours was the limit, that 30 minutes was insufficient time for Rio to attend, and that there was to be no discretion on the matter? Doubtless they are very busy people, but why could the testers not have waited a few more minutes for Rio to arrive, given the gravity of a failure to attend? FA General Secretary Graham Kelly reports that the FA only later drew up 'revised procedures to include this two-hour stipulation'.

Next, we can point to many inconsistencies in treatment of individuals. In 2002 FIFA allowed the FA to let off Billy Turley, who had tested positive for nandrolone. Edgar Davids and Jaap Stam were both banned by UEFA for five months for testing positive for nandrolone, whilst Rio got eight months for a failure/refusal followed shortly by a negative test.

The harsher treatment of Rio may be related to the aim of making an example of a high-profile player − of setting the standard for future cases. Two members of the three-man tribunal that convicted Ferdinand sat in a case involving the little-known Manchester City player Christian Ngouai, who committed the same offence earlier in the year, and who received only a £2,000 fine. Ngouai, also, was allowed an hour's grace to complete the test.

Even the UEFA guidelines currently suggested a minimum six month ban for a first offence, but at the time FIFA was in discussions with WADA. So the harsher treatment may also be related to the national and international politics of football. The FA had recently appointed a new chief executive who, it could be argued, used the high profile of Ferdinand to set an example for a firmer stance on disciplinary issues.[31] At the same time, the IOC and WADA were struggling to persuade governments to contribute their share to the funding of WADA, and to persuade some of the more influential and powerful international sports federations to agree to the WADA code, so as fully to internationalize its provisions and to render clear its guidelines and coherent its punishments. FIFA president Sepp Blatter's calls for a greater punishment for Rio attest to the growing rapprochement of FIFA with WADA, since FIFA was a notable non-signatory to the WADA code. Blatter was working with Dick Pound, chair of WADA, towards an agreement whose importance to them both can be assessed by the fact that it was announced at a special ceremony at the FIFA Centennial Congress in Paris in May 2004. At that time, IOC president Jacques Rogge praised Blatter for FIFA's compliance, noting that the agreement sends a clear signal to other governments and international sports organizations.

Finally, we should record the many inconsistencies in rules and their application across sports. The IAAF controls athletics, and issues a two-year ban for a first drugs offence, and a life ban for a second. All of the footballers discussed would have been banned for two years if they had been athletes. It could be said that such inconsistencies are a direct result of the powerful professional federations of football, tennis and cycling protecting their valuable assets, their professional athletes, and calculating their financial losses over an extended ban. In addition, their athletes are willing and able to defend themselves in the courts, so the federations fear bankruptcy if successfully sued by their own athletes.

The athletes have a right to know what to expect from the disciplinary process.[32] On the evidence of prior cases, Rio had every right to conclude that any punishment would be nugatory. If he (or anyone advising him) had reason to believe that an eight-month ban was even a remote possibility, the whole event might have been differently managed.

5.   *Player Protection – The Role and Responsibilities of the Club and Others*

Rio Ferdinand should have been better advised and protected by those around him. Sebastian Coe said:

> But how could a club with their wealth and resources allow this situation to develop? Once the truth emerged, they were outraged that they couldn't shut up shop. But this was not just an impertinent question from a journalist that could be slapped away. Beyond missing his test, I don't necessarily think Rio was guilty of anything more than being involved with a club who could not see the importance of this issue. Manchester United ... implied that random testing is some sort of personal intrusion. They're living in la-la land.[33]

WADA was set up in 1999 to develop international co-operation in the fight against doping. It is now backed not only by the IOC, but also by more than 70 governments, and most of the International Sports Federations. It wants a two-year ban for a first drugs offence, and a life ban for a second, as in athletics, and a strict liability policy. Why did those in charge of football in England, and those whose well-paid responsibility it was to protect the player and the club's asset, not see this coming?

Outcome

Since Rio is palpably innocent of taking any performance-enhancing substance, and the temporary amnesia argument is unconvincing, a not unreasonable supposition is that he deliberately evaded the test because he wished to avoid detection of some non-performance-enhancing substance in his system. The irony is that it is not clear why such a substance should be any of the business of UK Sport, the FA, or his club.

He has been punished because failure to attend = test refusal = presumption of guilt of using a performance-enhancing drug. Although we can be pretty sure that he was innocent of that, because of the subsequent negative test, nevertheless the UK Sport anti-doping system ground out its result. If he was merely seeking to avoid the club's disciplinary procedures for the use of a social drug, or to preserve his privacy over a medical matter, he nevertheless ran foul of the performance-enhancing drug detection machinery.

As it is, the consequences were very serious indeed. Not only did a player in his prime – some think the best defender at the 2002 World Cup – spend many months in enforced idleness, but also his club suffered badly. A few weeks after his ban, Manchester United had the worst defensive record in the Premier League, dropped 12 points behind the leaders, and eventually lost their champions title. And although his country put up a fair performance at the Euro 2004 championship we can't really estimate the consequences of his absence.

Rio is now back playing for club and country, the FA has improved its procedures, and FIFA has signed up to WADA. But it is hard to believe see how the FA, the PFA, MUFC and Rio's agent and advisers come out of this with any credit at all.

GREG RUSEDSKI

The Case

In 2002, the Czech tennis player Bohdan Ulihrach was found to have taken the steroid nandrolone and was banned for two years by the Association of Tennis Professionals (ATP). However, other players who gave samples at around the same time also showed elevated nandrolone levels and an enquiry by an IOC-accredited laboratory in Montreal revealed that all these cases had a 'common analytical fingerprint' – that is, were likely to have come from the same ingredients. These ingredients were mineral supplements and electrolytes that had been provided by the ATP trainers to players on the ATP tour. Ulihrach's sentence was quashed, and charges were dropped against six other unnamed players.

On 23 July the British tennis number two, Greg Rusedski, tested positive for the steroid nandrolone on the ATP tour in Indianapolis. His was one of 47 positive samples from the top 120 players, all of which demonstrated the 'common analytical fingerprint', such as was unknown in any other sport, thus indicating a single source from within tennis. Of the 47 positive samples, 43 cases were not investigated further. However, Rusedski's sample was one of four taken two months after the trainers had been instructed to desist, and so the ATP moved to prosecution. Rusedski announced his involvement publicly, denied any wrong-doing and declared his intention to defend himself.

1.   Strict liability

If the principle of strict liability were to hold, the question arises as to why the ATP saw fit to quash Ulihrach's sentence and to drop charges against others. Many athletes, including Alain Baxter, as we have seen, have been able to tell a story that might have provided a good excuse for the existence of banned substances in their bodies – and yet they have still received punishments, presumably on the ground that any relaxation of the principle would open the flood-gates to imaginative athletes and clever lawyers.

The first point to notice, then, is that in the case of Ulihrach and others the ATP breached the principle of strict liability.

2.   Acknowledgement of a Wider Authority

The ATP would not have been able to do this if it had been willing to acknowledge a wider authority in doping matters. Here it is useful to ask what reason there is for more than one governing body in world tennis, over and above the obvious economic reasons. For the origins of this scandal lie not only in the incompetence of the ATP, but also in an arrogant isolationism, which presumably preserves its power over the game. The ATP were all at once: provider of the banned substance, provider of the agents who supplied the substance to the athletes, employer of the athletes, policeman, judge and jury.

Without outside checks or referral to any authority other than itself there is a rich context here for confusion and injustice. Some of this could surely have been avoided if there were a unified world administration for tennis, and if tennis had signed up to the provisions of WADA. The ATP could even have taken the issue to the Court of Arbitration for Sport in Lausanne in 2002, instead of trying to deal with it 'in-house'. It didn't do so, and thus the Rusedski case was an accident waiting to happen. This raises serious questions about the governance of tennis at the highest level.

Parsons reports that the International Tennis Federation, who deal with offences involving Grand Slam tournaments and Davis Cup matches, were furious at the ATP because their high-handed approach was bound to suggest that tennis does not take drug-testing as seriously as other sporting bodies,[34] whereas top professionals (for example, Agassi) argue that tennis is among the best-policed sports.[35]

3.   Equitable Estoppel

The ATP presumably realised that it had placed itself in an impossible position, having accepted that it had provided the contaminated supplements in the first place, and that at least the majority of its athletes who tested positive were not guilty of any intentional wrong-doing. Of course, this alone would not have been a defence against the strict liability rule, but Ulihrach's ban was overturned in July 2003 on the grounds of 'equitable estoppel', the legal principle that says that a person cannot be prosecuted for an offence that is shown to be the fault of the prosecuting authority.[36] Now we can see the importance of reference to authorities other than oneself, for the defence of equitable estoppel was available to the player only because the ATP was both an agent in the offence and the prosecutor. This is a direct result of tennis not signing up to WADA, and being policed by itself. Rusedski, too, relied upon this defence.

4.   Reliance on Science (of nandrolone in the body, and of quantities)

It is difficult to see how we can have good law if it is based on flawed or inadequate science. And, of course, less than reliable science also brings dope testing, and sport itself, into disrepute.

Dr Wheeler, from St Thomas' Hospital, London, is quoted as saying that there is evidence that after a competitive event or hard training, nandrolone levels go up above the limit. Nandrolone can also easily enter the body through contaminated hydrating substances or through contaminated meat; and legal dietary supplements are broken down by the body to produce the same substances created when nandrolone is broken down in the body. Also, nandrolone traces can persist within the body for up to 12 months. Finally, Wheeler states that 'the nandrolone research that was carried out was on a few individuals who were not athletes'.[37]

One ruling in 1999 of the Court of Arbitration for Sport in Lausanne supports these misgivings and said that, despite the WADA ruling that 4 nanograms of nandrolone per millilitre of urine should be the limit, 2 to 5 nanograms was a 'grey area', and that such a level 'could be the result of endogenous production of the human body'.[38] Such findings suggest that too strict an application of the rules might well result in injustice, and to avoid it we need to be as sure as we can be that we can rely on the science behind the rules.

5. Supplements

Since Rusedski's case rests on allegations of contaminated supplements, it raises the general issue of supplements. Richard Quick, a swimming coach who thinks of himself as someone 'on the cutting edge of what can be done nutritionally and with supplements' is quoted as claiming that his athletes can do 'steroid-like performances', trying to 'keep up with the people who are cheating without cheating'.[39] And there are other 'artificial' means of enhancing performance, such as the altitude chamber which, whilst not illegal, severely test our intuitions as to what should be permissible. 'A whole team of long-distance runners sponsored by Nike lives in a much more elaborate simulated high-altitude dwelling in Portland, Oregon.'[40]

So comprehensive and elaborate are the plans for nutrition, supplementation, enhancement and doping that, from the point of view of the athlete, it can be difficult to see where one begins and the other ends. There has also been some official confusion over the relative seriousness of a particular drug, for example in cases involving modafinil. When Kelli White, who was a training partner of Dwain Chambers, tested positive at the World Championships, the International Association of Athletics Federations (IAAF) classified modafinil as a mild stimulant.

> The classification meant White faced disqualification and losing her 100 and 200m gold medals – but no ban. The new WADA list of prohibited substances, published on Jan 1, however, includes modafinil as a major stimulant.[41]

So was she taking a mild or a major stimulant? Did she take it or was she given it to take? Did she really appreciate what she was doing and what the consequences might be?

> Kelli White . . . lost her medals and prize money after a drug test showed that she had taken the stimulant modafinil. 'After a competition', she said, 'it's hard to remember everything that you take during the day'.[42]

How revealing – this suggests a regime designed by a team of support staff, to which the athlete submits. Even 'clean' athletes take a cocktail of pills that they hope will compensate for the supposed advantages of the banned substances taken by the cheats who risk detection. Greg Rusedski took such a cocktail every day, with a detailed and systematic diary – and we should assume that this is the rule rather than the exception amongst elite athletes, many of whom tread a fine line between the legal and the illegal.

6.   The Effect on the Logic of a Competition

As with Rio, Greg Rusedski was free to continue playing competitive tennis until his tribunal, held eight months after his positive test. We have contradictory intuitions and traditions operating here. On the one hand, he's 'innocent until found guilty', and should not be penalized in advance of the tribunal. On the other hand, a serious charge often brings an immediate suspension from duty pending investigations. For, if guilty, he would have been allowed to play as a cheat.

In the Baxter case, his Olympic bronze medal had to be returned, and the next best competitor was elevated – but what can the organizers of a tennis tournament do if a cheat wins a tournament? In like fashion, the cheat's result could be expunged, and other players advanced in the rankings. But, in this case, not only would he have won the contest; but also he would have beaten players in earlier rounds who were then knocked out, so that they could not make their mark in further rounds. Someone might reasonably claim, as the England football team regularly does in the World Cup after meeting Brazil, 'If he hadn't beaten me in an earlier round, I might well have gone on to win'. To expunge not only his tournament win, but all of his results, would make a nonsense of the whole tournament.

Outcome

Rusedski was found not guilty at tribunal, and left without a stain on his character. Doubtless he will continue to keep a check on the supplements he takes, and will get them regularly tested for himself.

Conclusion

Sometimes, we want the law to be clear-cut and evenly applied, but what we have seen through a consideration of these cases is that there is often genuine complexity and difficulty in the context and in the detail of the particular case. Outcomes are often determined not just by the rule, but also in the interpretation and application of the rule, which requires reference to background moral principles. In turn, those principles can only themselves be applied with reference to empirical features of the case, and also to facts of the matter. Mitigation, too, is almost wholly determined by context and by the features of the particular case.

What we learn from this is that justice does not run on rails. There is no simple reading-off of the correct disposal of the case from the rules governing it. Rather, it is a matter of thoughtful judgement, the weighing of all the elements present, and the bringing to bear of wider moral principles. We also learn that, if we carefully consider a range of cases, we can test both them and ourselves for consistency of approach and consistency in application of principle, and thereby extend our capacity for thinking through cases and arriving at just disposals.

We need to be constantly vigilant that consistency across cases is preserved. In order to achieve this, we should be on the lookout for any more general outcomes that might be applied across cases, and asking whether any more systematic view is achievable.

Acknowledgements

In the preparation of this essay I would like to acknowledge the contribution of first year students on the Philosophy of Sport and Exercise component of their degree course at Leeds Metropolitan University in the year 2003–04.

It was teaching these students that made me look at these issues again, especially in detailed application to the four contemporary cases. I am grateful to all those Carnegie students who contributed their ideas to vigorous discussions.

An early version of the essay was read at the First Annual Conference of the British Philosophy of Sport Association in Cheltenham, May 2004, and the final version at the National Seminar on Ethics of Sport (part of the FIEP Congress), January 2005, in Foz do Iguaçu, Brazil.

Notes

[1] Tamburrini, 'What's Wrong with Doping?', 215.
[2] Schneider, 'Genetic Enhancement of Athletic Performance', 40.
[3] Davies, 'British skier stripped of bronze', *Reuters* (21 March 2002).
[4] Ibid.
[5] Ibid.
[6] For more information, refer to the World Anti-Doping Agency's website, available at http://www.wada-ama.org.
[7] Cairns, 'Drug Legislation and Related Issues', 121–2.
[8] Flint, 'The Regulation of Drug Use in Sport – E4.134', See, in particular, *Baxter v. IOC*, 955.
[9] Bell, 'Comment', www.guardiansports.co.uk, (5 Jan. 2004).
[10] Cairns, 'Drug Legislation and Related Issues', 122.
[11] Hart, 'Rusedski seeks Compensation', *Sunday Telegraph* (11 Jan. 2004).
[12] Hart, 'Chambers "in denial" over use of drugs', *Reuters* (26 Oct. 2003).
[13] Coe, 'No Room for Leniency on Chambers Drugs Ban', *Reuters* (10 Nov. 2003).
[14] Ashley, 'Doping by Design', 22–3. For a detailed account of the process, see Longman and Drape, 'How a New Steroid Was Decoded', *New York Times* (2 Nov. 2003).
[15] Pound, available online at http://www.wada-ama.org/en/t1.asp?p = 41275&x = 1&a = 89361.
[16] Knight, 'Chambers will plead innocent', *Reuters* (8 Nov. 2003).
[17] Ibid.
[18] Knight, 'Chambers faces new drug shame', *Reuters* (24 Nov. 2003).
[19] Knight, 'Athletics: WADA warn of long-term THG danger', *Reuters* (30 Jan. 2004).
[20] Mackay, 'Chambers warned of liver damage', *Guardian* (30 Jan. 2004).
[21] Knight, 'Chambers faces new drug shame', *Reuters* (24 Nov. 2003).
[22] Ibid.

[23] Ibid.
[24] Davies, 'FA admit to failings on drugs', *Reuters* (1 Dec. 2003).
[25] Hytner, 'Savage: We've no complaints', *Daily Express* (5 Feb. 2004), 75.
[26] Kelso, 'Record ban for Ferdinand', *Guardian* (20 Dec. 2003), 1.
[27] Kelso, 'Let's kick hypocrisy out of sport', *Guardian* (20 Oct. 2004).
[28] Thompson, 'Privacy and the Urinalysis Testing of Athletes', 315.
[29] Kelso, 'Let's kick hypocrisy out of sport', *Guardian* (20 Oct. 2004).
[30] Davies, 'FA admit to failings on drugs', *Reuters* (1Dec. 2003).
[31] McCarra, 'FA's tough line stuns United', *Guardian Sport* (20 Dec. 2003), 2.
[32] Hansen, 'Eight months is vicious', *Reuters* (22 Dec. 2003).
[33] McRae, 'We've tottered from one drug-ridden debacle to another', *Guardian* (26 Jan. 2004).
[34] Parsons, 'ATP take the blame for drug tests on players', *Reuters* (10 July 2003).
[35] Parsons, 'Agassi adds insight into debate over drug testing', *Reuters* (22 Jan. 2004). See also Shine, 'Agassi says tennis is "leading sport" in testing for drugs', *Independent* (14 Jan. 2004).
[36] Hart, 'Rusedski seeks compensation', *Sunday Telegraph*, 11 January 2004.
[37] Wheeler, 'Nandrolone information and steroid risks', *BBC News Online* (5 Aug. 1999).
[38] Goodbody, 'Discrepancy in dates means Rusedski has to do some explaining', *Times* (10 Jan. 2004), 42.
[39] M. Sokolove, 'The Shape to Come'. *Observer Sports Magazine* (8 Feb. 2004), 50–7.
[40] Ibid.
[41] Knight, 'Athletics: WADA warn of long-term THG danger', *Reuters* (30 Jan. 2004).
[42] Sokolove, 'The Shape to Come', 52.

References

Ashley, S. "Doping by Design". *Scientific American* 290, no. 2 (2004): 22–3.
Cairns, W. "Drug Legislation and Related Issues". *Sport and The Law Journal* 11, no. 1 (2003): 118–23.
Flint, C., Taylor, J. and Lewis A. "The Regulation of Drug Use in Sport – E4.134". In *Sport, Law and Practice*, edited by A. Lewis and J. Taylor. London: Butterworths, 2003.
Grayson, E. *Sport and the Law*. 5th edn. London: Butterworths, 1999.
Houlihan, B. *Dying To Win*. 2nd edn. Germany: Council of Europe Publishing, 2002.
Morgan, W. J. and K. V. Meier, eds. *Philosophic Inquiry in Sport*. Urbana/Champaign, IL: Human Kinetics, 1988.
Schneider, A. "Genetic Enhancement of Athletic Performance". In *The Genetic Design of Winners*, edited by C. Tamburrini and T. Tännsjö. London: Routledge, forthcoming.
Tamburrini, C. "What's Wrong with Doping?" In *Values in Sport*, edited by C. Tamburrini and T. Tännsjö. London: Routledge, 2000.
Tamburrini, C. and T. Tännsjö, eds. *Values in Sport*. London: Routledge, 2000.
Tamburrini, C. and T. Tännsjö, eds. *Genetic Technology and Sport*. London: Routledge, 2005.
Thompson, P. B. "Privacy and the Urinalysis Testing of Athletes". In *Philosophic Enquiry in Sport*, edited by W. J. Morgan and K. V. Meier. Urbana/Champaign, IL: Human Kinetics, 1988.
Waddington, I. *Sport, Health and Drugs – A Critical Sociological Perspective*. London: E & FN Spon, 2000.

The Japanese Debate Surrounding the Doping Ban: The Application of the Harm Principle

Yoshitaka Kondo

Representative Discussions of Doping in Japan

Doping has been banned since the Olympic Games of 1968 [1]. However, rather than disappearing during the following 35 years, doping violations and suspicions have been frequently reported. There have even recently been cases of the detection of new steroids (THG: tetrahydrogestrinone), which has led to allegations that well-known American professional and amateur athletes used banned substances [2]. In addition, the gold medalist in the women's 100 m and 200 m events at the World Track and Field Championships last year was compelled to forfeit the medals she won due to her use of the stimulant Modafinil, while also being banned from competing for two years [3]. There are a number of reasons why the doping problem seems to defy resolution and I would like to point out at least two of them here after first describing the main arguments used by four key individuals involved in the doping debate in Japan.

The imperative that 'doping is bad' is followed in Japan, and, as a result, most violations in the past arose from ignorance rather than intentional violations [4]. The most severely punished Japanese case was a candidate athlete, Ito Yoshitaka, who competed in the men's 100 m event at the Atlantic Olympics in 1996. He tested positive in an out-of-competition test (OOCT) during the training period and lost his eligibility to compete for four years. Subsequently, he received a severe punishment as he was unable to overturn the test results at his hearing, despite his desperate attempt to show that he had either accidentally or inadvertently used the banned substance. Thus, with only scattered cases of unintentional or inadvertent use, Japanese athletes are generally considered to be relatively clean [5]. However, given the fact that there are some 1,500 or more athletes around the world who violate doping rules every year,[6] one is led to believe that there are some athletes who have no intention whatsoever of observing the rules from the very start.

The assertions of four individuals involved in the doping debate in Japan provide context and background on how doping is viewed in Japan. The first, Ryuta Imafuku, demonstrates a negative view of doping prohibitions, particularly those that ban the use of stimulants in sport. He uses the doping-related disqualification of Diego Maradona prior to the 1994 World Cup as an example and points out the problems with prohibiting doping, noting that Maradona's skill and reputation as a fair player were marred by the doping charges levelled against him. The prohibited drug detected in Maradona was the stimulant ephedrine, which contributed to Imafuku's dismay that 'Maradona was branded as a disqualified sports champion by his action in violation of the rules' [7]. Imafuku is sceptical about the prohibition on stimulant use in sport and concludes that it is impossible to scientifically draw the line on the effects of stimulants, citing cases of ethnological findings.

Imafuku also notes 'the involvement of drugs in the creative activities of contemporary artists is a fact that anyone would recognize including the records left by the artists themselves' [8]. However, the natural endowments of athletes are assessed in a category different from those of artists. He sees a difference between the ethical assessment of artists and athletes, which is demonstrated by his assertion that 'there is no room for the ideology of fairness in sports to be set within the ambiguous subjective realm of artistic creation' [9]. Ultimately, even if they have the same natural endowments, athletes and artists are assessed differently. From the contrast between artists and athletes, he points out the ideological orientation that is concealed in the sports world:

> It must be said that, in the concept of doping, the body of the athlete is considered to be a purely uniform structure and that it is thoroughly imbued with a perspective that negates its artistic and fluid existence. It is this concept itself of grasping the body of athletes only as an impartial kinetic machine, the true essence of the ideology that is hidden in the background of the ouster of Maradona. Maradona, who was an 'artist' in the true sense of the word, was reluctantly consigned to oblivion under the name of fairness as an athlete [10].

Imafuku's patronage to Maradona may be judged as almost emotional. Imafuku's assertion also suggests the possibility of the emergence of a different value judgment in the doping problem depending on how you position the existence of athletes. This assertion presents the connotation that the shackle applied by the traditional ethical view of sports that exists only on the surface reduces by half the appeal of sports, which is a point that should be heeded attentively. After all, the present-day sports world ostracizes amateurism and, in a sense, has transformed athletes to consumer goods while removing traditional sports ethics at the core.

Imafuku's views differ from those of Koji Taki, who has made a name for himself as a thinker with his multifaceted philosophy regarding various problems in modern-day culture. In his book, *Thinking about Sport*, Taki takes sports as the subject of his research and attempts to penetrate capital, nationalism and the physical body. He asserts that present-day sports are subjected to various influences prompted by the introduction of massive capital, the development of technology and the refinement of timekeeping methods and, as a result, 'naturally, it means waiting for the development of an abnormal body, training methods are developed and doping (the use of drugs to fortify the body) is in wide use' [11]. Taki also puts forth the following analysis:

> the statement that doping is bad goes unchallenged, the fact that it is widely used is an open secret. De Coubertin's ideal that sports are for the purpose of achieving a sound physical and mental balance has been discarded somewhere along the way [12].

With this in mind, Taki comprehends the structure of the doping problem as indicated below:

> When records have extended this far and competition intensifies surrounding the issue of minute differences, the natural way of training the body is no longer able to keep pace. The biological evolution of the human body has already reached completion. However, sports as devised by humans have become a realm of sophisticated information and have begun to transcend physical nature. In order to compensate for this imbalance, it is not strange that the dependence on technology for the modification of the body has become the natural turn of events. This modification does not stop at the level of scientific training that I have already described. Doping, which promotes the strengthening of the muscles by using anabolic steroids and other drugs, extends out broadly [13].

Athletes utilize the power of technology in order to satisfy the consumption demands of sport spectators while reaching the limits of the natural training of the body. The sports world is swallowed whole by the theory of production and consumption of capitalistic society and technology itself is in an uncontrollable state without any ethical consideration given to body modification. Taki insists that doping is ultimately inevitable when sports scientists agree to take part in the unnatural training of the body and efforts are made to enhance the consumption value of athletes and sport.

Taki also looks back, from a historical perspective, at conditions that made doping inevitable. Doping, which started originally with racehorses and fighting dogs, was eventually applied to humans. However, after the Second World War, it gradually became treated as a problem both in medical and ethical terms, culminating in the enactment of rules prohibiting doping in 1968. However, he cites the point that 'the French sports physician claimed that doping statistics are unreliable'[14] and points out the uncertainty of publicly released data. Taki explains:

in his autobiography, Harald Schumacher, former goalkeeper of the West German soccer team, exposed the fact that the West German team was engaged in doping on an everyday basis and Zico, who is very well known in Japan, also spoke on TV about the careless doping checks that were conducted while he was playing in Italy [15].

Even though regulations to prohibit doping began to appear, the excessive power of those in control did not decline. Ultimately, modern sports are one facet of the culture of capitalist society and people consume sports as such culture.

Taki is pessimistic about the future state of doping. He is unconvinced that the current protocol used to combat doping in sport is effective:

> they have countered the ever increasingly long list of drugs by suspending the use of drugs for a certain period prior to the match to avoid being detected in the tests or by developing new drugs. As a result, the struggle of doping vs. anti-doping has turned into a cat-and-mouse game and, as long as humans continue to pursue new records or victory, there will certainly be no way to break loose from doping... Those who test positive in drug tests are not only stripped of their medals but generally are prohibited from further participation in sporting events for a certain period of time. This is clearly a form of ethical punishment. Yet it is no longer possible to bring an end to doping by appealing to morality. With records gradually reaching the limit, could we not assume that the overall realm of sports, obsessed by victory with a lineup of athletes demonstrating superb capabilities, urges on the development of drugs capable of not being detected in tests as well as dependence on drugs [16].

He even claims that the doping conditions have become totally lost in a maze and it is no longer possible to appeal to morality.

Taki also notes that an excessive force is nurtured by modern society and that this has changed the conventional view of the body. The principles of capitalism have intruded into the sports world and, in order to maintain a balance between the product value of sports culture and consumption value, technology, represented by sports science research, is introduced to natural training methods, which leads to the inevitability of doping. In short, the doping problem arose from within the sports world and was accelerated by the destruction of amateur rules. The doping problem is a production of commercialism. The changing view of the body in modern society furthermore spurred that on and society is steadily tolerating intentional body modification. We are living in an era when people decide for themselves how they treat their own bodies.

Taki's analysis of the doping problem based on this sort of commercialism and the change in the view of the body provides suggestions that are definitely worthy of attention. It is also a fact, however, that the ideal form of the sports world is not visible based on his assertion. Even if his analysis of the problem is indisputable, it is not able to lead us to that ideal. It is unclear whether we should try to halt commercialism or to change our views of the body. Though the analysis of the current state of doping is an important task, it is probably necessary to pursue a further examination of the direction in which it leads.

Naoomi Kusabuka, on the other hand, holds the view that doping is the ultimate disgrace of international sports. He notes two particularly problematic areas in sport: the first being the proliferation of doping on a global scale, and the second being the actual circumstances of top athletes and the approach of medical science. In regard to the widespread use of doping, Kusabuka astutely notes 'doping is expanding across national borders ... and this is not a situation that can be coped with by means of the norms and laws of single countries' [17]. He calls into question the grounds on which substances are banned, while noting the distinction between drug use and drug abuse [18]. He notes that situations exist where physicians can prescribe certain drugs to ordinary patients but not to athletes. If the physician is obliged to refrain from prescribing the best medication and select a different prescription, just because it is on the list of prohibited drugs, there is a possibility that damage to one's dignity as a human being or, in other words, a violation of human rights, might occur.

Overcoming this contradiction is one of the issues involved in the anti-doping movement. Kusabuka questions 'whether or not the anti-doping movement can overcome the differences in positive law and culture in each country and the justice of sports centred in fair play can be established as the common standard of humanity' [19]. This point is exemplified by the 'great doping incident' that occurred at the Nagano Winter Olympic Games in 1998 when Canadian snowboarder Ross Rebagliati tested positive for cannabis. The problem gives rise not only to the way each country treats cannabis but also the different responses by international sports organizations. For example, the International Ski Federation had set the standard for cannabis violation at 15 nanograms; however, the International Snowboard Federation had no rules at all for cannabis. Meanwhile, the medical rules (Chapter 2, Section III, Article B) of the IOC, merely stated that cannabis is 'a substance subject to a certain degree of regulation' and did not clearly define the standards for determining violations. Since the standards for violation were not clearly delineated, the IOC disqualified the athlete and stripped him of his medal, while the Court of Arbitration for Sport (CAS) decided to invalidate the treatment and return the medal to Rebagliati. Of course, the use of cannabis is prohibited in Japanese society; however, all countries do not respond in the same manner, to say nothing of the differences between international sports organizations. In this problem, not only positive law and sports norms (ethics) but also the relationship to the positive law and norms (ethics) of each country would probably be called into question.

Returning to Kusabuka's assertion, his stance toward the doping problem in Japan can be summarized with the following:

> if we do not form a consensus on fundamental standards for why doping is bad or why it is illicit, regardless of the measures that may be devised to fortify testing and penalties, the initiatives would probably not be effective [20].

Unless the doping problem is scrutinized by returning to the point of origin, it will probably be impossible to resolve using simple remedies.

The second factor pointed out by Kusabuka that complicates the problem is the actual circumstances of top athletes together with the approach of medical science. The age when athletes who participated in the Olympic Games and other international sports tournaments trained on their own or through friendly competition with their rivals as in the past has come to an end, and project teams are now being formed with the participation of the athletes as well as coaches, physicians, trainers, counsellors, dieticians and others. The very livelihood of the project depends on the performance of the athlete. The doping problem even has an impact on the subsistence rights of athletes and their support staff. Competitive sports involving the top athletes represent a very ordinary and secular world rather than an extraordinary or imaginary one. As Kusabuka notes:

> in that sense, it would not be possible to prohibit doping only for medical or health reasons. Even if drugs have after-effects that conspicuously damage health or cause various disorders, would it be possible after all to prohibit drugs if they were used with the approval of the athletes themselves?[21]

Thus, he raises the point that assertions based on subsistence rights weaken the legitimacy of doping bans.

For example, as stated above, there are cases in which professional dancers use self-managed drugs in order to carry out long performances and there have been cases of movie stars confessing to the use of drugs in the past. Thus, even if one argues persuasively that doping is harmful to one's own health, it would not be very persuasive to athletes who use drugs with their own approval, or go ahead with the use of drugs on the pretext of subsistence rights. However, Kusabuka states that 'the problem is not viewing athletes to be the same as artists but whether or not it is possible to tolerate "maniacal artists" or "diabolical arts"'[22], and continues, 'the most important thing is to lay the groundwork that would not permit or tolerate doping' [23]. Furthermore, assessing the current social climate, he comments that,

> as long as a moral tone exists that allows and openly tolerates the so-called 'she-males', who promote sex changes appearing shamelessly on television, would it ever be possible to eliminate 'sex change' as inhumane or degrading?[24]

If we follow this assertion of Kusabuka's, there can be no doubt that current social trends are transforming the sports world. Sensationalistic reporting by the media and spectators who engage in riotous behaviour can also be seen as factors that are amplifying the allure of doping.

Kusabuka warns that social trends are further spurring the present day conditions of top athletes and support staff. Still, there are many obstacles to be overcome in his conclusion, which restricts the doping problem within a specific value system. If his value system had been accepted, the doping problem would probably not have induced such serious circumstances. If we accept that there is a possibility of returning to the tradition of sports ethics, it would be necessary to clarify even the means for building consensus based on a specific value system. By merely presenting a value system, it probably would not function as a driving force in improving the current conditions.

The fourth Japanese perspective examined here belongs to Toshio Nakamura, who is concerned about lifting the ban on doping and the self-destruction of the sports world. His position is that accepting both damage to health and inequality as reasons for the ban on doping is problematic because 'besides the conjecture that the ban on doping may even be lifted in the near future, the problem of losing the cultural value of sports is also emerging' [25]. He assumes that the grounds for lifting the ban on doping will emerge when the 'damage to health' and 'inequality' issues are overcome. He thinks that using the damage to health issue as a reason for banning doping will no longer be valid if it were possible to restore abnormally trained bodies to their original form after two or three years of rehabilitation, and conjectures that 'this will more than likely be possible sooner or later given the current state of medical research' [26].

Nakamura cites the IOC, the International Sports Federation, and the Japan Sports Federation, as examples of organizations that are equally guilty of the same obsession that athletes have with doping. In particular, Nakamura criticizes the temperament of the IOC:

> This is substantiated by the fact that there are many who support of this absolutist structure that makes it possible for the chairman to continue serving by changing the organization's rules and it is possible to conjecture that, if this persists for a long time, it gives rise to corruption and approaches closer to decadence, thereby probably escalating the acquisition of material gain and doping[27].

He states the fact that the persistence of this temperament is a sign that sports are treading the path toward self-destruction and that 'they are following in the footsteps of ancient Rome' [28].

Nakamura analyses the doping problem from the starting point of equality, but he also offers a different novel perspective. If doping is the physical processing of the body, mental processing uses mental training or latent perception stimulation (subliminal method), which is a further improvement of that. Latent perception stimulation is a method that uses subliminal stimulation, which is stimulation at the subconscious level that cannot be sensed by the brain and, in the case of athletes, training and game messages are fed into the brain. Nakamura thus argues:

> mental training carried out in this manner ... is an attempt to intentionally manipulate the human mentality by an artificial and heteronomous means and, furthermore, in extreme cases, it has the possibility of 'inducing a hypnotic state in athletes through the use of wireless earphones' and it would therefore be more appropriate to refer to it as 'mental doping' that transcends mental training [29].

He also expresses concern about the possibility of the advance of method processing through technological advancement. He considers mental processing a behaviour that violates human dignity for the purpose of gaining victory. In the debate regarding the banning of doping, in the 1960s, hypnotism and other psychological methods were also prohibited as doping but the ban was eliminated because of the lack of a means to detect them. However, there is a need to closely scrutinize whether or not methods that apply manipulation at the subconscious level should be tolerated. As Nakamura points out, 'dignity is being forfeited for the sake of honor';[30] even if it is possible as a method for pursuing victory, there is probably a need for a close examination from the perspective of ethics or sports ethics regarding its applicability to athletes. Nakamura's arguments thus focus on the concept of equality advocated by modern sports.

The views of Imafuku, Taki, Kusabuka and Nakamura characterize and represent some of the dominant views on doping in the context of Japanese culture. I have approached the problem using such key words as 'the nature of sportsmanship', 'product of consumption society', 'return to sports ethical view', and 'equality' and, as a result, I have reaffirmed that there is a large accumulation of difficult issues that are still waiting to be resolved in the doping problem.

Why the Doping Problem Defies Resolution

One of the main reasons why doping violations take place globally is the problem of borderline results. Ambiguity is sometimes present in the standards used to distinguish between positive and negative results; hence the resulting possibility of false positive and false negative results can occur. The general understanding is that a positive result indicates an athlete has violated the rules and a negative result indicates an athlete has not. However, this is not always so. To be more precise, there are, of course, athletes among those who test negatively who did not indulge in doping but, besides that, there are also athletes who indulged in doping but managed to test negatively by not exceeding the established standards or by utilizing masking agents.

As we are all aware, acts that openly violate, or nearly violate, the rules during sport competition are referred to as professional fouls and are tolerated or even at times praised. The general line of thinking in the competitive sport world is that acts that violate the rules, or are borderline violations, are acceptable as long as the referees do not see them. This practice also applies to doping and is likely linked to the idea that there is no problem as long as what the athlete does is within the scope of the standards that determine violations. The dominant view that violations of the rules are a part of the game is probably one reason why the doping problem is so difficult to resolve.

Another reason is the idea that doping is probably acceptable as long as the athletes are fully aware of the adverse effects doping has on their health. This, in other words, is the approach of allowing them to make their own decisions regarding their own persons, leaving the individual to decide where to place his or her values and recognizing the values of each person's values in a relative manner [31].

The issue of individuality will probably be called into question with respect to health conditions [32]. That is, there is also the problem of whether or not the overall health of athletes who become involved in doping can be judged by the same standards as that of the general public [33]. It is generally said that the line separating normal and abnormal is a deviation of 95 per cent of the average value. Based on that, the world's top athletic competitors would probably be judged as abnormal. From the perspective of the individuality of health conditions, would it be possible to apply the same standards for treating disabilities and illnesses in leading athletic competitors with the standards of treating the general public who fall within the range of normality? In order to restore optimal performance as quickly as possible, for example, would it not perhaps be acceptable to use prohibited drugs, prescribed by a physician, if that were considered to be the best practice for treatment? We risk violating one of the basic human rights of athletes if we prohibit them from receiving the best treatments because the World Anti-Doping Code forbids the use of the most effective medications in sport. At the same time, since doping rules exist, there are also concerns regarding health damage when athletes resort to acquiring drugs on the black market or decide upon their own treatment without consulting with physicians or experts. There is thus a need for a reconsideration of the doping rules from the standpoint of the individuality of health conditions.

Furthermore, value relativism and the acceptance or tolerance of pluralistic lifestyles among individuals is now reaching new heights; consequently, universal values are viewed with suspicion. Present-day society in Japan recognizes intentional modification of the body for reasons other than medical treatment. For example, ear piercing, liposuction, breast augmentation, constraining or promoting growth in stature, cosmetic surgery, and other plastic surgery procedures, though not covered by insurance, are tolerated as a reflection of individual lifestyles in Japan. Thus, one's choice of conduct is respected as indicative of individuality, self-discipline and independence as long as the Harm Principle, the basic principle of a free society, is not violated.

I argue that the tendency toward tolerating intentional body modification in general society is more than likely linked to a tolerance of intentional body modification in the sports world. Even if limited to adults, total reliance on the right to self-determination probably promotes the collapse of both the social bond and people's commonsense. There is probably a need to re-examine the rising prominence of the excessive predilection toward value relativism from the perspective, for example, of Aristotelian morality and ethics or communitarianism [34].

To summarize this section, I argue that the way of thinking of the right to self-determination, the very core of the modern concepts of liberalism and libertarianism, is one of the factors that contribute to the lack of resolution of the complicated doping problem [35]. I have pointed out two items, namely, the tendency toward tolerating rules violations in the sports world and the application of the right to self-determination, as factors that render the solution to the doping problem more difficult. I would thus like, in the discussion below, to reconsider the reasoning behind the ban on doping from the perspective of the latter reason, the concept of the right to self-determination. I would like to define the right to self-determination here conditioned on the assertions of J.S. Mill in his work *On Liberty*, namely, (1) adults with the ability to make decisions; (2) circumstances surrounding one's own life, body and property; (3) conduct that inflicts no harm on others; (4) behaviour considered by others to be folly; and, as a result, (5) the ability to make decisions on one's own. Indicating each of them by a key phrase, they would be the qualifying criteria to make judgments, self-possession, non-infliction of harm, the right to act foolishly and the right to self-determination, respectively. In particular, when considering the doping problem, I would like to give thought to the argument regarding the ban on doping through a reinterpretation of the third condition of the non-infliction of harm.

The Categories of 'Self' and 'Other'

In the fields of philosophy and ethics, there are ways of thinking about things using relational concepts that make general distinctions or provide for opposites. Mental and physical, self and other, male and female all represent a way of thinking about things or situations based on a dichotomy of opposites. What is treated in this study is 'self and other', which is a way of thinking about things that distinguishes between self and not-self.

The categories 'self' and 'other' usually distinguish between self and everything that is not self; from that perspective, there are undoubtedly some who take note of the fact that 'self and other' also exists within oneself (internally). There are two types of internal voices, one that actively promotes the action that an individual is about to take and one that attempts to stop the person, if possible, from taking that action. The 'voice of the conscience', which tries to stop someone who is about to undertake an action knowing that it is somehow bad, is an easy example to comprehend.

The same phenomenon is also true in sports. For example, there is a voice that strongly urges one on during the game and another that urges one to give up. These internal voices come in turns and, at times, the voice urging one to give up may ultimately dominate, and perhaps may contribute to a wretched performance. American sports psychologist, W. Timothy Gallwey, explained this state of internal discord, which one can divide into Self 1 and Self 2, and advocated methods for overcoming this discord [36]. In his works, he states that in order to achieve sufficient performance, it is important to ignore Self 1, which instils distractions, by adopting methods of meditation [37]. Though I will not discuss it here since it deviates from the issue at hand, it need only be understood that there is an internal phenomenon that distinguishes between self and other in both mental and physical terms.

'Not Harming Others' and 'Not Annoying Others'

In this section I will begin with an explanation of the non-infliction of harm as a way of considering the doping ban argument based on the Harm Principle found in *On Liberty*. The non-infliction of harm highlighted here, in simple terms, means that your own conduct must not directly inflict harm on others, which is an extremely commonsensical approach. In modern society, you would not be permitted to strike another person because you did not like what he said or because you were treated in a derogatory fashion. Since you would normally only be permitted to strike the other person in justifiable self-defence, you would be found guilty of doing bodily harm if your violence caused injury in cases other than those considered justifiable self-defence.

However, even if it is not conduct that violates the law, behaviour that is annoying to others is often experienced in everyday life. Though it was possible, albeit exceptional, in the past to see women do their make-up while riding in the commuter trains in Japan, we now commonly see women openly and nonchalantly applying their entire make-up on the train during the morning commute. The train is a public space shared by all passengers and, as long as it remains so, it is necessary to refrain from conduct that satisfies one's own selfish ends. Shouting in a loud voice, talking persistently on mobile phones, and other behaviour that is annoying to others must be avoided to the utmost. Though doing one's make-up does no harm to others, it may potentially cause others discomfort. Doing direct harm to others is furthermore easy to understand while the standards for judging behaviour that is annoying to others seems to change with the place and time.

The punishment for inflicting harm on others is determined by law while annoying others is determined by morality. Being a matter of morality, there is no specific punishment but such conduct may be met by the disapproving glances of others, neglect, expressions of displeasure, or even ostracism. In Japan, ostracism is a traditional precept and, when imposed because local customs were ignored, it may at times be applied with more severe consequences than violations of the law.

Reinterpretation of 'Other'

First of all, we shall assume that, of the conditions indicated in *On Liberty*, the condition of the right to self-determination is satisfied as long as no harm is done to others. In order to determine whether or not doping is conduct that one may decide on one's own, I will attempt to reinterpret the meaning of 'other' in the expression 'doing harm to others'. To follow Mill's assertion, since self-determination is not permitted if it is conduct that harms others, one is not permitted to decide on one's own to choose to engage in doping behaviour.

Allow me to present two new choices.

1) The Future Self as Other

The principle of intergenerational ethics, an important issue in environmental ethics dealing with our ethical responsibility to future generations, informs this interpretation. Ethical responsibility here means that, since passing on the burden of environmental contamination from the present generation to future generations is tantamount to harm, arbitrary conduct that is environmentally destructive cannot be permitted [38]. I will set up a hypothesis using present self (I myself) as A and future self (I) as A1 while referring to the concept of the ethical responsibility to future generations.

Relationship between self and other – Interpretation I

A ---------------------> A1

Present (self)   Future (other)

When hypothesized in this manner, 'present A' and 'future A1' are different persons and the 'future I' then becomes 'other'. A self-other relationship comes into being with 'present I' as 'self' and 'future I' as 'other'. I will now consider the reasons for the prohibition on doping based on this hypothesis.

There are already concerns that doping causes serious damage to athletes' health. There are clearly concerns of drug-induced health problems (after-effects), even if, for example, an athlete considering the use of an illicit drug ('present I') asserts that he or she has the right of self-determination because it is a personal matter. However, the fact that doping is obviously a behaviour that will adversely affect the health of 'future A1' ('other') should nullify a person's right to make such a decision. If 'future I' is assumed to be a different person, the right of self-determination that is essentially self-seeking no longer applies to the conduct of 'present I' who inflicts damage on the 'other'. The ethical responsibility to future generations impedes such conduct.

This is easy to understand when viewed in terms of the relationship between adults and minors. When considering the example of adults and minors, it is unclear who will be required to take responsibility for 'future A1' as a result of the decision of 'present A'. Normally, in the case of responsibility for adults, the condition of qualifications for self-determination with respect to 'future A1' are satisfied and thus one would take responsibility oneself. With 'future A1', if a minor were unable to take responsibility for him or her self, another person (guardian) would take responsibility. Conventional wisdom would allow for a tolerance of paternalism toward 'future A1' if the ability to make rational decisions were lacking or weak. If we hypothesize about 'future A1' in this manner, we expand the scope of decisions that one can make alone.

This point is the same as Brown's argument tolerating paternalism toward minors. In other words, Brown's assertion is based on libertarianism, which holds the highest regard for human liberty; however, even if banning the use of such drugs were appropriate because young people, who lack decision-making capabilities, do not have the ability to make choices regarding the use of illicit drugs, he claims that adults cannot be prohibited from using illicit drugs [39].

Brown is, of course, not advocating the active use of illicit drugs. This is an assertion that adult athletes must make for themselves. Nevertheless, since youth have not adequately acquired the capability to make this type of decision, the use of illicit drugs should not be included among their choices. Brown states, on the other hand, that as long as adult athletes are recognized as having the ability to decide the majority of the conduct of their own lives, they should be allowed to decide on their own whether or not to use drugs rather than being forced to accept a meddlesome doping ban.

As indicated above, if intergenerational ethics, that is, ethical responsibility to future generations, is to be realized, a prohibition on doping would be justifiable as long as it can stand up to objections based on self-determination and one can show that doping is harmful to future generations ('inflicts harm on others').

2) 'Other' Cannot be Subjected to Self Control!

Another choice is the method of hypothesizing the 'other' within oneself. This, in other words, is the idea that there is conduct one can control through his or her own will (a) and conduct that one cannot control this way (a1).

Relationship between self and other – Interpretation II
A (self) (a/a1)
(a) Controllable (self)
(a1) Not controllable (other)

One can call into question our responsibility for acts of negligence that we execute through our own free will; however, responsibility would be lessened, or may not, at times, be questioned at all, if one can establish that an individual committed the act in a state of mental incompetence or feeble-mindedness. If this principle is assumed, perhaps only the conduct that one can control on one's own is within the scope of 'self' while, conversely, conduct that one cannot control on one's own is within the scope of 'other'.

If one accepts this hypothesis, acts that are beyond one's control (a1) become 'other' and conduct that inflicts harm on others could naturally no longer be deemed self-determined conduct. In other words, if we assume the existence of otherness within the self in the sense of being uncontrollable, the scope of the right of self-determination becomes restricted and the prohibition of specific conduct becomes a possibility.

Doping could be prohibited within the framework of controllable conduct 'self' and uncontrollable conduct 'other'. Thus, one cannot decide on one's own to use illicit drugs since the self (a1) cannot control the body's biological reactions to illicit drugs. Decisions that one can make are limited to conduct that can be controlled by the self. As everyone has experienced, one cannot control his or her reaction to drugs once they enter the body. For example, antipyretics that are taken when one has caught a cold and has a high fever automatically reduce the fever regardless of the will of the individual to lower the fever.

The dichotomy of the self-controllable (a) and the not self-controllable (a1) explains why blood doping is prohibited but high-altitude training is an acceptable alternative. In short, in the case of blood doping, the use of another person's blood is rarely carried out because of blood group incompatibility but, even if it were your own blood, the biological reaction caused by a blood transfusion into the organism clearly falls under the purview of 'not self-controllable' conduct (a1) since the injection of additional red blood cells will enable the athlete to deliver more oxygen to his or her muscles despite his or her will to do so. On the other hand, high-altitude training is 'self-controllable' conduct (a) because of the way the organism acclimatizes its body and controls its reaction. If acclimatization were not possible and the conduct could not be controlled by the self, the training itself would not be continued. Thus, as long as the self cannot control the drug reaction as a rational, moral agent, who controls his own training programmes by himself, it cannot be considered conduct subject to self-determination [40]. Prohibition, consequently, is probably justifiable [41].

The Ban on Doping Inflicts Damage on Others

I reinterpret 'other' based on this 'self-other' dichotomy and utilize my reinterpretation to present a new argument for the prohibition of doping. As my initial interpretation, I hypothesized that the 'future self' would become 'other' when seen from the perspective of the 'present self'. Thus, even if the present self acknowledges that doping might involve drug-induced health damage and the possibility of causing serious damage to the future other, this conduct should be avoided based on the principle of ethical responsibility to future generations. Since it is said, in particular, that the dosage needed to work effectively as doping is far greater than treatment prescribed by physicians,[42] it is easy to envision an adverse impact in the future. Doping thus comes under the heading of infliction of harm and is conduct that is probably not applicable to self-determination.

Secondly, I replaced 'self-other' with self-controllable/not self-controllable. Uncontrollable conduct is thus deemed to be 'other' and beyond the scope of self-determination. Primarily, doping based on the use of illicit drugs is a state in which the self's essential control capabilities are take over by the automatic control of the drugs (a state in which control by the self is not possible). In the case of ordinary training, the athlete would be reduced to a state of exhaustion if a given level is exceeded, rendering continued training itself impossible. If illicit drugs are used, however, it would become possible to exceed the self-controllable limits. Doping conduct, which commits control to an uncontrollable other, corresponds after all to the infliction of harm and probably is beyond the scope of determination by the self.

Notes

[1] Wilson and Derse (eds), *Doping in Elite Sport: The Politics of Drugs in the Olympic Movement*, 68–9.
[2] An excellent summary of the events that transpired can be found online at http://www.nikkansports.com/ns/sports/sportsnow/03112.html.
[3] "K. White's Suspension", *Chunichi Shimbun* (20 May 2004).
[4] Since external pressure applied by the 'public' functions as the norm in Japan, even if there is the possibility of violation due to ignorance, it is thought that there are no athletes or other concerned parties who would become involved in intentional or planned doping. The norm based on this external pressure of the public has been nurtured as an element of the unique spiritual culture of Japan and a study from the perspective of the 'public' that exists between the individual and society holds the promise of providing a valuable vantage point with reference to the doping problem, though I will leave it for another day.
[5] Doping violations thus far in Japan are limited to only a few cases, including the use of cold medication by a male volleyball player in the Los Angeles Olympics in 1984, the use of cold medication by a female alpine skier in 1989, and the use of methyltestosterone

(contained in tonic medicine) by a male billiard player in the Asian Games held in Bangkok in 1998.

[6] According to data of the Mitsubishi Kagaku Bio-Clinical Laboratories, Inc., (http://www.mbcl. co.jp/) the only doping detection organization in Japan recognized by the International Olympic Committee and World Anti-Doping Agency, the ratio of positive test results for doping to negative ones over the past few years has been 1.5 per cent, which corresponds to a total of about 1,500 athletes per year.

[7] Imafuku, *Beach of Sport*, 141.

[8] Ibid., 142.

[9] Ibid.

[10] Ibid.

[11] Taki, *Thinking about Sport: Body, Capital and Nationalism*, 21.

[12] Ibid.

[13] Ibid., 142.

[14] Ibid., 144.

[15] Ibid.

[16] Ibid., 146.

[17] Kusabuka, 'Can Doping be Prevented by Moral?', 38.

[18] Ibid., 39.

[19] Ibid.

[20] Ibid.

[21] Ibid.

[22] Ibid., 40.

[23] Ibid.

[24] Ibid.

[25] Nakamura, 'The New Turning Point of Sport', 26.

[26] Ibid., 27.

[27] Ibid.

[28] Ibid.

[29] Nakamura, *Sport Culture*, 160.

[30] Ibid., 162.

[31] For example, see Brown, 'Paternalism, Drugs, and the Nature of Sports', 'Ethics, Drugs, and Sport', and 'Practices and Prudence' as well as Hata *et al.*, 'Criticizing Doping Issues'.

[32] Nakagawa, *Philosophy and Medicine*.

[33] Kato, *Invitation to Environmental Ethics*.

[34] MacIntyre, *After Virtue: A Study in Moral Theory*.

[35] There are various views of doping by researchers specializing in sports philosophy and ethics. To provide a simple summary, Simon approaches the problem of drug doping from the standpoint of the essential nature of sport, while Brown, who has already been mentioned in this study, raises doubts about rules that prohibit doping from the standpoint of libertarianism, which holds autonomy and the right of self-determination in high regard. Fraleigh considers the doping problem from the standpoint of rule-utilitarianism and communitarianism, while Schneider and Butcher consider the reasons for prohibiting doping in terms of both the athlete (individual) and society. Arnold applies MacIntyre's concept of practical application to sport and pursues the problem from the vantage point of Aristotelian morality and ethics. Please refer to the references for their various assertions.

[36] Gallwey, *The Inner Game of Tennis*, 13–17.

[37] Ibid., 21.

[38] This concept is discussed in Kato, *Invitation to Environmental Ethics and Ethics for Making-Agreement and Rule*, as well as in Kondo, 'A Study on the Teaching Methods Advocated by W.T. Gallwey'.

[39] Brown, 'Ethics, Drugs, and Sport', and 'Practices and Prudence'.

[40] While this holds for distinguishing blood doping from high altitude training, one might object that it does not appear to be universally applicable in differentiating other forms of doping from permitted practices that produce similar effects. For example, an athlete is prohibited from injecting his or her thigh with a banned steroid to gain strength and power but is free to increase his or her strength and power by lifting weights, through muscle stimulation or via other permitted procedures. An elite athlete does not gain muscle strength, power or endurance simply by injecting steroids; hence, if an athlete ceases to train and becomes stationary while taking steroids, he or she will not gain much, if any, advantage. The athlete thus has to choose to train while using the drug to get the effect, unlike with blood doping where the effect will be manifested inside the body, despite what the athlete wills, once the banned substance enters the system.

[41] Simon's argument serves as the basis for this view of drug reactions (Simon, *Fair Play: Sports, Values, & Society*). However, he uses it to justify the ban on doping due to his desire to avoid having sport become a competition of the drug reactions of athletes, a clearly different point of view from that presented in this study in which drug reactions are described in the sense of infliction of harm.

[42] Burkett and Falduto, 'Steroid Use by Athletes', 69–74 and Bever and Lower, 'Anabolic Steroid Use in Weight-Trained Athletes', 157–60.

References

Arnold, P. J. "Sport as a Valued Human Practice: A Basis for the Consideration of Some Moral Issues in Sport". *Journal of Philosophy of Education* 26, no. 2 (1992): 237–55.

Bever, D. L. and D. R. Lower. "Anabolic Steroid Usage in Weight-Trained Athletes". *Health Education Research* 2, no. 2 (1987): 157–60.

Brown, W. M. "Ethics, Drugs, and Sport". *Journal of the Philosophy of Sport* 7 (1980): 15–23.

Brown, W. M. "Paternalism, Drugs, and the Nature of Sports". *Journal of the Philosophy of Sport* 11 (1985): 14–22.

Brown, W. M. "Practices and Prudence". *Journal of the Philosophy of Sport* 17 (1990): 71–84.

Burkett, L. N. and M. T. Falduto. "Steroid Use by Athletes in a Metropolitan Area". *The Physician and Sportsmedicine* 12, no. 8 (1984): 69–74.

Fraleigh, W. P. "Performance-Enhancing Drugs in Sport: The Ethical Issue". *Journal of the Philosophy of Sport* 11 (1985): 23–9.

Gallwey, W. T. *The Inner Game of Tennis*. Translated by S. Goto. Tokyo: Nikkan Sport Publisher, 1978. Originally published as *The Inner Game of Tennis*. Toronto, New York, London and Sydney: Bantam Books, 1974.

Hata, T., Kimura, M., Kondo, Y. and Inagaki, M. "Criticizing Doping Issues". *Taiiku-Genri-Kenkyu* 33 (2003): 115–32.

Imafuku, R. *Beach of Sport*. Tokyo: Kinokuniya Shoten, 1997.

Kato, H. *Invitation to Environmental Ethics*. Tokyo: Maruzen, 1991.

Kato, H. *Ethics for Making-Agreement and Rule*. Tokyo: Maruzen, 2002.

Kondo, Y. "A Study on the Teaching Methods Advocated by W.T. Gallwey; Critical Consideration of his "Inner Game Theory"". *Japanese Journal of Sport Education Studies* 3, no. 2 (1984): 19–27.

Kusabuka, N. "Can Doping be Prevented by Moral?". *Taikuka Kyoiku* 46, 1(1998): 138–41.

MacIntyre, A., *After Virtue*, 2nd edn. Translated by S. Shinozaki. Tokyo: Misuzu Shobo, 1993. Originally published as *After Virtue: A Study in Moral Theory*. Notre Dame, IN: University of Notre Dame Press, 1984.

Mill, J. S., *A Theory of Liberty*. Translated by K. Shiojiri and T. Kimura. Tokyo: Iwanami, 1971. Originally published as *On Liberty*. London: John W. Parker and Son, West Strand, 1859.

Nakagawa, Y., ed. *Philosophy and Medicine*. Tokyo: Kobundo, 1992.

Nakamura, T. *Sport Culture*. Tokyo: Taisyukan Shoten, 1981.

Nakamura, T. "The New Turning Point of Sport". *Taikuka Kyoiku* 46, no. 1 (1998): 26–8.

Schneider, A. J. and R. B. Butcher. "The Mésalliance of the Olympic Ideal and Doping: Why they Married and Why They Should Divorce". In *Sport: The Third Millennium. Proceedings of the International Symposium, Quebec, Canada, May 21–25, 1990*, edited by F. Landry, M. Landry, and M. Yerlès. Sainte-Foy, Quebec: Les Presses de L'université Laval, 1992.

Simon, R. L., *Introduction to Sport Ethics*. Translated by Y. Kondo and H. Tomozoe. Tokyo: Fumaido, 1994. Originally published as *Fair Play: Sports, Values, & Society*. Boulder, CO: Westview, 1991.

Taki, K. *Thinking about Sport: Body, Capital and Nationalism*. Tokyo: Chikuma, 1995.

Tateiwa, S. *Private Property*. Tokyo: Keiso Shobo, 1997.

Wilson, W. and E. Derse, eds. *Doping in Elite Sport: The Politics of Drugs in the Olympic Movement*. Champaign, IL: Human Kinetics, 2001.

Doping and Anti-doping in Sport in China: An Analysis of Recent and Present Attitudes and Actions

Fan Hong

It is now common knowledge that the Chinese Communist Party used sport to gain international recognition. Consequently, Western media and some academics and observers claimed that Chinese athletes were caught up in a state-run drug programme like that of in the East Germany. This essay examines the factors that caused doping in sport in the context of Chinese history, culture and ethics. It analyses the Chinese government's anti-doping policy and practice from the 1990s. It concludes that there is no systematically state-run drug abuse sports programme in China and that drug-use is not only a political problem, but also moral, educational, economic, medical, social and cultural problem in the global society.

Historical Perspective

For the ancient Chinese the important aim for their lives was to search for long life and immortality. Longevity symbolized the basic tenet of a good life and it has retained its place in the hearts of the Chinese. Most of the Chinese festivals, celebrations or greetings of best wishes contain the wish for long life.

The quest for longevity is evident as early as 219 BC when the First Chinese Emperor Qing Shi Huang ordered Xu Fu, a physician, to take 3,000 virgin boys and girls with a fleet to search for the three magic islands in the east where the immortals were believed to live. The aim of the mission was to bring the secret pill of immortality back to him. It was said that Xu Fu never found the magic islands and feared being punished if he came back empty handed; he and the three thousand boys and girls settled down on an island that is now part of Japan.[1] After Qing Shi Huang, emperors of different dynasties continued their search for magic pills of immortality for more than 2,000 years of feudal China.

For the ordinary Chinese the search for long life was from traditional Chinese medicine. The extensive use of herbs for the alleviation of the symptoms of disease and for long life can be traced back to the book *Shen Nong Ben Cao Jin* [The Herbal Classics of the Divine Plowman] of approximately 100BC. According to this book, Shen Nong, the Divine Plowman, tested and recommended a total of 365 herbs, one for each day of the year. The book includes 365 kinds of herbal medicine.[2]

Later in the sixteenth century, Li Shi Zhen (1518–93) spent more than 30 years of study and field investigation before publishing the famous pharmacopoeia, *Ben Cao Gang Mu*. Li's work consisted of a total of 52 volumes and comprised 1,898 drugs. Among them, 350 were derived from minerals, 1,099 from plants and 443 from animals. A total of 11,096 recorded prescriptions were included. Li classified 'herbs' originating from plants according to their habitats, shapes and the part of the plant that was used. He also classified 'agents' according to their nature, shade and growth based on their mineral, botanical or animal origins, for example, swallow's nest, rafter dust, child's urine and human faeces. *Ben Cao Gang Mu* is held in high esteem among Chinese medical practitioners.[3]

The prescription format used by traditional Chinese parishioners has remained unchanged for a thousand years. They tend to prescribe four or more herbs together, believing that drug interactions synergize the major action of the principal herb or smooth its possible side effects. In 1986 the Oriental Healing Arts International Bulletin listed more than 700 formulas of Chinese herbal combinations including some secret formulas from ancient times and some from renowned practitioners.

Some herbs that contained multiple active and stimulant elements, like Ginseng, were used to stimulate man's energy and increase longevity. Ginseng was called a 'dose of immortality' and the 'spirit of man and the earth'. For thousands of years Ginseng has been used by the common people as a tonic, in emergency as medicine to rescue dying patients, and by the rich as a rejuvenating and revitalizing agent. There were many scholarly and literary writings on how it could stimulate sexual desire and bring sexual happiness.[4]

In addition, vegetables like mushrooms were greatly favoured, as were vital parts of animals that were believed to have lived for a very long time. Cranes, turtles and tortoises were particularly esteemed and were thus to be found cooking gently in the pots of shamans.

Some plants imported from foreign lands, such as opium poppy and cannabis (or hemp, marijuana) grown in Southwest China were never mentioned in the Chinese pharmacopoeia as hallucinogenic or psychotomimetic agents, but the pollen from these plants was used in Chinese medicine as a purgative herb.[5]

The Chinese idea of immortality was primarily the eternity of both the spirit and the body. Without the body there could be no immortality. Therefore, the quest was not just for meditation release from the constraints of life and death, but for the transformation of the physical body into an eternal vehicle for the spirit. Thus traditional Chinese immortality, especially Taoists' immortality, involves not only meditation and development of the spirit but also the hunt for the magical pill, elixir or method which would ensure that the body would be transformed into an everlasting human frame capable of bearing the spirit and of being united to the One origin and to Heaven and Earth for ever.[6]

Furthermore, the ancient Chinese believed that the world contained materials that were imperishable, such as gold, jade or mercury. If the flesh body could be transformed or replaced progressively by such imperishable materials then immortality would ensure. When people who sought immateriality took small quantities of jade, flakes of gold, or mercury into their diets, their bodies would absorb the imperishable materials and transformation would gradually be achieved.[7]

The most significant figure in the establishment of the alchemy tradition of Taoism was Taoist Guo Hong. Guo was born in 284 AD and lived to be 79, a long life in his time. During his life he compiled a study of Taoist practices called *Bao Pu Zi* [the Book of the Preservation-of-Solitary Master]. It consisted of 70 volumes, drew material from many different schools and contained different methods of making pills. It was a guide to all the known ways of becoming an immortal in the fourth century.[8] Guo himself was a master of the use of jade, gold and mercury to make pills for eternity.[9]

Joseph Needham in his volumes on *Sciences and Civilization in China* has commented that the experiments on the materials, which preceded these diets, led the Chinese into making some very fundamental early scientific discoveries.[10] However, many of these experiments failed to achieve the intended result and instead caused illness and death. A lot of people died in great agony and pain from metal poisoning. Martin Palmer commented: 'It is probably true to say that in no country other than China have so many people poisoned themselves into early grave in the search for long life and immortality!'[11]

Although China has a long history of producing and practicing stimulant herb medicine, magic formulas and pills, there is no evidence to suggest that ancient Chinese people used them for sports and exercise purposes. This is in contrary to the ancient Greeks, who used stimulants to strengthen their bodies and to enhance their physical performance at the Ancient Olympic Games in the third century BC.[12] Rather, the Chinese used stimulants to shape their perishable bodies and achieve immortality.

Nevertheless, the cultural tradition, which used drugs to seek the transformation of the body, and the herbs and prescriptions, helped to achieve the desired transformed body in a magical way and influenced Chinese sport in modern times.[13]

Drug Use in Modern Chinese Sport

Up until the 1970s drug abuse was virtually unknown in Chinese sport. The reasons are, firstly, China was isolated from the international sports community. China withdrew from the IOC and 11 other international sports federations in 1956 due to the 'two Chinas' issue. China split from the Communist community including the Soviet Union and Eastern European countries during the 1960s and 1970s. Drug use in sport outside of China did not affect Chinese sport until the 1980s when China opened its door and rejoined the international sports community. China attended the 1984 Olympic Games in Los Angeles after an absence of 32 years, won 15 gold medals and came fourth in the medal table. The victory did not stir any suspicions of drug abuse in Chinese sport.

The first case of drug use in Chinese sport was reported in 1988 when two female athletes tested positive at an international competition before the 15th Winter Olympic Games. They argued that they had taken some Chinese traditional medicine for their relaxation at the recommendation of their relatives. However, they were disqualified from the Winter Olympic Games. The report was sympathetic and general public did not pay much attention to this case.[14]

It was in the same year when the Chinese female swimmers collected 12 gold medals at the World Swimming Championships in Rome that suspicions of drug use in Chinese sport arose. Commentators drew particular attention to the masculine physique of many female swimmers. Four positive tests were recorded around the time of the Rome World Championships.[15]

In 1994 when the Asian Games took place in Japan, 11 athletes including seven swimmers tested positive for the steroid dihysrotestosterone. In January 1998, when the World Swimming Championships took place in Perth, one swimmer was found to be carrying a flask containing thirteen glass vials of Human Growth Hormone on arrival at Sydney airport. Following this incident, four Chinese female swimmers tested positive.[16]

In September 2000, before the Olympic Games in Sydney, China dropped 30 athletes, coaches and officials from its Olympic team after seven rowers failed their blood tests. In April 2002, two Chinese swimmers, one of whom was a member of China's world-record-setting 4x100 freestyle team, tested positive for an anabolic steroid. In 2004, 40 athletes, coaches and officials were axed from the Olympic team due to suspicious blood test results. Ma Junren, the famous athletic coach, and six of his runners, were among them.

Table 1 indicates the number of doping tests conducted by the COCADC (Chinese Olympic Committee Anti-Doping Commission) from 1990 to 2004. In general, 60 per cent of tests were out-of-competition tests. For example, in 2003, 60.8 per cent of tests were out of competition and in 2004 the number was 67 per cent. The number of tests increased from 165 in 1990 to over 4,009 in 2004. The rate of positive cases in the Chinese national doping control testing programme dropped to 0.4 per cent in 2004 which was far below the international average of 1.6 per cent.[17] Athletes who tested

Table 1 Statistics of Athletes' Doping Test in China 1990–2004

Year	No. of Tests conducted by the COCADC	No. of Positive Cases	Positive (%)
1990	165	3	1.82
1991	731	5	0.68
1992	938	5	0.53
1993	1,357	21	1.56
1994	1,292	13	1.01
1995	1,914	13	0.68
1996	2,080	11	0.53
1997	3,540	21	0.59
1998	3,044	15	0.49
1999	3,505	16	0.46
2000	3,204	13	0.41
2001	5,121	23	0.43
2002	4,975	20	0.42
2003	4,896	18	0.36
2004	4,009	17	0.40

Source: COCADC

positive came from the following sports: swimming, athletics, weightlifting, football, rowing, body-building, judo, taikuando, boxing, skiing, shooting, cycling and football.

The Chinese sports authority keeps a particularly close eye on the following three sports: swimming, athletics and weightlifting. For example, in 2004, 352 swimmers from 25 squads throughout China had 794 tests during and out of competition. Of these the COCADC conducted 724 tests and FINA and WADA conducted 70. These tests included blood tests. There was no single positive case. From 2001 to 2004 China conducted 3,100 doping tests in swimming, more than any other country in the world. Only one case tested positive in 2003. The Chinese Athletic Association stated that the COCADC tested 918 athletes and 5 were positive in 2003.

In 2004 at the Athens Olympics Chinese athletes were tested more than 150 times and they were all negative. China won 32 gold, 17 silver and 14 bronze medals. Their 32 gold medals put China above Russia and second to the USA. Shi Kangcheng, the Deputy Secretary General of the COCADC, proudly claimed after the Athens Games that China has won a gold medal for doping control in sport, which was more important than the other gold medals China had won at the Olympic Games.

Anti-doping Policy

China's success in doping control stems from its determination, policy and centralized management system. Between 1988 and 1998, some 52 Chinese athletes competing at international level have tested positive for anabolic steroids. This number includes 23 swimmers. As mentioned earlier, at the 1998 World Swimming Championships in Perth, Australia, four Chinese swimmers tested positive and the Chinese were humiliated by rival nations and condemned as a team of 'cheats and liars'.[18] Some coaches and the Western media claimed that the Chinese systematically drug athletes, especially young females.[19] Following the publicity given to former East German coaches in China in the 1990s, many observers believe that Chinese athletes are caught up in a similar state-run drug programme.[20]

However, this belief is perhaps more political than factual. It certainly is the case that drug-use is an international problem. To assume a Chinese/East German link is purely circumstantial. There is no direct evidence to prove that there is a systematically state-run drugs programme based on an East German system. In fact, the Chinese authorities regularly and consistently condemn drug-use in sport publicly. More than 30 decrees and regulations have been issued against drug abuse in sport between 1989 and 2005.

In August 1990 the Sports Ministry, for the first time, announced the 'three principles: seriously banning, strictly testing and severely punishing those who use drugs in sport'. It issued the 'Regulation of Anti-doping in Sports Competitions' in 1995. On 19 January 1998 the Sports Ministry issued the 'Urgent Notice on Ban on Drug Use in Sport'. On 1 October 1995 'The Sports Law of the People's Republic of China' was issued. It stated:

> Athletes, coaches, referees and organisers of sports competitions should obey sports ethics and anti-doping regulations . . . Those who use drugs in sport will be punished according to law.[21]

On 1st March 2004, after three years preparation, the State Council issued the *Code of Anti-doping in China*. It demonstrated the Chinese government's determination to fight against drug use in Chinese society in general and in sport in particular. It provided a coordinated policy and an overall framework in which doping controls organizations, including customs control, medicine supervision, legal systems and sports organizations, could take place.

In the meantime, progress was being made towards joining the international anti-doping policy and organizations. China has been a WADA Foundation Board member since 2000. China signed the Copenhagen Declaration and accepted the World Anti-Doping Code in 2003. The Code was translated into Chinese in February 2004 and the information was available for athletes and public review. It also co-operated with Norway, Sweden, Australia, Britain and France to exchange information and establish the doping quality control system. After ten years' effort China has established its National Doping Control Quality System, received the international standard certification in 2004 and won international credibility.

Management System

The COCADC was established in 1990. It is directly under the leadership of the Chinese Sports Ministry and the Chinese Olympic Committee. Its major function is to implement regulations and rules of anti-doping in sport and promote drug free sport in China. There are two divisions in the COCADC: Testing Division and Administration Office. Testing Division is responsible for carrying out the national testing programme, developing the annual testing plan, conducting testing distribution and producing training programmes for doping control officers. By 2004 there were 273 doping control officers (male 120 and female 153) in China, of which 173 were in Beijing and the rest were in provinces. They will be a major resource for the 2008 Olympic Games. The Administration Office is responsible for administration of the COCADC; producing anti-doping education programmes; co-operation with international organizations; and acting as a watchdog of the Chinese Sports Ministry for its overall anti-doping policy and practise.

The COCADC is not an independent organization. It under the direct leadership of the Sports Ministry and the Chinese Olympic Committee and facilitates its co-ordination with national sports associations from grassroots to senior management levels. Every sports association is required to provide its calendar each year to the COCADC. The COCADC organizes an annual meeting with high-risk sports associations to discuss with them the total number of intended tests. The sports associations could suggest testing numbers, but the decision will be made by the COCADC according to the sport's profile and participation numbers.

Athletes in high-risk sports, such as swimming and athletics, are required to report their whereabouts and contact information to their sports associations when they are leaving their permanent residence or regular training venue for more than 48 hours. This does not apply to low-risk sports, such as badminton and martial arts. Major national sports teams have their permanent and concentrated training camps. Athletes and coaches and managers stay there for most of the training time. This sports association officials visit them regularly. So do the COCADC.

Under the Chinese Sports Ministry and the Chinese Olympic Committee there are 20 individual sports associations and management centres in Beijing and 32 provincial sports committees. All of them must follow the rules set up by the Sports Ministry and the COCADC. However, some major associations such as the Athletic Association, Weightlifting Association, Swimming Association and Football Association and some provincial sports committees, such as Jiangxi, Shanxi, Fujian and Anhui, also have their own rules to demonstrate their determination to end drug abuse in their particular sports.

The China Doping Control Centre was set up in 1989 and has passed the International Olympic Committee's annual examination from 1989 to 2002 and WADA accreditation since 2003. It is responsible for analysing all doping samples collected by the COCADC in China. The centre participated in the joint research project to develop EPO (Erythropoietin) detecting methods with Australia, France, Canada and Norway.

In short, the Chinese government and sports authorities have taken measures to combat drug taking in sport at every level and conferred severe punishments on drug cheats – athletes, coaches, team doctors and officials.[22] They understand that efficient enforcement of these measures is vital if China wants to improve, not damage further, its sports image on the international stage.[23]

The statistics in Table 2 and Table 3 after the endnotes show how Chinese authorities enforced the anti-doping laws in 2002 and 2003. Heavy punishments have been meted out to athletes and other relevant people including coaches and team doctors. Athletes were banned from competition from six months to two years and fined from 4,000 to 15,000 RMB. Table 4 after the endnotes shows that from 2004 the punishment also extended to the team, the club or the sports organization where the athletes came from.[24]

The Reasons for Drug-use in China

Gold Medal Ambitions

Decrees, regulations and punishment are effective ways to stop some athletes and coaches' attempts to use drugs, but cannot completely solve the problem. The ambition of the government, the medal craze of the nation and the rewards available to athletes make drug use almost irresistible. In 1990 the government set a target of becoming 'a top world sports power by the end of the century'. In 1993 and 2001 China bid twice to host the Olympic Games. The success of the bid to host the 2008 Olympic Games stimulated a set of new objectives in China. As Jiang Zemin, the Communist Party General Secretary between 1989 and 2003, stated:

> The success of the bid will advance China's domestic stability and economic prosperity. The Olympics in China has the objective of raising national morale and strengthening the unity of Chinese people both in the mainland and overseas.[25]

The Olympics, of course, are the best place for China to present its credentials as a superpower.

Towards fulfilling this goal, in July 2002 the Party and the Central Government issued a document on 'Strengthening and Progressing Sport in the New Era' (Zhonggongz-hongyang guowuyuan guanyu jinyibu jiaoqiang he gaijin xinshiqi tiyu dongzuo de yijian).[26] It emphasized that hosting the 2008 Olympic Games is the priority not only for Beijing but for the whole country. China must grasp this opportunity to display itself to the world and to make the Beijing 2008 the best Olympic Games ever. The Sports Ministry immediately drew up two important internal documents: 'The Outline Strategy for Winning Olympic Medals 2001–2010' (Aoyun zhengguang gangyao 2001–2010) and 'The Strategic Plan for Winning Olympic Medals in 2008' (2008 Aoyun zhengguang jihua). These two documents comprise an action plan to ensure China achieves the victory they expect: challenging the Americans and becoming the global athletic superpower. This puts officials, coaches and athletes under enormous pressure.

Financial and Political Rewards

At the same time, money plays its part. In modern commercialized China, the reformed sports system encourages financial rewards and corporate sponsorship. Medal winners receive huge sums from the state and sponsors. For example, while the Chinese average wage is about 1,000 RMB per month, the state rewarded gold medal winners with 8,000 RMB in 1984, 18,000 in 1988; 80,000 in 1992 and 150,000 in the 2004 Olympics respectively. In addition, the winners received money from various sponsors and commercial channels. For example, Liu Xiang, an Olympic hurdles gold medallist, received more than 1,500,000 RMB from various sponsors and media agencies after the Athens Games. Winner's coaches and officials also receive rewards from the state and sponsors. Those sports officials pay particular attention to their athletes' performance at national and international competitions, for their career promotion is directly linked to it.

Easy Access to Drugs

Drug use is not simply a problem for sport but a problem for the nation. When the People's Republic was established in 1949, the Communist government banned drug use in China, especially opium. 80,000 people who smoked opium were jailed and more than 20,000,000 people finally gave up opium. It was forbidden to plant poppies anywhere in China. It was not until the 1980s when China opened its door that drug-use among Chinese people started again. Yunnan and Guanxi provinces are close to the drug production area – 'the gold triangle'. They gradually become a route to import and transport drugs into China and to other Asian countries.

In November 1990 the State Council set up the National Anti-doping Committee. The People's Parliament issued 'The Decree of Anti-doping' in December 1990. In January 1995 the government issued the 'Regulations of Anti-doping by Force'. To implement the Regulations 695 rehabilitation centres were set up by 1997 and 650,000 drug users were sent for rehabilitation by police. From 1984 to 2004 1,140,400 people from 2,000 counties and cities were registered as drug-use regulars and of them 70 per cent were youths.[27]

Beijing Sport University conducted a survey in 2004 involving 4,500 middle school students in 14 provinces and big cities. The results were shocking: more than 10 per cent of the students admitted that they used perform enhancement drug in order to pass the PE test in the annual national university entrance examination.[28] The percentage of positive cases is higher than that among athletes. The media also revealed that some drug dealers openly sold drugs outside the examination stadium.[29] Wang Baoliang, a senior sports official of the Sports Ministry, suggested that the Higher Education Committee should consider having drug tests in its university entrance examination and that the Sports Ministry would provide necessary support.

Drugs can now be bought in the open market and on the Internet. They provide easy access to drugs. In addition, some companies and individuals even come to sports training centres and teams to sell drugs under the name of nutritional supplements to coaches and athletes in the open. They give the people who buy their drugs a large commission. There are stories of the drug dealers and the people who buy the drugs both becoming millionaires in a short time. A head coach of the national athletic team stated:

I am very disappointed by the current situation. Many coaches now don't pay attention to how to enhance their athletes' performance by scientific and hard training but by taking drugs. They spend a lot of time to learn which drug is more effective for their athletes.[30]

Is Drug-use in Sport Ethical?

International debate on gene-doping is not a Chinese concern yet. Their immediate concern is the drugs on the list of WADA. It is generally acknowledged by official statement and educational material that using drugs in sport, especially the banned drugs on the list of WADA, is unethical. It gives athletes an unfair advantage and is cheating. It also damages athletes' bodies. A senior sports official in Beijing stated:

International competition now is not the competition between athletes, but doctors and biochemists, and modern technology. The real victims in this drug-using sport are the athletes, especially those from the Third World.[31]

There is also another perspective: 'what constitutes drug misuse?' As mentioned earlier Chinese people have a long history and culture of using herbs, animals and secret formulas to regenerate energy. It is natural for athletes and coaches to use some traditional Chinese medicine to achieve the desired transformation of their bodies in a magic way. Therefore, it should not cause surprise when a head coach of the national swimming team claimed that his swimmers drank turtle soup everyday and a head coach of a national athletic team said that his athletes drank crane soup and soup made of animal testosterone. A football team of the first division was required to eat 'sea slug' every day to ensure they could run faster and better endure fatigue during its training and competition sessions. Some ordinary people injected cock's blood to make them feel more energetic.

Since the great majority of Chinese medical materials originate from plant and animal sources, the lack of research and proper quality control compromises the reputation of Chinese medicine and put athletes' reputations in danger. Take Ginseng for example: it contains multiple active elements, not just a single active ingredient. The chemical structure of some of the components has been studied and recognized, but many are not yet fully understood.[32]

There is a clear indication that some Chinese athletes were cheating to win and there is also an indication that some Chinese athletes used medicine, by mistake, which they can commonly buy over the counter. There is heavy punishment for drug users by law, but there is no law to protect those athletes who misuse drugs for health reasons or to protect young athletes who are forced to take drugs. Neither are there independent advisory bodies to advise Chinese athletes about their rights of defence, nor their appeals, when they test positive. In 1998, for the first time when two female rowers from Wuhan city tested positive at the 3rd Chinese Cities Competition, they took their case to the court and claimed it was their coach and team doctor who forced them to take drugs. However, the case was dropped without any explanation.[33] Fifteen athletes were accused of taking drugs at the 9th National Games in Guangzhou in 2001 and they lost their titles and were banned from competition for one or two years as punishment. None of them appealed against the decision. It is not clear whether they had been given sufficient advice and help on the rights of appeal or they simply gave up. The current policy and system still focuses on catching and punishing those who use or misuse drugs in sport, but not educating and protecting athletes. The lack of an athlete's voice or of any organization other than the government is now at the centre of the ethical debate in China.

Case Study – the 10th National Games

The National Games in China originally was a national gathering to show national unity. It required all the provinces and big cities, like Beijing and Shanghai, to form their own team to compete in the games. The 1st National Games took place in 1959 and was more political and entertaining than commercial. Since the 1980s, along with the growth of gold medal fever and commercialisation of sport, the National Games became a money tree for athletes, coaches and sports officials. In addition, the Games closely linked to the promotion of sports officials at every level, for they were the measure of their success. Furthermore, the National Games since 1987 have become a training and test ground for the Olympic Games. It takes place at the same interval as the Olympics.

The 10th National Games took place between 12 and 23 October 2005 in Jiangsu province. The Games were called the mini-Olympics. It included all the Olympic sports: 28 sports and 357 events, using all the rules of the Olympic Games. It was the test ground for the Olympics in Beijing in 2008. 9,922 athletes from 46 sports organizations participated and all the Olympic athletes competed at the Games. Liu Peng, the Minister of Sport and the Chairman of the Organizing Committee of the Games, pointed out: 'the Games is an important step to show that we are ready to host the 2008 Olympic Games in Beijing. . . . It symbolises the image of the Beijing Olympic Games, the image of Chinese sport and China's international reputation.'[34] More than 30 IOC officials and international federations watched the Games, including Dr Rogge, the IOC President.

Liu Peng announced publicly that anti-doping in the Games was one of the priorities and that the Chinese sports authority must show its zero tolerance to doping offences. More tests would be conducted and the athletes who took drugs would be seriously punished. Between January and September 2005 the Sports Ministry issued three documents to emphasize its anti-doping policy. It focused not only on the tests during the Games in October, but also those before the Games. All the sports associations and management centres had to inform the test centre of their athletes' training grounds. Failure to do so would result in punishment for the teams and the associations. The athletes would be disqualified from the Games.

In the meantime, all sports associations reminded their athletes that the 10th National Games was different from the previous ones, which were called 'the competitions of drugs'. This time China must show the world a new image. In April 2005 the Chinese Swimming Association held its anti-doping conference in Herbin. Luo Xuejuan, the Olympic gold medallist, proposed that all the athletes must believe in their strength and prove themselves through their hard work and true ability.[35]

During the games 47 drug control stations were set up and 362 people were involved and participated in the doping control tests. The COCADC sent 80 experienced doping control officers to supervise the tests. The Laboratory received between 110–200 samples and worked 24 hours each day. A three-person delegation from WADA was present at the Games at the invitation of the Chinese Sports Ministry. The delegation visited the doping control facilities, observed the operations at some doping control stations and provided the COCADC with suggestions from the improvement of doping control practices in China. According to the statistics, the 10th National Games conducted 1,615 drug tests before and during the Games. Among them there were 1,615 urine tests of which 1,373 were in competition and 242 were pre-competition. EPO tests were also conducted. About 3–8 athletes from each event were tested at the Games.[36]

As early as January 2005 12 female weightlifters of Hubei provincial team were caught cheating in an out-of-competition test. In June, the Sports Ministry announced that the 12 female weightlifters were banned from competition for two years and the whole team including male and female weightlifters was banned from competition for one year. Their coaches were banned for life and lost their positions as head-coach and coach.[37]

In March 2005 one athlete from Hebei provincial skiing team was banned from competition for one year. The COCADC announced that he violated the regulation of anti-doping in sport by avoiding the out-of-competition drug test.

Another case also took place in March. A female cyclist from Fujian provincial team tested positive at an out-of-competition test. She was banned from competition for two years and fined 4,000 RMB. Her coach, an Australian, was banned for four years from working in China and fined 5,000 RMB. The Fujian Cycling Association was given a warning and was fined 20,000 RMB.

Then in September, just before the Games, two female athletes from Chongqing tested positive at out-of-competition tests. They were banned from competing at the Games and also banned from all competitions for two years and fined 5,000 RMB.

The last case was Sun Yingjie, the best long-distance runner in China at present. Sun won the Beijing International Marathon championship three times and the bronze at the 9th World Athletic Competition in Paris in 2003. She was regarded as one of the Chinese prospects to win a medal at the 2008 Beijing Olympic Games. At the 10th National Games, Sun won the marathon championship on 16th October and her drug test was negative. She then attended the 10,000m the next day and came second but her drug test was positive. The Organising Committee of the Games immediately announced that Sun was banned from continuing to attend the Games and demanded she return her silver medal. Her coach and other relevant people would be punished later.[38]

The Chinese sports authority was disappointed about Sun's case but generally happy about its doping control practise at the Games. The experience at the 10th National Games has given China confidence about its ability to control and test drug-use in sport in 2008. Shi Kangcheng, the Deputy Secretary General of the COCADC, claimed:

Over the first ten years, our priority was to increase the number of tests, during the last five years our focus was on the quality of the tests. Now we are better equipped to conduct more tests.[39]

Towards the Beijing Olympic Games

The Chinese sports authority has made great progress in the fight against drugs in sport at the 10th National Games. It now plans to carry out 4,500 doping tests during the 2008 Olympic Games. That will be more than at the 2000 Sydney Games, which conducted 3,000 tests, and the Athens Games in 2004, which had 3,500. The China Doping Control Centre will work 'around the clock' during the Games. Dick Pound, the WADA President, has claimed that WADA will work with China to make sure its anti-doping apparatus is adequate.[40] David Howman, the WADA Director-general is pleased about China's commitment to the anti-doping policy and practise. He has praised: 'We are very pleased with the support by the Chinese government. The quantity is increasing, the quality is improving and their commitment is undoubted.'[41]

However, the desire to be the best in the world is still the dream for most of the Chinese and the government. To realize the dream, the medal targets at the Olympic Games are set; competitions are getting tougher; unethical practices are encouraged by some sports officials and coaches; huge financial rewards are irresistible; the development of the national and international doping markets in China give sports administrators and athletes easy access to drugs, and there is a traditional Chinese culture of using drugs for transformation of the body. All these factors probably still tempt some athletes, coaches and officials to take short cuts by using drugs. Drug-use in sport happens in China as well as in other countries. It is not only a political problem, but also a moral, educational, economic, medical, social and cultural problem in China and in the world.

Notes

The author wish to thank Yuan Hong of the COCADC for providing her with some information and Ying Cui, who worked with the COCADC and now works with WADA, for providing her with some information and invaluable suggestions for this essay.

[1] Feng and Li, *Pill, Medicine and Prescription*, 5.
[2] Ibid., 54. See also, Kee, *The Pharmacology of Chinese Herbs*, 3.
[3] Feng and Li, *Pill, Medicine and Prescription*, 103–6; Kee, *The Pharmacology of Chinese Herbs*, 3 and 12.
[4] Kee, *The Pharmacology of Chinese Herbs*, 17–19.
[5] Ibid., 4.
[6] Palmer, *The Elements of Taoism*, 91.
[7] Ibid., 95.
[8] Ibid., 97; Feng and Li, *Pill, Medicine and Prescription*, 63–5; Kee, *The Pharmacology of Chinese Herbs*, 10.
[9] Chinese Society for History of Sport, *The Ancient Chinese Sport History*, 23.
[10] Needham *et al.*, *Clerks and Craftsmen in China and the World*, 263.

[11] Palmer, *The Elements of Taoism*, 91.

[12] Verroken, 'Drug Use and Abuse in Sport', 29.

[13] Palmer, *The Elements of Taoism*, 91–5.

[14] Interview with Cao Yuchun, reporter of New Sport in 2004 in Beijing. See also Yang and Jin, *Say No to Drugs*, 23.

[15] Houlihan, *Dying to Win*, 55.

[16] Ibid.

[17] Chinese Olympic Committee Anti-doping Commission (COCADC) in Beijing, in April 2005.

[18] Craig Lord, 'Expulsion Calls after Four more Chinese Test Positive', *The Times* (15 Jan. 1998), 44.

[19] Anita Lonsbrough, 'Australian Coach Wants Total Ban on China's Liars', *The Daily Telegraph* (15 Jan. 1998), 36.

[20] The relevance of this criticism is related to the Eastern German swimming coaches' confession that their swimmers had used anabolic steroids in the 1970s and 1980s. When the Communist countries in Eastern Europe collapsed, a number of East German sports doctors and coaches went to work in China.

[21] *The Sports Law of the People's Republic of China*, 2.

[22] Ibid.

[23] See Wu Shaozu's speech, 'We must Ban Drug-use in Sport in China', *Tiyubao* [Sports Daily] 20 (22 Jan. 1998).

[24] Tables 2–4 follow References.

[25] Hong, Wu and Xiong, 'Beijing Ambitions', 514.

[26] *Renmin ribao* [People's Daily] (22 Aug. 2002), 1.

[27] 'Drug Users in China have reached 1,050,000 and 70% was youth,' www.people.com.cn (2 Dec. 2003).

[28] In China, all the secondary school students who attend the annual national university entrance examination must pass general physical education tests, such as the 200m run and high jump, to enter normal universities. Students who want to go to sports universities or physical education institutions are required to pass general physical education tests and tests for their specialized sports, such as swimming or football.

[29] 'Some people sell drugs outside the national university entrance examination stadium', *Southcn.com* (1 April 1995).

[30] Wu Ping, 'Current Situation of the Chinese athletics', *Titan zhoubao* (22 Oct. 2000).

[31] Interview conducted in Beijing in 2003 by Fan Hong.

[32] Kee, *The Pharmacology of Chinese Herbs*, 19.

[33] 'There is no ending to fight against drug abuse in sport?' www. Xinhuanet.com (29 June 2005).

[34] 'Liu Peng emphasises the importance of the National Games', *sport.org.cn*(19 Sept. 2005).

[35] 'Luo Xunjuan, the swimming champion, condemns drug abuse in sport', *http://www.olympic. cn/news/olypmic-comm,2005-04-14/537618.html*.14 April 2004.

[36] Drug test for the 10th National Games and no of tests increased 20% than the 9th Games', *http://www.olympic.cn/China/doping/2005-4-29/550554.html*. 29 April 2005.

[37] 'Hubei female weightlifting team was punished by the Sports Authority', *Southcn.com* (24 June 2005).

[38] 'The decision of the Organising Committee: Sun Yingjie's 10,000 silver medal returned and she was banned from competition', *http://sports.sina.som.cn*. 21 Oct. 2005.

[39] 'China gets tougher in anti-doping before the Olympics', *http://www.cocadc.cn/english/sanji/ sJ01.php?id = 186.*

[40] 'WADA to help China keep it clean for Beijing 2008', *http://www.cocadc.cn/english/sanji/ sjo1.php?id = 189.*

[41] 'China gets tougher in anti-doping before Olympics', *http://www.cocadc.cn/english/sj01. php?id = 186*; and 'WADA senior official praises anti-doping at the 10th National Games', *http://news.xinhuanet.com/sports/2005-10/14/content_3617585.htm*.

References

Chinese Society for History of Sport. *The Ancient Chinese Sport History*. Beijing: Beijing Sport Institute, 1989.

Feng, Hanyong and Dianyuan Li. *Pill, Medicine and Prescription: Chinese Traditional Medicine and Immortality*. Chengdu: Sichuan renmin chubanshe, 1993.

Hong, Fan, Ping Wu, and Huan Xiong. "Beijing Ambitions: An Analysis of the Chinese Elite Sports System and its Olympic Strategy for the 2008 Olympic Games." *The International Journal of the History of Sport* 22, no. 4 (2008): 510–29.

Houlihan, Barrie. *Dying to Win*. Strasbourg: Council of Europe Publishing, 2002.

Kee, Chang Huang. *The Pharmacology of Chinese Herbs*. London: CRC Press, 1999.

Lin, Boyuan. *Chinese Sport History*. Beijing: Beijing Physical Education Institute Press, 1989.

Needham, J. *Clerks and Craftsmen in China and the World*. London: Cambridge University Press.

Palmer, Martin. *The Elements of Taoism*. Shafterbury: Element, 1993.

Qiao, Keqing and Guan, Wenming, *Chinese Sports Philosophy*. Nanzhou: Gansu Minzhu Press, 1993.

Report on Drug use in Sport, *Tiyu wensh* 2 (1986): 17.

The Sports Law of the People's Republic of China. Beijing: Renmin tiyu chubanshe, 1995.

Verroken, Michelle. "Drug Use and Abuse in Sport." In *Drugs in Sport*, edited by David R. Mottram. London: Routledge, 2003.

Yang, Tianle and Jin, Jichun (eds.). *Say 'No' to Drugs: Anti-doping Education Text Book*. Beijing: Beijing Sport University Press, 1998.

Table 2 Punishments for Drugs Taken in Sport, Statistics of 2002

Name	Sex	Team	Sport	Punishment to the athlete	Punishment to relevant people
Gao Mingming	Female	Jinan	Judo	Banned from competition for 2 years and fined 4,000 RMB	Coach Wang Wei was banned from coaching for 1 year and fined 5,000 RMB
Wang Rui	Female	Heilongjiang	Weightlifting	Banned from competition for 2 years and fined 4,000 RMB	Coach Guo Weiru banned from coaching for 1 year and fined 8,000 RMB
Cui Shuling	Male	Jiangsu	Rowing	Banned form competition for 3 months	Coach Wang Yong banned from coaching for 3 months and fined 2,000 RMB
Ling Lengmei	Female	Fujian	Athletics	Banned form competition for 2 years and fined 10,000 RMB	Coach Chen Hua banned from coaching for 2 years and fined 10,000 RMB
Liu Fuyuan	Male	Shanxi	Athletics	Banned form competition for 2 years and fined 5,000 RMB	Coach Feng Hui Banned from coaching for 1 year and fined 5,000 RMB
Zhang Shinan	Female	Beijing	Weightlifting	Banned from competition for 2 years and fined 4,000 RMB	Coach Hong Jiaxing banned from coaching for 1 year and fined 5,000 RMB
Zheng Hui	Male	Heilongjiang	Athletics	Banned from co mpetition for 2 years and fined 5,000 RMB	Coach Liu Gang banned from coaching for 1 year and fined 4,000 RMB
Lin Na	Female	Liaoning	Athletics	Banned from competition for 2 years and fined 10,000 RMB	Coach Zhang Juan banned from coaching for life and fined 4,000 RMB
Chen Qian	Female	Jiangsu	Modern Pentathlon	Banned from competition for 6 months	Researcher Lu Suinan fined for 10,000 RMB

Table 3 Punishments for Drugs Taken in Sport, Statistics of 2003

Name	Sex	Team	Sport	Punishment to athlete	Punishment to relevant people
Li Chengbo	Male	Shengyang	Skiing	Banned from competition for 6 months	Coach Liu Suming fined 2,000 RMB
Chao Lei	Male	Hebei	Wrestling	Banned from competition for 2 years and fined for 8,000 RMB	Coach Jin Guisheng banned from coaching for 1 year and fined from 8,000 RMB
Liu Chunya	Female	Shanghai	Weightlifting	Banned from competition for 2 years and fined for 4,000 RMB	Coach Zhou Hongjun banned from coaching for 1 year and fined for 8,000 RMB
Dai Wenbin	Male	Fuzhou	Athletics	Banned from competition for 3 years and fined 80,000 RMB	Coach Han Cao banned from coaching for 3 years and fined for 80,000 RMB
Wang Yanli	Female	Heilongjiang	Cycling	Banned from competition for 2 years and fined 4,000 RMB	Coach Xia Chunxiao banned from coaching for 1 year and fined 4,000 RMB
Wang Weihua	Male	Guangdong	Athletics	Banned from competition for 2 years and fined 15,000 RMB	Coach Sui Li banned from coaching for 2 years and fined 10,000 RMB
Wanh Hua	Male	Shanghai	Weightlifting	Banned from competition for 1 year	Coach Hu Huibing fined 5,000 RMB and team doctor Peng Bo fined 5,000 RMB
Zheng Yongjie	Male	Gansu	Athletics	Banned from competition for 3 years and find 80,000 RMB	Coach Yang Jianming banned from coaching for 3 years and fined 80,000 RMB
Li Huiquan	Male	Heilongjiang	Athletics	Banned from competition for 3 years and find 80,000 RMB	Coach Guan Bo banned from coaching for 3 years and fined 80,000 RMB
Yuang Xiaoxia	Female	Liaoning	Rowing	Banned from competition for 6 months and find 5,000 RMB	Coach Xiao Jingming banned from coaching for 6 months and the team doctor Xiao fined 5,000 RMB

(continued)

Name	Gender	Province/Team	Sport	Punishment	Official punishment
Li Rong	Female	Shanxi	Athletics	Banned from competition for 6 months and fined 5,000 RMB	Coach Li Aifeng banned from coaching for 6 months and fined 5,000 RMB
Ge Wei	Male	Shandong	Rowing	Banned from competition for 2 years and fined 10,000 RMB	Coach Yu Huitao banned from coaching for one year and fined 5,000 RMB; the team doctor Wang banned from practise for 1 year and fined 5,000 RMB
Li Ning	Female	Guangzhou Army's team	Swimming	Banned from competition for 2 years and fined 10,000 RMB	Coach Liu Guangtan banned for life and fined 5,000 RMB
Zhang Shuai	Male	Beijing Guoan FC	Football	Banned from competition for 6 months	Coach Yang Zuwu banned from coaching for 6 months and fined 5,000 RMB; the team Doctor Suang banned from practise for 6 months and fined 5,000 RMB
Dragon Race (horse)		Guangdong-Dongwan	Horse racing	Banned from competition for 1 year	Coach Beng Chi banned from coaching for 2 years and the jockey banned from competition for 1 year
Swift (horse)		Guangdong-Dongwan	Horse racing	Banned from competition for 1 year	Coach Mo Zexi banned from coaching for 2 years and the jockey banned from competition for 1 year
Xu Jiening	Female	Chongqing	Weightlifting	Banned from competition for 2 years	

Table 4 Punishments for Drugs Taken in Sport, Statistics of 2004

Name	Sex	Team	Sport	Punishment to athlete	Punishment to relevant people	Punishment to the team, club or sports organization
Zhang Qiang	Female	Heilongjiang	Athletics	Banned from competition for 6 months and fined 5,000 RMB		
Ding Haifeng	Male	Ningxia	Weightlifting	Banned from competition for 2 years and fined 10,000 RMB	Coach Wang Chengji banned for life and fined 10,000 RMB	The Weightlifting Team banned from the competition and fined 60,000 RMB
Su yan	Female	Ningxia	Weightlifting	Banned from competition for 2 years and fined 10,000 RMB		
Ma Wenhua	Male	Ningxia	Weightlifting	Banned from competition for 2 years and fined 10,000 RMB		
Dang Zhiyong	Male	Beijing Mahua Fitness Club	Bodybuilding	Banned from competition for 2 years and find 20,000 RMB		The Club fined 20,000 RMB
Zhong Xin	Male	Xinjiang Fitness Association	Bodybuilding	Banned from competition for 2 years and fined 20,000 RMB		The Association fined 20,000 RMB
Sheng Jian	Male	Hainan Olympic Fitness Club	Bodybuilding	Fined 15,000 RMB		The Club fined 20,000 RMB
Xia Tian	Male		Bodybuilding	Banned from competition for 2 years and fined 25,000 RMB		
Meng Liya	Female	Zhongti Beili Fitness Club	Bodybuilding	Banned from competition for 6 months		The Club fined 10,000 RMB

(continued)

Liu Min	Female	Beijing Yuanzhong Athletic Club	Athletics	Banned from competition for 2 years and fined 10,000 RMB	Coach Xu Jiping banned from coaching for 2 years and fined 10,000 RMB	The Club fined 20,000 RMB
Han Zengfeng	Male	Army's team	Wrestling	Banned from competition for 2 years and fiend 10,000 RMB	Coach Da Lai banned from coaching for 1 year and fined 10,000 RMB	The Team fined 20,000 RMB
Zhao Xinyu	Male	Liaoning Weightlifting Team	Weightlifting	Banned from competition 2 years and fined 10,000 RMB	Coach Feng Changqian banned from coaching for 1 year and fined 8,000 RMB	The whole team was banned from competition for 1 year and fined 20,000 RMB
Zhao Qingbao	Male	Beijing Athletic Team	Athletics	In process		
Yao Ye	Male	Jiangsu provincial Shootinh Team	Shooting	Banned from competition 3 months	Coach Ma Jun fined 8,000 RMB	The Team was fined 14,000 RMB
Liu Jiansheng	Male	Liaoning Zhongyu FC	Football	Banned from competition for 2 years and fined 50,000 RMB	Coach Cheng Qiang banned from coaching for 1 year and fined 10,000 RMB	The Club fined 28,000 RMB
Zhang Ke	Male	Shengyang Jinde FC	Football	Banned from competition for 1 year and fiend 5,000 RMB	Coach Duan Xin fined 5,000 RMB	The Club was fined 14,000 RMB
Liang Zhuanliang	Male	Beijing Cycling Team	Cycling	Banned from competition for 2 years and fined 10,000 RMB	Coach Liu Jizeng banned from coaching for 1 year and fined 4,000 RMB	The Team was fined 20,000 RMB

Source: COCADC, 2005. US$1 = 6 RMB, Chinese currency

Anti-doping in Sport: The Norwegian Perspective

Runar Gilberg, Gunnar Breivik & Sigmund Loland

Introduction

The Norwegian attitude to doping has always been clear. The use of performance-enhancing substances has not been publicly acknowledged by anyone. Norway is called 'the homeland of preambles' and has adjusted to a self-defined role as a moral leader with regard to sports ethics in general and the attitude to doping particularly.

Doping was discussed as a problem in sport for the first time in a study published by the European Council in 1964. Norway responded quickly and followed up the study by suggesting measures to the other Nordic countries and UNESCO. The Norwegian Olympic Committee and Confederation of Sports (NIF) passed the first anti-doping resolution in 1971. Five years later, the same body carried out control measures against anabolic steroids and started to perform doping controls in sports federations. In 1978 doping controls were conducted in all NIF's member associations. In 1980 controls at any time were expanded to include substances and methods registered on the IOC doping list.

However, NIF wanted to introduce more frequent doping controls and impose stricter sanctions nationally than were required by the international rules set by the IOC and international associations. For the controls to be most effective, it was also considered important to perform unannounced testing and out-of-competition testing.

Efforts to establish a Norwegian doping laboratory started in 1985. In 1988 the IOC accredited the section for doping analyses, at the Hormone Laboratory at Aker University Hospital, as an official doping laboratory.

The NIF Assembly was not content just with introducing strict regulations in Norway, but aspired to work offensively to make the Norwegian standard applicable internationally. In addition to addressing the doping issue at international sports federations, political efforts were made at the European Council. Even though this work did not have an immediate effect, some international and national sports bodies gradually accepted 'Norwegian regulations' such as unannounced testing and the use of blood tests and urine samples.

In the 1990s, Norway was also pushing for an independent international 'doping police', which would be able to test the athletes at any place and at any time. This proved to be a difficult task. When the World Anti-Doping Agency (WADA) was established in 1999, an important step was taken. WADA introduced the World Anti-Doping Code in 2004. This code is to ensure that the rules and regulations that apply to the anti-doping programme are the same, irrespective of where the athlete lives or in which sport s/he participates. All athletes at international level must have an obligatory certificate documenting the tests taken, as well as stating where they are situated at any time.

This essay attempts to describe and understand the Norwegian anti-doping work over the last decades with a particular emphasis on its preventive aspects. Firstly, we will look at the ethical justification of the Norwegian anti-doping work. Secondly, we will discuss the argumentation specifically used here. Thirdly, we will look at whether anti-doping work has been successful with regard to attitudes as well as to the prevalence of doping among Norwegian athletes. Fourthly, we will comment on investigation into motives and reasons for Norwegian athletes who have used doping. Finally, we will discuss whether the clear Norwegian guidelines against doping have been followed up with the same clarity in action. How has Norwegian sport during the past 15 years been able to combine a high level of performance with a plain 'no' to the use of performance-enhancing substances? And what about the so-called 'grey zones' or the zones in which there are no obvious rights and wrongs as in the case of the use of so-called 'altitude houses' or 'hypoxic chambers'?

Fundamental Values in Sport

For the past three or four decades, Norway has promoted sport without doping. Several reasons are given, and the two most important ones are the health aspect and the quest for fair play. However, behind both of these arguments lies what one could call 'sports values'. An understanding of sport as a carrier and mediator of values has a long tradition in Norway. Sport has never been conceived of as a neutral sphere.

Throughout history, Norwegian sports authorities have constantly considered sports values to be threatened. Thus, it has always been considered necessary to protect them. This is clearly described in NIF's long-term plan for political work in sports of 1991:

> The external pressures on sport today are putting its values to the test. We are forced to ask: Where do we want to go with sport? Which norms and values would we like sport to be based on? What kind of sport can give meaning and create values?

This attitude indicated the basis and direction for NIF's work on ethics and values during the period from 1991 to 2003.

The justification for working with values was partially idealistic – sport was meant to have a positive impact on the individual and the community. It was also partially pragmatic and a 'value makeover' was required in order to maintain public and financial support. Both attitudes were predominant in the plans presented by NIF's working group for ethics and values in sport, which was established in 1991. In the group's long-term strategic plan for 1992–98, the following main targets were listed: 'that the sports movement will survive and produce positive values for individuals and society and thus strengthen its position as a people's movement and a motivator in society'.

As a result, working with sports values became an important area of commitment in the 1990s. A campaign was called: 'Sport is too valuable to be ruined.' It consisted of a workbook that discussed some of the value problems as well as fundamental values in sport. Moreover, campaign letters were sent to all the 12,000 sports clubs in Norway.

One primary goal behind the campaign was grassroots engagement. This was supposed to be a bottom-up approach: values ought to be defined by those primarily engaged. In order to reach as many people as possible, the campaign was also run in the media. Several surveys were conducted with regard to what values sport represented and should represent and what challenges to these values sport was facing. Among other things, four surveys on attitudes to moral dilemmas were conducted among the Norwegian population, NIF members, elite athletes and sports managers. A survey was also carried out among sports federations and sports districts in NIF.

This survey, 'Report on Values',[1] showed that there were concurrent views from all groups in most areas. The participants in the survey agreed that sport represented important values in and outside of sport. They expressed a great concern that sport's inner and experiential values would be undermined. The greatest value challenges for the future were considered to be: performance pressure, commercialization, unfair play, doping, differing sets of values, early specialization, demanding attitudes, unfortunate alcohol culture, eating disorders, salaries given without tax declarations ('dirty money'), sports injuries and spectator violence. In addition, a restrictive attitude was seen with regard to the use of alcohol and doping. However, the focus on performance and sport success was very strong with a certain willingness to cheat to gain an advantage.

In 1994, based on the value campaign and its results, NIF chose joy, health, community and fair play as its fundamental values. The debate that took place regarding values resulted in a Sports Value Manifesto that described the consequences of the different values on elite sport, competitive sport, recreational sport and sport for children and youth respectively. The following value model presents summarized values in the different groups (see figure 1).

The four basic values are different but are considered to share the characteristic that they can raise the threshold for using doping.

- A sport distinguished by *joy* stands in contrast to serious sport that only focuses on results and thus it is easier to use illegal substances in order to perform better.
- A sport that focuses on *community* will make it harder for athletes to use illegal substances because participants will have empathy with their competitors and regard them as friends.
- A sport that focuses on *health* and healthy living will give athletes internal barriers against using medical drugs that on a short or long-term basis will damage their health.
- An *honest* athlete will not cheat but play fair and follow the rules and regulations.

This list of values was in the short run intended for elite athletes. However, in the long-term programme against doping, it was important also to include people in recreational sport and sport for youth.

One of the main challenges along the way was to make the values something more than 'paper values'. The aim was that athletes, coaches and managers would claim ownership to sports values – the values ought to be internalized and guide action.

> The individual manager, coach and athlete must be aware of the fundamental values in sport and know how these are lived up to in practical life. The organization's expressed values must be in accordance with their members' actions.[2]

FUNDAMENTAL VALUES	JOY	COMMUNITY	HEALTH	HONESTY
Elite sport	… from performance and entertainment	… working to achieve a joint target	… by a minimalized risk of injuries	… by fair play
Competitive sport	… from excitement and competition	… working together to prepare for competition	… by healthy habits	… by fair play and amateur spirit
Recreational sport	… from individual improvement	… in open, social companionship	… by preventive activity	… by respecting other people
Sport for children and youth	… from play and mastery	… through social training	… by establishing healthy habits	… by upbringing

Figure 1 Value model for various forms of sport in Norwegian sport

Words and Action

The long-term plan for the period from 1992 to 1998 was called: 'From Words to Action.'[3] It served as the strategic plan for the NIF's newly established Department of Ethics, Sports Medicine and Anti-doping.

A recurring issue in the plan was the work to achieve a higher degree of conformity between ideals and reality. One of the main objectives was to promote increased knowledge about, and understanding of, the basic values in sport, and the main strategy was to focus on elite sport and sport among children and youth. Managers, coaches, referees, sports medical personnel and teachers at schools became the secondary target group. An important aspect in this work was to define good and bad actions in sport, and secondly, to reward good actions and rectify the bad ones. Attempts were made to make elite athletes aware of their position as role models as well as working with schools regarding value issues.

In the last half of the 1990s, a number of initiatives were made to strengthen value consciousness in sport. Campaigns were carried out against doping and the use of drugs, and seminars were held to raise the awareness among sports physicians. A system of fair play prizes was also introduced for athletes who had acted in accordance with the basic values in sports. In 2000, the prize was named 'Sports Values Award', and was from that point on a national prize which given to a sports club that had excelled with its value awareness.

In 1998, a new long-term plan about NIF's work on ethics and values was drawn up which will be applicable to 2010. Again, this plan was called: 'From Words to Action.' The superior goal was as follows: 'All members of Norwegian sport must have a strong, positive relationship to the fundamental values in sport, and these values will be founded on practical and specific actions'.[4]

The primary target group for this objective was expanded to everyone who was associated with specific sports activities. In other words, support networks, medical personnel and parents were included.

Measures and Strategies

A number of different measures and strategies were outlined in the plan. A free and independent 'Value Forum in Sport' was established, appointed by NIF with the intention to stimulate a debate about values in sports and society. This forum's work received much publicity in the local and national media. 'The Sports Value Seminar' was established as an annual event.

The financing of the work initiated at NIF's Department of Ethics, Sports Medicine and Anti-doping in 1992 was made possible through targeted subsidies from the Ministry of Cultural Affairs. From 1991 to 2002, the department spent NOK 13 million on the work on ethics and values; on average NOK 1.1 million a year (wage costs are *not* included in these figures).

From 1999 to 2002, NIF also cooperated with the Department for Alcohol and Drugs and the Department for Tobacco Control at the State Directorate for Health and

Social Affairs. Particular drug and tobacco-related measures became an integral part of the general ethics and values work through the agreement with these departments.

The most characteristic point in NIF's work on ethics and values was a large scale of measures directed at a number of various target groups (in line with the strategic plans mentioned earlier). Measures with specific themes and target groups were implemented along with measures of a more general character, measures internally in the NIF administration, and measures on practically all levels in Norwegian sport.

Anti-doping Work

At the same time, and as a part of the general work with values, NIF had more specific anti-doping work on the agenda. In 1992, the doping section at NIF formed a general plan for NIF's anti-doping work for the period 1992–95.[5] The main objective for NIF's anti-doping work was 'All Norwegian sports shall be free of doping'.

The work to achieve this goal was meant to be long-term, determined, systematic, built on co-operation and always ahead of new development. The areas of commitment were divided into two: controls and supervision on the one hand, and preventive work (the theme of this essay), on the other hand.

From 1988 to 1995, there already existed a general plan. The plan for 1992–95 was therefore to be considered as a follow up. The main principle was to carry out intensive campaigns directed against selected target groups each or every other year as well as current, less resource-demanding, measures towards all target groups.

In 1992, two anti-doping campaigns were carried out. One of the campaigns was directed towards health personnel, and the other campaign was of a more general nature and addressed the general public. The market research agency MMI examined the effects of the anti-doping campaign directed towards health personnel and argued that it had made an impact in attitudes. In 1993, an anti-doping manual was put together for managers and employees at clubs, federations, districts and others. The manual was continuously updated and redistributed. One year later, after the 1994 Lillehammer Olympic Games, a new anti-doping campaign was carried out: 'You can have sport success without drugs.' This campaign was run at the same time as another campaign: 'Norwegian elite athletes against drugs.' As of 1995, several seminars were held for sports physicians. The seminars discussed the role of sports physicians, adverse effects and symptoms of abuse, athletes' safety, doping tests and controls.

Several other measures were initiated, directed at coaches and young athletes. In 1997, the project 'Anti-doping in schools' was set into motion. Educational material was distributed to all Norwegian high schools and a selection of junior high schools. Former athletes who had abused drugs held lectures at schools. Advertising campaigns were run with slogans such as: 'Doping does not always kill', 'Doping drove me mad', and 'The least dangerous part of doping is getting caught'.

Around the millennium, the Internet became an important asset in the anti-doping work and the general work with values. An anti-doping handbook for athletes was also produced and distributed to elite athletes, recreational athletes and schools.

An extensive anti-doping campaign called 'Play clean, play fair, play true' was developed together with WADA and carried out in 2002. The material comprised three posters and postcards with information. As in earlier campaigns, the arguments included fair play and health. This was put into plain speaking in the last campaign: 'Doping is illegal based on two main reasons: because it gives an unfair competitive advantage and because it is dangerous to one's health.' A third reason was also emphasized: 'Doping is illegal by sports regulations.'

On a critical note, the Norwegian anti-doping campaigns have to a smaller degree focused on the deeper reasons why athletes – both elite athletes and amateurs – use doping. In such an extended perspective it would be sensible to observe the use of doping in relation to the development in society in general. Increased societal emphasis on performance, body image and appearance has opened up for an increased use of bio-chemical and pharmaceutical means and methods. In elite sport, the logic of performance has become the hegemonic logic that in many cases overrules laws and regulations. Traditional anti-doping work can to a certain extent be said to work with the consequences and not with the symptoms of the doping problem.

The Fair Play Argument

In the campaign 'Play clean, play fair, play true', fair play is defined as: 'An expression for a fair competition – a competition on equal terms with no cheating.' It is also claimed that 'it is possible to obtain good results without cheating'.

In order to strengthen the ethical considerations, these questions are asked, first and foremost to young athletes

- Why do you think that doping is illegal in sport?
- Why do you think that people use doping?
- How do you interpret the expression 'fair play'?
- What is the most important you can do to win in a fair way?

Basically, athletes' responses were as follows:

- Doping is illegal for two main reasons: Because it gives a competitive advantage and because it damages one's health.
- Individuals use doping because they do not believe that training over time will provide as good a result as if they use doping. They want fast results and have the ambition of being the best, no matter the costs.
- Fair play expresses fairness in competition and takes into consideration that the competition shall be free of any forms of cheating or illegal means.
- Determination, beliefs and patience will help you to reach your goals in an honest way.

Critics point to the argumentation as a bit idealistic and naive. The answer to the second question: 'People use doping because they do not believe that training over time will provide as good a result as using doping' expresses implicitly that it is possible to perform just as well without doping as with doping. Only it will take longer. This may be considered throwing dust in young athletes' eyes. One could argue that no matter how patient you are, you cannot compensate the advantage in performance that you will have in blood doping, for example. Maybe it would have been better to indicate that in many sports, doping agents boost performance more efficiently than is the case without such agents? Should not the choice of doping or not really be presented as a moral choice that might even have performance costs?

The Health Argument

In the Norwegian anti-doping campaigns, the focus has always been on the medical adverse effects of doping agents and methods. This is a general emphasis in the anti-doping struggle. WADA also considers the health aspect to a great extent when the agency methodically reviews and revises its doping list. As it is said in information material, the list is intended to protect athletes against themselves, but also against ambitious, irresponsible coaches, managers, sports physicians and others who might be attempted to be medically irresponsible.

There are three types of adverse effects in health that have been argued: Physical, psychological and social adverse effects:

Physical Adverse Effects: The physical adverse effects will vary depending on the type of substances that have been used. In several campaigns, one of the arguments has been that anabolic steroids affect women's femininity and men's masculinity. Abuse can also result in hepatic injuries, jaundice and cardiovascular diseases, to mention a few. The use of central stimulants can, in the worst case scenario, cause cardiac arrhythmic disorders, cardiac arrest and sudden death, and there is also a risk of adverse effects such as spasms, convulsive fits, insomnia and weight loss. Blood doping using e.g. EPO will increase the viscosity of the blood. This will not only increase the oxygen intake, but also the risk of thromboembolism and sudden death.

Psychological Adverse Effects: There has also been a focus on psychological adverse effects in doping during the anti-doping campaigns. The use of anabolic steroids may for example lead to increased aggressive behaviour, depressions, addiction and withdrawal symptoms, plus changes in the perception of reality, hallucinations, uneasiness and anxiety.

Social Adverse Effects: The social adverse effects in doping have to a greater extent become the centre of attention in doping campaigns. One of the main arguments has been that anabolic steroids, often combined with alcohol, may cause an aggressive and violent behaviour. Since drugs must be bought illegally, abusers will easily be involved in criminal actions. The link between using drugs in sport and drugs as narcotics will also be apparent.

Critics have argued that the focus on the adverse health effects has been close to (irrational) propaganda to create fear. By focusing on negative effects to this extent, it is claimed that athletes will not identify themselves or their friends with these images.

There is a general acceptance that long-term abuse and large doses are dangerous, but it is possible to use performance-enhancing drugs in controlled ways and without real health risks, and there are many other health risks involved in especially elite sports. Why single out doping as the only health problem?

Reasons for Doping

The use of performance-enhancing substances and methods must also be viewed on the background of the general development in society. With values such as individualism, performance, progress, pushing the limits and the use of technology and science, sport coheres with and strengthens key values in modern society.[6]

Sport, elite sport in particular, has a clear cut performance ethos. Managers, athletes and coaches are constantly evaluated based on the results that are achieved. Coaches and managers who fail must resign or are fired. Athletes who have had a bad season may lose sponsorship agreements and their role on the team. The demand for victories, improvement and records has become more merciless in sport than anywhere else.

The gain by winning – both fame and income – is so huge that the temptation of taking shortcuts is hard to resist, particularly knowing that performance-enhancing substances and methods will be effective in a number of sports. There will always be athletes and support networks willing to use them, illegal or not.

As in the anti-doping work in general, Norwegian anti-doping campaigns have not addressed specifically the question of whether the logic of the elite sport system is a contradiction to the logic of moderation and anti-doping. The Norwegian attitude has in many ways been aiming for both performance and morality. However, in the 1999 Action Plan for Anti-doping Work in Norway, this problem was raised. A survey showed that only seven out of 1,252 Norwegian elite athletes claimed to experience a strong or moderate pressure to use doping. This may imply that the general focus on performance is not considered as a pressure to use illegal medication. The majority has a distinct negative attitude to the use of doping, both from a fair play perspective and a health perspective. Athletes also consider effective controls and strict sanctions to be the most important measures to prevent the use of doping in organized Norwegian sport.

Improving Bodily Appearance

The doping problem is not exclusive to elite and competitive sport. It also exists in environments with less competitive training and exercise and with a stronger focus on body appearance. In fitness and bodybuilding, doping is used to enhance performance, but most often doping is used in order to obtain the 'ideal body'. Doping is a means not only in the pursuit of a muscular and well-proportioned body, but also in pursuing a social identity. Fitness and body building sub-cultures that organize doping use often have a well-developed use of symbols and rituals in its communication with the outside world. These environments are often very private and hard to access for outsiders because the knowledge about, and the use of, doping becomes such an important part of the environment's protective ideology.[7] At the same time, the cultures have to a certain degree become a channel for doping to sports such as powerlifting, weightlifting and throwing disciplines in track and field events.

The same body ideal that is found in many health studios has become more and more a general ideal. The images are everywhere, in the media, movies, fashion industry and commercials. Muscular men and slim, fit women are dominating the scene. In this context, sport and training become very interesting arenas. Different sports provide different opportunities to shape the body. Most forms for training will lead the body closer to the ideal.[8] Many people work hard to meet the ideal in order to become attractive as well as the desire to perform. The body ideals may enforce what Johanson calls 'the logic of discontent'.[9] With regard to body shape and looks, enough is never enough. The fitness and body sculpturing industry are constantly offering new means – in the form of training methods, diets and drugs. Moreover, anti-doping is facing the challenge of increased medication in the population, and the use of pharmaceutical products is becoming increasingly common both in society in general, and also in several sports environments. The anti-doping message is met by strong counterforces.

It has been difficult for anti-doping campaigns to deal with this focus on body image or recreational drug use. There is a lack of organization here, and there is a lack of possibility to enforce sanctions. It has also been quite vague who has the responsibility of anti-doping work in unorganized environments. While the Norwegian Ministry of Church and Cultural Affairs has been responsible for anti-doping in sport, drug use in the rest of the population has been considered a general health problem and the responsibility of the Norwegian Ministry of Social and Health Affairs.

A general law against doping has been discussed at the Ministry of Justice and by the Police on several occasions, but has so far not been implemented. The current legislation allows the use of doping, while the distribution and storage of these drugs are illegal.

The lack of conformity between sport regulations and Norwegian legislation may complicate the anti-doping work. In Sweden, all use of doping has been criminalized since 1999, and a similar Norwegian legislation would give the anti-doping work much stronger impact, especially when meeting with users of doping in unorganized sports. The current situation provides unorganized sport with no legislation to follow or sanctions to fear as long as they stay away from distribution.

Norwegian Attitudes towards Doping

Sport in most Western countries appears to be diversified, representing many values and attitudes. The development in Norway seems to be going in the same direction.[10] In 1993, members of sports organizations participated in a Norwegian survey about attitudes to certain values and dilemmas.[11] In a comparative study from 2003, the same questions were asked of similar groups.[12] The survey dealt with people's opinion about what should be the most important values in sport in general and in specific parts of sport; children's sport, recreational sport and elite sport. The survey also included questions about attitudes to specific dilemmas regarding values in different aspects of sport.

The panel included two groups: NIF members between the ages of 15 and 24, and elite athletes. In the 2003 survey, a group of coaches participated as well. Norwegians from the general population were also asked questions in order to get a basis for comparison.

The survey dealt with different ethical dilemmas in elite sport and sport for children and youth. The respondents were asked which solution they would have chosen if they were faced with various dilemmas and what they thought most others people performing the same sport would have done in the same situation. One of the themes was the attitude to doping. These are difficult issues to deal with in terms of a survey, and responses cannot be taken at face value. However, they are still good indicators of attitudes, and we will provide some examples here.

Most questions were linked to scenarios such as the following:

> You are an elite athlete and are going to participate in the Norwegian National Championship. The three best athletes will qualify for the Olympic Games. Participation in the Olympic Games will give you sports scholarships and sponsorship agreements. You are told that there is a drug that will enhance your performance by up to 30 per cent if you use it on a daily basis over six months. Many of your foreign competitors use this drug. The drug is difficult to detect in doping controls. Without using this drug, your chances of qualifying for the Olympics are minimal. What would you do in this situation?

The answers showed that only 1 per cent of the youth groups in 1993 and 2003 would use the drug in this particular situation. However, nearly 25 per cent answered 'I don't know' in 1993 as well as 2003. No elite athletes, neither in 1993 nor in 2003, stated that they would use doping and practically no one from the two coach groups from 2003 answered 'yes'. When directly asked, all groups disapproved of illegal performance-enhancing substances.

The next question in the survey followed the first question and asked: 'What do you think that most of the athletes within your sport would have done?'

Here, 10 per cent of NIF's members from 15 to 24 years old answered that they believed that most other athletes in their own sport would have used doping. This applied to both surveys. A small number of elite athletes in 1993 and 2003 answered that they thought most other athletes would have used doping in the given situation. Among the coaches there were also a few who thought that other athletes would have used doping.

There are hardly any differences in the attitude towards the use of doping in 1993 and 2003, despite the fact that other Norwegian surveys show a greater support of modern, materialistic values, less respect for the law and authorities.

This latter development is particularly typical for youth. It goes against the values that sport wants to represent, and a reasonable interpretation of the concurring results may be that NIF has managed to resist social processes that go against its own sets of values.

It is also worth noting that there were more people who believed that other athletes in the same sport would have used doping than the people who said they would. This was not surprising because most people want to be associated with what they see as the ideal (yes-saying). Questions about what respondents assume others do are less 'dangerous' and may therefore be more reliable. But believing that other people use drugs may also create a more open attitude to using drugs themselves.

It is interesting to note that young people to a greater extent than elite athletes and coaches believed that illegal drugs are used in sport. One of the explanations may be that young people are influenced by the increasing acceptance for medication in society in general.

The Use of Certain Drugs

The survey also included questions regarding the attitudes to certain types of drugs used in doping. A selection of results is given below. The Monitor groups refers to a representative sample of the Norwegian population above 16 years of age.

> Among elite athletes, several types of performance-enhancing substances are used in addition to physical training. There is a list below of substances that in different degrees enhance body performance. Which of them do you think should be accepted/approved of and which ones should be banned? (Figure 2)

A total of 72 per cent of the general population (monitor groups) answered that the use of EPO (Erythropoietin) was unacceptable. NIF members were even more opposed and the strongest opposition group was among elite athletes where 97 per cent answered 'cannot be accepted'.

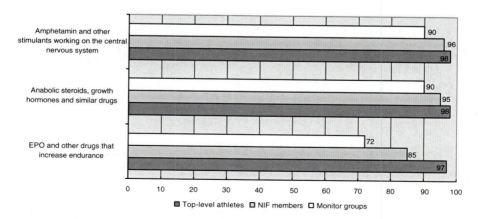

Figure 2 Percentage of the different groups who answered 'cannot be accepted'

With regard to anabolic steroids and growth hormones, the variance between the groups was smaller. Between 90 and 98 per cent of all groups replied that these drugs were unacceptable. Anabolic steroids represent the classic drug in doping and were among the first substances that were prohibited and tested for. Most people outside and inside sports are aware that these are illegal drugs.

The attitude to the use of amphetamine and similar substances was very much the same as the attitude towards the use of anabolic steroids. The respondents in all groups opposed the use of doping such as blood doping, anabolic steroids and amphetamine. The small percentage that stated they accepted this use (1–5 per cent) is hard to evaluate.

Considering the thesis on the medicalization processes of society,[13] results showing strong opposition against the use of performance-enhancing substances in sport are interesting. However, the results may also be understood in the light of the increasing differentiation and specialization of modern society where the use of drugs in everyday life seems to have another meaning and purpose than the use of drugs in sport. The use of performance-enhancing substances in sport is associated with cheating and immorality while general use of drugs in society is to a greater degree considered a part of modern life.

Furthermore, the survey showed that young people in general were more positive to use performance-enhancing substances than older people. This trend was characteristic for all types of substances. The reasons for this may be many. Youthful openness and curiosity towards new things may play a part here. Young people grow up in a society that has a lower threshold for the use of drugs. Thus, it is reasonable to believe that they will develop and maintain a more liberal attitude to performance-enhancing substances than the current adult population who grew up under quite other conditions. If the apparently liberal attitude among youth towards performance-enhancing substances is an omen of a real change of values in society and not just a generation difference, this may have challenging consequences for the work with anti-doping in sport in the long run.

Elite athletes were most clearly opposed to the use of these substances. The reason for this may be that most individuals in this group have been socialized into a pronounced anti-doping culture. Furthermore, the costs of getting caught are very high. Previous surveys have shown that to give a positive doping test without having used doping on purpose is one of the things that Norwegian athletes fear the most.[14] It is no wonder, then, that elite athletes are sceptical.

Attitudes to Anti-doping Work

The 2003-survey[15] showed that people in sport and the general population were positive about spending money on anti-doping work:

> The Norwegian Sports Assembly spends a lot of money to prevent doping in sport. Do you think this work should expand, be run on the current level, be reduced or stopped? (Figure 3)

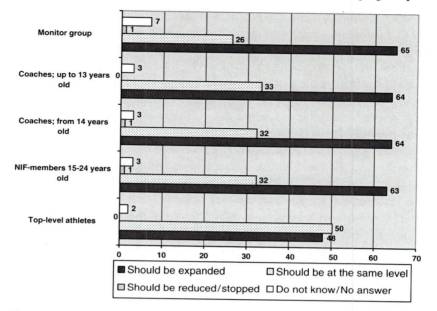

Figure 3 Attitudes to NIF's anti-doping work. The figures show percentages

Figure 3 shows that a distinct majority in all groups thought that anti-doping work ought to be expanded or at least kept at the current level. Half of the elite athletes suggested that it ought to be at the current level while 48 per cent suggested that it should be expanded. A total of 64 per cent answered that resources in anti-doping work should be expanded. No one replied that it ought to be reduced or stopped.

The fact that so many people in the general population and the sports groups were of the opinion that anti-doping work not only should be kept at the same level but be expanded, may be a result of the idea that doping is fairly common in elite sport. Elite athletes did not share this view to the same extent. This group has better knowledge of anti-doping work and perhaps the prevalence of drug use, and might think that the control mechanisms are sufficient.

Doping in Norway

Even though active anti-doping work has been on the agenda in Norwegian sport since the 1970s and this work seems to have been successful, it does not mean that Norwegian athletes have not used doping. Now and then, there are Norwegian positive tests in doping controls.

The first known Norwegian doping case was in 1977 when the discus-thrower Knut Hjeltnes tested positive on anabolic steroids. Unlike most other athletes who have been caught later, he admitted having used illegal substances.

From 1977 to 1985, 24 Norwegian athletes have been found guilty of doping. In comparison, the corresponding figures from 1998 to 2002 were considerably higher − 38 convicted athletes in less than half the time. However, considering that the number of controls has been multiplied, the increased number of positive tests does not give any indications on increased use of drugs. A total of 1.2 per cent of all urine samples collected by athletes organized in NIF in the period of 1977−95 were positive.[16] Surveys among athletes indicate that 1.3−1.4 per cent of athletes in Norway use or have used drugs,[17] compared to more than 5 per cent in Canada and the US. The extent of doping is most common in power sports such as powerlifting and throwing disciplines in track and field events.

Neither the number of positive doping tests nor the number of participants in surveys who claim they use doping, is synonymous with the number of athletes who actually have been using illegal substances. In surveys, under-reporting must be expected, and several illegal substances, e.g. growth hormones and EPO, have for a long time been impossible to track in tests. It has also been possible to use doping at times where the chances of getting tested have been small.

It has been even harder to map the extent of doping outside of organized sports. About 2 per cent of people who use fitness centres in Norway say they use doping, but when NIF has conducted doping tests at fitness centres, a total of 20.4 per cent of the tests have been positive.[18] One of the reasons behind this high percentage may be that the tests in fitness centres are conducted on the basis of suspicion and tips primarily. However, there are reasons to believe that doping is more common outside than inside organized sports.

Motives for Doping

While NIF Sports Assembly's arguments against doping have mostly dealt with justice (fair play) and health (doping damages your health), the motives for having used doping among individual athletes differ substantially. A survey carried out among athletes who tested positive from 1998 to 2002 gave the following explanations:

> The most common reasons for using doping are illnesses or injuries. However, there is no clear definition of illnesses/injuries in these arguments. Some athletes explain that they have been injured and therefore have not been able to meet the demands for qualification to different championships without cheating. For some of these athletes, the use of doping has been the last resource in order to meet the demands. The other explanation is that many athletes have been ill and failed to check the doping list before taking medications that afterwards have turned out to contain substances on the list.[19]

Both explanations may be linked to NIF's two strategies to fight doping. Athletes who have been injured experience this fact as unfair. Fate has inflicted them with a handicap, and in order to compensate they must use substances that will get them well faster in order to compete on equal terms with athletes who have not been injured. To push it to extremes: the (rationalized) wish for fair play pushes them to use doping.

The second explanation may seem to be in accordance with NIF's health argument. You are injured, there are medications, also illegal, that can make you injury-free, and if health and healthiness are desired values, it would be wrong not to use the means that will repair the injuries. Some people will even say that it is a hazard to your health doing elite sport and not using drugs. They use the *Tour de France* as an example to argue that the bodily strain is so huge that without taking hormones and other drugs the cyclists will be at risk of collapsing.

The second-most common explanation given by the revealed doping users was taking 'contaminated' dietary supplements. Some of the athletes defend themselves by saying that the use has been negligent and admit that they should have checked the content of the supplement more closely and compared it to the doping list.

This explanation may also be based on the health aspect. Dietary supplements are used to strengthen the body and immune system in order for the body to endure extensive and hard training. Some dietary supplements – the ones that are contaminated – are a little too effective, enabling the body to build from hard training instead of breaking it down. Even if the athletes claim that they were unaware of the fact that the supplement contained illegal substances, they achieved what they were looking for: a supplement that had an effect on body and performance. Some athletes who test positive for illegal substances admit readily that they wanted to enhance their performance.

When going through these explanations, we see that NIF's arguments for the use of doping can also be turned around – as an argument to use drugs. This does not mean that NIF has been wrong or failed to reach out with their arguments in their campaigns. There will always be people you cannot reach, people who will go their own way no matter what, and some will always interpret things according to self-interest.

Nevertheless, as we have discussed, it may be of value to problematize the fair play argument as well as the health argument. Attitudes must be based on conviction and belief in the better argument, and counterarguments always have to be taken seriously. What is, and when is it – fair play? What if the majority of the other competitors use doping? How about compensating the disadvantage if you get an injury that will set you back? The same goes for the health argument. What about the substances on the doping list that will not damage your health? What if, in a given situation, it may be a danger to your health not to use some of these substances?

The Norwegian Perspective

Norway has in many ways been a pioneer country in anti-doping work. For more than three decades there has been a continuous, consistent and value-based effort to prevent doping. Are there special aspects of Norwegian sport that have made this possible?

A Uniform Norwegian Sport

The way Norwegian sport has been – and is – organized, has no doubt made it easier to have an active anti-doping policy. In Norway, there is a joint Norwegian sports confederation where elite sport, mass sport and recreational sport are united. The fact that Norwegian sport is organizationally one unit has made it possible to reach a uniform attitude to the doping issue, and the Norwegian model has also made it easier to coordinate the campaigns between different disciplines in sport and at different sports levels.

The Role of the Norwegian State

It should not be forgotten that the Norwegian state authorities exert significant influence in Norwegian sport. Norwegian sport has received significant financial support from two Ministries to operation and facilities. However, with these funds there has also been a requirement that sport should be based on morality and values. The attitude to the use of doping is in many ways a barometer of the healthiness and moral status of sport.

However, even though the close relationship to public resources has imposed some regulations including the doping issue, the influence has by no means been one-sided. The requirement of a doping-free sport has been just as strong within sport. As the surveys above clearly indicate, there is a more restrictive attitude to doping inside of sport than in society in general.

Dedicated People Involved

In the development of Norwegian anti-doping work, certain individuals have played key roles as well. Mr Hans B. Skaset is perhaps the most important one. In his long life in sport he has played most roles; from a track and field athlete and coach on the national team to professor at the Norwegian University of Sport and Physical Education, from the manager of NIF to Director General of the Department of Sport Policy at the Ministry of Cultural Affairs. In most of these roles he has been interested in the doping issue and has had much influence on the Norwegian anti-doping work. In the early stages of the 1970s and 1980s, he was the spokesperson for a practical and realistic attitude to fight doping. According to Skaset there was no point in making ideal principles that were impossible to enforce. Instead, there ought to be definite rules and regulations with appropriate and harsh penalties.[20]

Mr Skaset has also played an important role internationally with building up uniform and efficient control measures. He has been critical of what he has considered a certain laxitude of Norwegian attitudes and the development of acceptance for so-called grey areas. As the Director General at the Ministry of Church and Cultural Affairs, he openly criticized Norwegian elite sport for the lenient line showed towards Norwegian athletes who tested positive during the Sydney Olympics in 2000, and towards the use of grey zone means such as altitude chambers. Not long after this, Mr Skaset left his job at the Ministry in order, among other reasons, to protest what he considered inadequate public and sport strictness in its attitudes towards doping issues. It is hard to see, however, that this is a general trend of Norwegian anti-doping work. At an international WADA-sponsored seminar in Oslo in the spring of 2005, a report was launched indicating that Anti-doping Norway is among the more efficient national anti-doping organizations in an international, comparative perspective.

Grey Area Debate

And it is exactly this grey area debate that has characterized the Norwegian doping debate the past few years. Is everything legal that is not put on the doping list? What is natural and what is artificial enhancement of performance? When staying in altitude chambers that have the same physiological effect as the use of EPO, what is the moral difference between using the two methods?

In the aforementioned surveys[21] there were almost the same number of people (between 20 and 30 per cent in all groups) who answered that the use of altitude chambers were 'acceptable' as those who answered 'unacceptable'. It was evident that people in and outside sport experienced grey areas and much uncertainty with regard to moral status. Opinion polls for the main Norwegian subscription newspaper *Aftenposten* confirmed that the population was sceptical to altitude houses. A total of 37 per cent of the population in 2001 stated that they disapproved of this method. Both the population in general and the organized athletes were divided on this issue.

Even though there were no rules in the doping regulations that prohibited the use of altitude chambers, one of the sport districts managed to get the majority at the Sports Assembly to pass a resolution that banned Norwegian athletes from using such means. This resolution came despite the unanimous Board of Sports and elite sports management's stand that favoured the possibility of using an altitude room as an instrument in the continuous battle for medals.

Norway considers itself a pioneer country in anti-doping work and it has, as many other countries, acknowledged the Olympic motto: *citius, altius, fortius*. The goal of Norwegian elite sport prior to the 2004/2006 Olympic Games was to become the third best European nation in the summer and Winter Olympics as a whole. Considering the country's small population, this is setting the bar high. In this respect, it is possible to question the realism of the goal and perhaps the double communication when, on the one hand, supporting continuous and, to a certain extent, extreme progress in performance and, on the other hand, advising against the means that at least some see as necessary to succeed. Maybe the anti-doping work to a greater extent should dare to problematize the performance culture that seems to permeate elite sport? In much of the Norwegian anti-doping material practically no conflict is raised between a clear 'no' to doping and a clear 'yes' to performance on a high level. We do not say by this that elite results depend upon doping – we sincerely believe that there are possibilities in most sports without doping – but the issue should be critically addressed, also in anti-doping material. One never escapes that at its core, a choice of anti-doping is not a pragmatic but a moral choice that might have short-term costs and might go against narrow self interest.

Conclusion

Norwegian anti-doping work has been massive and complex. Along with controls and sanctions, considerable amounts of resources have been put into working on attitudes. Some of the earliest campaigns in particular gave the impression of propaganda with exaggerated focus on adverse effects on health and attitudes. The focus has gradually been centred on fair play and the disapproval of cheating.

Based on the surveys that have been carried out, we can draw the tentative conclusion that the anti-doping information has reached its audience and made an impact. Among the general population and more strongly among elite athletes there are clear attitudes against the use of doping.

However, this does not imply that doping is not used in Norway. Ever since the testing started, some Norwegian athletes have now and then tested positive. Still we believe that the anti-doping work has had a significant effect. Even though some parts of it can be criticized, this work has been characterized by an impressive continuity and consistency.

Notes

[1] NIF, 1993.
[2] Ibid.
[3] NIF, 1994.
[4] Ibid., 2.
[5] NIF, 1992.
[6] See for example Guttmann, *From Ritual to Record*, Hoberman, *Mortal Engines*, Heikkila, "Discipline and Excel" and Østerberg, *Det moderne.*
[7] Barland, *Gymmet.*
[8] Duncan, "Sport Photographs and Sexual Differences".
[9] Johanson, *Den skulpturerade kroppen.*
[10] Breivik and Vaagbø, *Utvilingen i fyisk aktivitet i den norske befolkningen.*
[11] NIF, 1993.
[12] Loland *et al.*, *Evaluering av etikk og verdiarbeidet i NIF.*
[13] Waddington, *Sport, Health and Drugs.*
[14] Breivik and Gilberg, *Gjennom slit til stjernene.*
[15] Loland *et al.*, *Evaluering av etikk og verdiarbeidet i NIF.*
[16] Bahr and Tjørnhom, "Prevalence of Doping in Sports".
[17] Bergsgard and Tangen, *På sporet etter dopingmisbrukere.*
[18] Bahr and Tjørnhom, "Prevalence of Doping in Sports".
[19] Antidoping Norge, *Rapport.*
[20] Olstad and Tønnesen, *Norsk Idrettshistorie.*
[21] Breivik and Vaagbø, *Utvilingen i fyisk aktivitet i den norske befolkningen*; Loland *et al.*, *Evaluering av etikk og verdiarbeidet i NIF*; Seippel, *Idrett og sosial integrasjon.*

References

Antidoping Norge. *Rapport: Kjennetegn ved dopingsaker i organisert idrett.* Oslo: Antidoping Norge, 2002.
Bahr, R. and M. Tjørnhom. "Prevalence of Doping in Sports: Doping Controls in Norway, 1977–1995." *Clinical Journal of Sport Medicine* 8 (1998): 1.

Barland, B. *Gymmet: en studie av trening, mat og dop.* Oslo: Doktoravhandling Norges idrettshøgskole, 1997.

Bergsgard, N.A. and J. O. Tangen. *På sporet etter dopingmisbrukere. Utprøving av et undersøkelsesopplegg for å avdekke mulig dopingmisbruk blant eliteidrettsutøvere i 8 norske særforbund. Arbeidsrapport nr. 6/95.* Bø: Telemarksforskning, 1995.

Bergsgard, N.A. and J. O. Tangen. *Avvikende atferd i konkurranseidrett. En undersøkelse av dopingmisbruk og vektregulering på klubbnivå innen to idretter i Norge. Rapport nr. 141.* Bø: Telemarksforskning, 1998.

Breivik, G. and R. Gilberg. *Gjennom slit til stjernene. En studie av norske toppidrettsutøveres levekår og livskvalitet.* Oslo: Norges idrettshøgskole/NIF, 1999.

Breivik, G. and O. Vaagbø. *Utvilingen i fysisk aktivitet i den norske befolkningen 1985–1997.* Oslo: NIF, 1998.

Duncan, M.C. "Sport Photographs and Sexual Differences: Images of Woman and Men in the 1984 and 1988 Olympic Games." *Sociology of Sport Journal* 7 (1990): 22–43.

Guttmann, A. *From Ritual to Record. The Nature of Modern Sports.* New York: Colombia University Press, 1978.

Heikkila, J. "Discipline and Excel: Techniques of the Self and Body and the Logic of Competing." *Sport Sociology Journal* 10 (1993): 397–412.

Hoberman, J. *Mortal Engines – The Science of Performance and the Dehumanization of Sport.* New York: Free Press, 1992.

Johansson, T. *Den skulpturerade kroppen. Gymkultur, friskvård og estetik.* Stockholm: Carlssons, 1998.

Kulturdepartementet. "Kontaktutvalget for anti-dopingarbeid." *Handlingsplan for anti-dopingarbeid i Norge.* Oslo: Kulturdepartementet, 1999.

Loland, S., P. Kristiansen, and O. Vaagbø. *Evaluering av etikk og verdiarbeidet i NIF, 1993–2003.* Oslo: Norges idrettshøgskole, 2003.

NIF. *Idrettens verdigrunnlag. Strategiplan 1992–1998.* Rud i Bærum: NIF, 1992.

NIF. *Rammeprogram for Norges idrettsforbunds antidopingarbeid 1992–1995.* Rud i Bærum: NIF, 1992.

NIF. *Verdirapport 1993. Sammenfatning av fire rapporter fra undersøkelser om idrettens verdier, utført i 1992–1993.* Rud i Bærum: NIF, 1993.

NIF. *Avklaring om idrettens verdier, 1992–1994. Rapport fra arbeidet med idrettens verdigrunnlag 1992–1998.* Rud i Bærum: NIF, 1994.

NIF. *Fra ord til handling, 1994–1998. Strategiplan for idrettens verdiarbeid.* Rud i Bærum: NIF, 1994.

NIF. *Idrett og samfunn. Saksdokument til Idrettstinget 1994.* Rud i Bærum: NIF, 1994.

NIF. *Idrettens verdimanifest. Dokument utarbeidet av NIFs arbeidsgruppe for idrett og etikk og NIFs idrettspolitiske utvalg (NIPU).* Rud i Bærum: NIF, 1994.

NIF. *Fra ord til handling 1998–2010. Strategiplan for idrettens verdiarbeid.* Rud i Bærum: NIF, 1998.

NIF. *Idrettspolitisk dokument. Saksdokument til Idrettstinget 1999.* Rud i Bærum: NIF, 1999.

NIF. *Referat fra Idrettsstyrets strategimøte 29. og 30. august.* Oslo: NIF, 2003.

Norges idrettshøgskole. *Evaluering av etikk og verdiarbeidet i NIF 1993–2003.* Oslo: Norges idrettshøgskole, 2003.

Olstad, F. and S. Tønnesson. *Norsk Idrettshistorie, 1939–1986.* Oslo: Aschehoug, 1986.

Østerberg, D. *Det moderne. Et essay om Vestens kultur 1740–2000.* Oslo: Gyldendal, 1999.

Schneider, D. and J. Morris. "College Athletes and Drug Testing. Attitudes and Behaviors by Gender and Sport." *Journal of Athletic Training* 28, no. 2 (1993): 146–50.

Seippel, Ø. *Idrett og sosial integrasjon.* Oslo: Institutt for samfunnsforskning, 2002.

Tjørnhom, M. *Dopingkontroll i Norge. En beskrivelse av Norges Idrettsforbunds kontrollvirksomhet i perioden 1975–95.* Oslo: Hovedfagsoppgave Norges idrettshøgskole, 1997.

Waddington, I. *Sport, Health and Drugs. A Critical Sociological Perspective.* London: Spon, 2000.

Ethics in Sport: The Greek Educational Perspective on Anti-doping

Nellie Arvaniti

> To present yourself and contest in the stadium of Olympia you must be perfect. – What does perfect mean teacher? Asks Filinos the athlete.
> – The body, Filine, is cultivated with exercise, the soul with music and the mind with knowledge. This is the only way to make beauty. In beauty is tightly preserved the idea of man. Man is not only he who has a strong body, but he who has at the same time a beautiful soul and mind. Thus beauty is the expression of this completeness, and this perfection is the virtue. He who has virtue is perfect.
>
> Pindaros (ancient Greek poet and writer)

'Sports have been created by people for people.'[1] Sports are joy, health, well-being, young people's character building and with their multicultural character, sports bring people closer together and promote a truce throughout the globe for the creation of a peaceful and better world, as the *Olympic Charter* expresses.[2]

The balanced body-mind cultivation, the cultivation of friendship, equality, social solidarity and anti-racism are all values that sports promote, while the respect for the defeated, the recognition of the most competent and even the ensuring and providing of equal opportunities for every one in an environment of justice, democracy, fair play and rules constitute the basic functions and development conditions of sports. Sports are conditioned by values and rules in order to function, while the existence of a specific structure is indispensable.

Consequently, sports, with their organization and through specific structures and rules, are called to serve high objectives. But what is actually happening? Are sports fulfilling their mission today and preserving their ethics? Sports are considered today an activity system that moves and develops inside society. They are fed by the social environment. Various agents, foundations, organizations, individuals and governments are interested in, and contribute to, sports. Organization, principals and values conditioning sports, as well as the axes on which they move, are affected by society's structures and changes (political, economic and cultural) in the course of time. As such, 'One of today's socioeconomic activity characteristics, and maybe the most dominant, is competition, which finds in the area of sports all the possibilities for application and proliferation'.[3] On the other hand, sports' great effect on public opinion and the intense presence of commercial television have significantly increased the opportunities for financial profit within sport. This situation has attracted the interest of sponsors and professionals who understand that high performance sports, due to their spectacular character, can ensure great profit.[4] Therefore, in many cases, winning and achieving a good performance appears to become a necessity and the sole objective of the athletic environment. The pursuit of records is a reality.

Exhausting training characterizes the athlete's daily schedule. The passion for winning medals makes athletes train in an inhuman way from young ages, interpreting wrongly the principal *citius – altius – fortius*. But is training, in every case, what is needed to bring new and constantly better performances? Can the athlete constantly 'break' his record and surpass himself?

Given the fact that the need for higher performances exists, science comes in, in many cases, to support the athlete with technical means, supplying him with substances that will increase his performance. That way, the athlete obtains high performances with 'crutches', and the doping phenomenon becomes a scourge.

Identifying what constitutes doping can be a challenge, as

> The definition of doping has evolved over time. In fact it is so difficult to find a definition which captures the reality of it in all its complexity that, for a long time, doping was defined as using products which were written in the forbidden list. It is only with the adoption of the anti-doping code of the Olympic Movement, in 1999, that the IOC elaborated the following definition of doping:
>
> (1) The use of an expedient (substance or method) which is potentially harmful to athlete's health and/or capable of enhancing their performance, or
> (2) The presence in the athlete's body of a Prohibited Substance or evidence of the use thereof or evidence of the use of a Prohibited Method.[5]

The World Anti-doping Code's approach is quite similar[6]

Article 1 defines doping as the occurrence of one or more of the anti-doping rule violations set forth in Article 2.1 through Article 2.8 of the Code.[7] Doping alters an athlete's behaviour in many ways:

> According to legislation, doping alters the genuineness of the athletes' result and effort, endangers the athletes' health, is opposite to the fundamental Olympic

principals, the principals of fair play and medicine ethics and it is, of course, forbidden. It is a complex and comprehensive phenomenon and it is a plague for the Olympic spirit and the Athletic Family. It is even a fact that, as years go by, changes appear in the international 'stage'. These changes appear in: 1) the form (in that way from known substances we have passed to synthetic, variations, 'masks'); 2) the methods (biological, genetic etc.); 3) the way of channelling them in the market (internationally and organized); 4) the personal characteristics of users (younger athletes resource to them) and 5) the way to deal with them both through internal as well as international legislation.[8]

It is a common agreement that doping must be eradicated; it is a disaster for sports, the Olympic Movement, and for society in general. But is it so simple that we can be optimistic this will happen?

The contemporary athletic system can be expressed in two forms. The first of these forms is:

'Sports for more people.' Objective? Social association, freedom of expression and creation, preservation and improvement of a person's good health, fighting stress, possibility for distinction through mild forms of competition, cultivation of a positive attitude for exercise throughout a person's life and a healthy way of life. It is addressed to people of different age and social groups. It takes place in different social environments, spaces and other environments, like community, gymnasiums, clubs, work, family etc.[9]

Furthermore,

It can have a competitive spirit or not. These kind of athletic expressions are characterized, in a big percentage, by spontaneous, unpretending personal choices, while the element of the game is evident. None the less, even in these cases the use of doping substances appears, for various reasons. Research shows that the use of doping substances and practices are spreading in areas where millions of citizens exercise, while statistics from USA research reveal that 11 per cent of children between the ages of 11 and 12 use anabolics in a regular basis.[10]

The second form is competitive sports, which has a connection in most cases to significant material interests. The dominant characteristic is the intense competitive spirit, which is demonstrated at sport meetings of every level, with the Olympic Games being the top-level, followed by international and national championships, school championships and youth athletic games between clubs. Everyone's pursuit is not participation but winning and, in some cases, winning at all cost.

This is the point where an athlete might use unfair means to improve his or her body's capabilities. Cases of athletes who have used doping substances and methods have been observed and are constantly observed in athletes of all ages and levels. Is it possible to stop all this evil that threatens sports and the Olympic Movement?

Education is the answer to doping in sports in the long run, as Richard Pound, President of the World Anti-Doping Agency (WADA) stressed in Ancient Olympia, in 2002, during the 41st International Session of the International Olympic Academy.[11] Doping will be stroked out of sports only if all those concerned uphold the rules of fair play, as Gunther Heinze, member of the International Olympic

Committee (IOC) for the Olympic Program points out. He stresses the importance of education in fighting doping with the assertion:

> The right education, the proper advice and the promotion of positive values, are as important as sanction is, for developing the practice of sports without doping. Information and education can not be dissociated from sanctions that may appear necessary to inflict in case of violation of sports' ethical and deontological rules, of deliberate deceit, lack of respect for the opponent, violation of the principals of a fair game.[12]

But what is Anti-doping Up-bringing and Education and Where does it aim?

> We can characterize it as an educational process based on scientific principals and methods, that uses programmed learning opportunities, in order to offer an individual the possibility to make decisions that are negative towards doping, using as criteria the sports ethics and the respect of the athlete's health.[13]

> As a result, education's basic objective is the social adoption of a negative attitude towards doping by all athletic agents involved. Through properly designed educational programs and learning procedures it aims at preventing and coping with the use of doping substances and methods by athletes. With the application of indicative-quality programs targeted to matters of sports ethics and individual health it's goal is to provide the athlete with all the necessary knowledge and information around doping and to help him develop critical, communicative and other capabilities that will lead to the conscious abstinence from doping.[14]

In addition, N. Nisiotis argues that understanding sport as a game can be a great help in dealing with the threats that challenge the Olympic spirit today. According to Nisiotis:

> Hard training as well as the use of unethical means for the achievement of an Olympic distinction can be overcome by the conception of the game in sports. Because this conception reminds high competition athletes that the beginning and the main objective of their occupation with all kind of sports, that requires hard and mechanistic training, must lie in the necessity to enjoy life in its fullness and creativity, releasing themselves from any form of psychological and social oppression. The game is the symbolic expression of the first natural, biological and mental tendency of man to create something new and to take pleasure by his creation as a result of his freedom. Sports as a game overcome boredom and fatigue throughout training and transform enemies to partners and collaborators.[15]

Even the deep philosophical regarding of sports, their changes through time, and in connection with socio-cultural alterations and sports ethics, must be studied to redefine the aims of the Olympic Movement. Athletes need education on how doping alters their bodies and their performance, the ethical dilemmas and health repercussions associated with doping, how doping control procedures are carried out and sanctions imposed, as well as their responsibilities as athletes and sports agents.

Who should be Educated? Who do Anti-doping Programmes Concern?

The answer is: all involved in the athletic 'system'. The athletes and their supportive environment, that is to say:

- Athletes of all levels
- Students – athletes
- Sport agents
- Sport scientists
- Parents and the athletes' family environment
- Journalists of sports mass media

Sports executives, trainers, physicians, physiotherapists and also athletes themselves and their parents, must become crusaders in this difficult fight, as Lampis Nikolaou, former President of the Greek Olympic Committee and Vice President of the International Olympic Committee, pointed out in Athens, in 2003, during the International Meeting – Hellenic Olympic Committee, Fight Against Doping.[16]

How and Where can Education be Placed?

A. In Universities

University students are a potential active athletic population. Through university education, where a large number of athletes, and future trainers, teachers and sports agents study, it is extremely important and possible to develop programmes and to promote actions against doping. They may be funded, regardless of the study programme, or incorporated in it.

It is necessary to include in the curriculum of the departments of physical education and sports science anti-doping programmes focusing on the ethical, medical, legal and educational sides of the matter. The study programmes should include information on substances, methods, controls, sanctions, the World Anti-Doping Code, research results and the consequences to all involved. After all, the students' participation in national and international educational programmes will sensitize them more and will help them develop, in the future, collaborations with agents and promote politics against doping. Athletes, future teachers, trainers, sport experts and parents are today's, but also tomorrow's, athletic environment.

B. In Schools

Education (School Education) as a system and a social agent forms a system of values, principles, and new conceptions of the way of life.

> School offers an important opportunity for systematized and continual education. Its goal is to help the young individual to form an opinion on matters that concern his life directly (social values, drugs, alcohol etc.) and to adopt positions that will help him in future decisions, this way preventing the formation of negative positions and behaviours of the young individual, which will be difficult to change later.

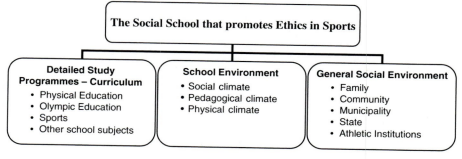

Figure 1

Furthermore, the student, being the connection between school and society, carries messages from school outwards (family, social environment).[17]

School gathers a large number of student-athletes who participate in competitive sports, as well as in other mild forms of athletic programmes (sports for all). As a consequence, the school environment is a suitable place for communication and promotion of sports ethics. Although school is recognized as the most suitable place to promote social issues to young people, the results will not be those expected if a supportive social environment is not available.

Fundamental conditions needed for the cultivation and development of sport ethics is the existence of the proper school climate; that is to say in a social school, the sufficiency of classes, the propitious educational environment and the cooperation of the school community with sports agents and the State .

Detailed Study Programmes – Curriculum

The following are included in the detailed study programmes and curriculum to promote anti-doping among athletes:

- Physical Education
- Olympic Education
- Sports (All day School)
- Other Classes (Subjects availability)
- Papers drawn on various sciences

Through all of the school's cognitive subjects, but mainly through the instructional characteristics of Physical Education, through Olympic Education and Sports, the sports' and Olympic Movement's aims are being redefined and the athletic and social models are being determined in order to form young peoples' complete personalities. Some of the values encouraged are:

- Sports are health. It is contradictory for an individual to be fit and not healthy (healthy versus fit).

- Sports are a part of our lives and not our whole life.
- Basic desire and pursuit is the perfection of individual limits and not beating the opponent.
- Acceptance of sports laws and rules (among which are anti-doping rules).
- Team spirit and mutual help.

School Environment

- Social climate. Through the various cultural, athletic and every kind of social school activities organized and realized within the school environment, social values are being promoted. These include respect of the rules, equal opportunities for all students, recognition of the most capable, respect for the opponent, acceptance of the individual's dissimilarity et cetera.
- Educational climate. The expression of athletic morals, the substantial relationships and the students – tutors, communication, the advice to students for self-respect and respect of the opponent, the knowledge of the real reasons of a young person's occupation with sports, the development of an enjoyable educational-athletic process, the rewarding of students-athletes for the demonstration of fair play spirit and sport performance, the encouragement of students with particularities and disabilities to participate in athletic programmes, the facilitation of student-athletes that are training for championships, the right organization of school champion-ships, the competent formation of Physical Education teachers on sports developments, these are some of the basic parameters for the promotion of ethics in school sports.
- Physical climate. The Physical Education teachers in all school units and for both levels of education, the correct and adequate material and technical athletic school infrastructure facilitate the Physical Education Detailed Study Programme application and, as a consequence, school sports are developed. The capability to participate in championships, of all schools, regardless of the geographic location, the size or anything else and the rewarding of the best student-athletes not only for their performance, but also for their ethos, will help cultivate the proper athletic behaviour.

General Social Environment

School and society are communicating vessels. Education and the entire athletic system are affected by society. This is the reason why social developments for the formation of rules of ethics in sports must be taken into consideration, as well as the adequate educational strategies that will promote ethics. In order for benefits to exist, continual collaboration between the school, the athletic agents and the state is necessary, as well as connections between schools and out-of-school sports.

Economic and educational assistance of school sports, ethic recompense, rewards of the best students-athletes and those who play a 'good game', social facilitations to students-athletes, according to the athletic spirit and generally the enactment of the right motives (ethical and material) by the state, are important success components. In addition, all of the above will contribute to the formation of a position of 'exercise for life', which is a position that is considered necessary nowadays when the 'sedentary' way of life governs, along with the mutated pollution and unhealthy nutrition, the constantly increasing environment pollution, as well as the rising intercultural needs and cultures.

Ways of Incorporation

The instructive and methodological approach of ethics and doping matters varies between countries. It depends on the educational system, the school schedule and every country's needs, as well. But all programmes and classes have the same objective and move on the same axes. Specifically, the anti-doping programmes application can be realized directly by:

Detailed Study Programmes

All school Study Programmes and curriculum are affected and must be readjusted to the social needs. Doping in sports, an acute social phenomenon, must find its place inside the school environment and become an issue for study and process from many angles, in order to illuminate it in a multiprismatic way, to push forward its relationship with reality and to find ways of containment. In more detail, sports ethical dimension and anti-doping action can be promoted through:

1. The class of Physical Education with an experience-kinetic approach, but also with speeches, research and drawing up of small studies. The student-athlete is educated with the timeless values of the Olympic spirit, the value of participating and not necessarily winning, 'fair play', the joy of the game and competition.
2. School sports, pursuing, strictly, the observance of sports ethics rules. School sports, moving inside the proper athletic framework and with its amateur character, has the ability to become a positive model for high level sports.
3. The rest of the cognitive subjects, as part of their subject-matter, with the condition that studying doping becomes the class's objective.
4. The all-day school, which is called to promote, through its programmes, educational as well as social aims. 'Sports', one of the all-day school's classes, is an excellent educational field for the cultivation of athletic messages.
5. The athletic and cultural school activities of various contents (athletic, musical, painting exhibitions, theatrical performances et cetera).
6. Olympic Education programmes. Olympic Education must include in its subjects the radical changes in sports in the course of time and in connection with the elements of modern civilization, and how high-level competition has formed a new competitive scene. In that way, subjects related to political influence, commercialization, gigantism, nationalism-chauvinism, inequalities between

countries from the aspect of athletic infrastructure, Mass Media dominance, and the lack of knowledge and sensitization on Olympic philosophy, as well as doping use by athletes as a consequence of many of the parameters mentioned above, must be examined and become conversation topics by teachers and students.

7. Health Education programmes. Cultivation and consciousness of health (physical and mental) as the most important human possession, knowledge of doping and the risks it involves, but also cultivation of personal dexterities in order to avoid doping, these must become subjects for process and analysis by students. These subjects' study must have a spiral form, that is, teaching should be repeated frequently and systematically, in order to bring the desired results.

Outside the School Programme

1. Inter-school athletic programmes.
2. Inter-cultural activities.

The cooperation of schools and local administration for the realization of the campaign against doping in sports, as well as the organization of multicultural athletic activities, is considered positive and with perspective. The contribution of athletes' parents and the mass media can also bring results.

The Greek Experience

During the last decade in Greece, there have been many efforts, searches and questions asked about matters of social education, sports ethics and anti-doping policy, as the substance of Physical Education and Olympic Education, under the guidance of the Greek Ministry of Education, the Greek Olympic Committee, the International Olympic Academy, the Foundation of Olympic and Sports Education, in addition to other agents, with the objective of cultivating a critical position and conscience on issues of Sports and the Olympic Movement.

With the undertaking of the 2004 Olympic Games by Greece, this tendency was strengthened and proper ground was created for the development of the targeted Olympic Education programmes and their connection to the educational system. This way, during the school year 1998–99, the Greek Ministry of Education Pedagogical Institute designed the first Olympic Education pilot programme, with the main subject being sports ethics and fair play. The programme was incorporated in the school schedule and applied in 30 grammar schools. Its success led the Ministry of Education to expand the Olympic Education pilot programme, based on the same philosophy, objectives and goals.

Approximately 400 grammar schools and 135 appropriately trained Physical Education teachers 'teach' the Olympic and Sports Idea to young students. The programme is observed by experienced teachers and is well received by all. And it continued: from the year 2000 until 2004, the Greek Ministry of Education gradually employed 2,000 Physical Education teachers who, after being trained, staff school units of Primary and Secondary Education within the Olympic Education framework.

The programme spread widely and is included in approximately 7,500 schools, that is 99 per cent of the country's schools. One million Greek children participated in the programme. Multiple activities of a pedagogical, athletic and social character targeted at cultivating a healthy sports position and conscience took place during that period. The Ministry of Education observed them with great interest, appreciated and funded many of them. Culture, sports, social education and the values associated with each are cultivated within the school environment by participants in both the school community and in the local community, as well. The programme was also used after February 2003 in all the organized school units in Cyprus and the Greeks abroad.

At the same time, the Organizing Committee for the Olympic Games in Athens 2004, in collaboration with the Greek Ministry of Education, used the Collaboration Memorandum and the Operational Project to contribute to, and participate in, teachers' formation as well as to publish significant instructive books (Olympic and Paralympic instructive books package) on the Olympic and Paralympic Games. Some difficulties and problems arose in the processes that were merely the consequence of the programme's breadth and its application at the national level. The crown of this effort is the recognition and reward of the programme, at the European level, through the Commissioner of the European Union, Ms Vivian Reding.

Of course, young peoples' formation and education through sports, the promotion of athletic and Olympic values through practices and games without discrimination, fair play and spirit are the main goals of the Physical Education class. All classes can promote sports ethics and anti-doping policy on the condition that these matters are their subject's objective and part of their teaching. In this case, an inter-science approach between different classes as well as cooperation between students and teachers is suggested. In Greece, during the last two years, a Unified Inter-subject Study Programme Framework has been developed. It involves both study levels (Primary school, Junior high school-High school) and School Study Programmes are designed under an inter-science conception. That is to say, the cultivation of education values, such as the value of human life, social solidarity and 'fair play' will exist, as common subject matter, in different cognitive subjects of the same class. They appear frequently in cognitive subjects of various classes. All of these will be connected to the basic objectives of education and will lead to the development of inter-subject activities. The instructive manuals of all cognitive subjects and both education levels were written according to this philosophy. A subject about sports ethics has been already incorporated into the educational material of Physical Education, for Secondary Education and more specifically Junior High School.[18]

Since doping is a very complex social phenomenon, agents, like the penetration of market mechanisms in sports territory, the excess knowledge and the consequent alterations in assuming, interpreting and dealing with reality, the school's connection with society makes the student population vulnerable to doping substance use. The school community must contribute effectively to the fight against doping, appreciating that the school environment is the most appropriate territory for the promotion of anti-doping policy. In order to design and develop educational and prevention programmes and sensitize the student-athletes, or to modernize the already-existing programmes, it is necessary to conduct research to determine the appropriate tools and contribute substantially toward this direction. Programmes working on this framework include the Greek Ministry of Education (Athens Secondary Education Counselors' Office) and the Athens Economic University Statistics Department (October 2004–January 2005), with the participation of High School students and Physical Education teachers.[19] The results of this research are presented below.

The research's objective was to detect, in a reliable and authentic scientific way, positions, knowledge and behaviours of students and teachers on the issue of doping, as well as their opinions for the school's intervention capability on this matter. The research was conducted using anonymous questionnaires: a) for a sample of 1,400 teenagers (53 per cent boys, 47 per cent girls) randomly selected from five cities in Greece: Athens (37 per cent), Corinth (24 per cent), Argos (15 per cent), Nafplio (14 per cent), and Ioannina (10 per cent), and b) for n a sample of 150 Physical Education teachers (45.5 per cent men, 54.5 per cent women) randomly selected from eight cities in Greece (64 per cent from the Athens area). The largest percentage (61 per cent) was between the ages 30–40, with previous employment and experience in Education up to ten years (62 per cent).

From the students' questionnaires a tendency to the following was ascertained: 65 per cent exercise systematically and 52 per cent participate in sport unions. Specifically: football (28.6 per cent), basketball (18 per cent), tennis (8.3 per cent), volley-ball (7.7 per cent), athletics (7.5 per cent), swimming (6.2 per cent), martial arts (5.8 per cent). In addition, the scientific facts showed that young people consider doping a social phenomenon (63.4 per cent) that concerns all countries (68.5 per cent) and all sports (60.9 per cent). The overwhelming majority of students were opposed to doping substance use in sports (91 per cent). The majority also recognized that substances can damage the human organism, and furthermore 56.7 per cent believed that it is possible that they can cause death. Additionally, 10 per cent stated having used forbidden substances on their own responsibility (35 per cent), their trainer's (17 per cent), and their parent's (11 per cent). Finally, 74 per cent thought it was false that without doping substance use Olympic and international records cannot be achieved.

As far as knowledge on forbidden substances goes, a considerable percentage of students surveyed did not know which substances were banned in sport. Many falsely included creatine (49.1 per cent), caffeine (19.3 per cent) acetylsalicylic acid (18.6 per cent) on the banned list, while many failed to identify ephedrine (47.6 per cent) and growth hormone (27.1 per cent) as banned substances. Young people state that they know some facts on the doping issue (85 per cent), but they confess that their information comes mainly from the mass media (72.4 per cent), compared to learning this information at school (19.8 per cent). Nonetheless, teenagers believe that school must sensitize, form and properly educate student-athletes and future trainers and sports agents.

From the teachers' questionnaires a tendency to the following was observed: 71 per cent were employed or continued to be employed in a sports union mainly as a trainer (67 per cent) or a gym instructor (24 per cent). 69 per cent stated they were active in sports before entering the Education field, in athletics (49 per cent), football (17 per cent), volleyball (10 per cent), basketball (9 per cent). The results of the research also revealed that 83 per cent of teachers consider doping a social phenomenon that concerns all countries (67.7 per cent) and all sports (60.7 per cent). Almost everyone surveyed (94 per cent) was opposed to athletes using banned substances. The teachers recognized that doping substance use causes damage to the human organism and 80 per cent even believe that it can cause death. As far as ways to deal with the phenomenon, 74 per cent of teachers support the need of formation and education to increase students' knowledge of doping, as well as everyone implicated in the sports system. A considerable percentage (52 per cent) appreciated the need for repressive methods (doping controls) for student-athletes. As far as scientific sufficiency for the realization of educational programmes and doping matters where teaching is concerned, 64 per cent of Physical Education teachers surveyed feel they have not been formed and trained up to now in order to realize the educational task, but 90 per cent indicated a willingness to be educated and to educate others. Nonetheless, and because of the importance of the issue, 56 per cent has discussed doping in the school class. With their pedagogical capacity and the proper formation they can contribute effectively in the fight against doping. The sensitization, experience and know-how (instructive and methodological) obtained by teachers, in the process, and the school's interconnection with society and its problems, are experiences and educational practices with added value for the school population and the educational system. By turning to advantage the instructive and educational experience of teachers within the proper educational environment, having instructive material as tools, unobstructed work for the promotion of education's objectives and the school's operation as a modern Social Unit can continue.

Therefore, it is necessary to form strategies for a positive intervention and for the Greek Ministry of Education to examine the possibility of including doping prevention programmes within the Physical Education class framework, which will be addressed to all Junior High and High Schools students in Greece.

C. In Athletic Agents

- In International Sports Federations
- In National Sports Federations
- In Trainers – Judges – Referees Associations
- In the Olympic Champions Association
- In Athletes Unions
- In major Sports Clubs
- In Municipal Sports Organizations
- In Foundations and Companies related to Sports

International Sports Federations design and develop doping information and sensitization programmes for their athletes. They produce printed and electronic material. The International Athletics Federation bases its programmes' philosophy on four axes: education, information, control and research. The above-mentioned agents' cooperation is indispensable for the exchange of material, experience and know-how. At annual seminars for trainers, referees and judges, at athletes' rewards festivities, at Pan-Hellenic championships, and at science conventions under the auspices of Federations, opportunities are given for recommendations, interventions and general information on matters of forbidden substances and their consequences on the athletes' health, doping control procedures, principals and politics against doping, and sanctions in positive cases.

D. In the International Olympic Academy

The International Olympic Academy (IOA) is the educational foundation of the international Olympic Movement and is recognized by the International Olympic Committee for its work in the study of subjects and matters pertaining to the Olympic Movement and the diffusion of Olympic Education at the international level. Sessions are hosted at the IOA annually and include international participants from the athletic field at the main sessions, and academics at the annual postgraduate seminar who all promote future Olympic education in their respective countries. Included in its educational programme are:

- The Olympic Studies Postgraduate Programme
- The International Session for Young Participants
- The International Session of National Olympic Studies
- The International Session of Teachers and Staff of Physical Education Institutions of Higher Education
- The special Athletic-Medical Foundations and Organizations Conventions

Personalities from the international athletic field attend sessions at the IOA with the objective of exchanging opinions with others and promoting Olympic Movement issues. These programmes must include in their content, systematically, matters of sports ethics.

Conditions

In order for all of the above-mentioned to succeed and for the goals of anti-doping policy to be achieved, basic and necessary conditions must exist. Briefly, these include:

- The rallying of all powers fighting for the battle against doping in sports and the promotion of the Olympic Idea. The International Olympic Committee (IOC), The World Anti-Doping Agency (WADA), the International Sports Federations, the Ministries of Education, the International Olympic Academy (IOA), government agents, National Sports Federations, national anti-doping organizations, Athletic organizations and of course mass media must cooperate in the programming and promotion of anti-doping policy, on a national and international level.

- The interconnection of all efforts and programmes so that there is no overlapping, financial waste or inertia.
- The exchange of know-how and experience from agent to agent and from country to country.

Several countries have drawn up excellent educational programmes. With the proper adjustments they can be incorporated into the athletic environment of another country. To this purpose, a recording and evaluation of national and international anti-doping educational programmes must be done.

- Evaluation of every educational programme. The constant self-evaluation and evaluation of others is indispensable in any educational action and process. This improves strategies targeted to perfection as well as maximizes the result.
- Research. Designing effective programmes will be possible only when athletes' needs in what concerns knowledge and necessary information are imprinted, as well as the athlete's psychological-ethical support. Moreover, first of all science and medicine must contribute drastically in the battle against doping, because medicine knows better than any other science that doping impairs health and may even lead to death. The promotion of research in this field can lead to recording studies of the negative consequences of doping on the athletes' health. Because, as G. Rontogiannis stresses, 'The knowledge of undesired actions, observed today, by the athletes' use of methods and substances considered as doping, is mainly based on clinical observations and research on guinea-pigs. But the description of the athletes' risks is based, relatively, on a very limited number of observations and on a limited number of autopsies of athletes' that passed away prematurely.'[20]
- Teachers' formation. People responsible for the realization of information and sensitization programmes against doping in sport must know the educational methods and procedures with which they will approach these matters. The adequate teachers' formations, as well as the existence of sufficient instructive materials, are important success parameters.
- Common coordination of all actions and agents. The WADA could help in this direction, particularly through the Ethics and Education Committee, which works for the coordination, programming and realization of athletes' information and sensitization programmes, around the globe, with clear objectives and procedures. The WADA's action framework includes the *Outreach Programme*, an athletes' information and sensitization programme, the *Athlete's Passport*, a sensitization and information programme for high level athletes and *e-learning*, an educational programme through the internet.

- Mass media cooperation. Mass media contribution in these matters is catalytic and their contribution valuable, for their influence is known. The promotion of every effort and action in the battle against doping is necessary.

How Optimistic can we be? Up to where can we reach?

It would be ideal if athletes completely stopped using performance-enhancing substances and methods that are illegal and dangerous to their health, but is this possible? Sport, as a spectacle, provokes and stimulates the system around it. The higher the level of sport, the higher the demands are from those who ensure the spectacle and profit from sport, so the athletes find themselves trapped in this situation.

Ensuring equal opportunities for all athletes is a parameter that can contribute in a positive way. As G. Rontogiannis points out:

> But more than any one else, every athletic agent who has the mission to direct, encourage the athlete's effort for further and better athletic performance, but also who can protect his health, can help to this direction. This person must have a firm negative attitude against doping. The same of course applies to physicians and, especially, to sport-physicians who are authorized with the caring and maintaining of athletes' health.[21]

We find ourselves at a critical point for the political battle against, and management of, doping. The establishment of the World Anti-Doping Agency (WADA), and the cooperation of government and athletic agents towards the adoption of a World Anti-Doping Code where the same weights and measures for all athletes will be in effect, are a turning point for the Olympic Movement.

Olympic champions and 'clean' high-level athletes who are positive role models for the athletic family can also contribute substantially to the anti-doping movement. Great emphasis must be given as well to lower athletic categories, where sports have a purely amateur character and the athletes are younger and more likely to change their behaviours. The reduction of positive doping cases must become a pursuit and an objective for us all. The partial containment of this phenomenon is not impossible and in that direction we should aim. The athlete's health protection and his right to participate in 'clean' games is the world athletic community's duty.

Notes

[1] Schneider, 'Ethics and the Challenges of the Potential Use of Genetic Technology in Sport'.
[2] IOC, *Olympic Charter*.
[3] Panousis, 'Alteration forms of the Olympic Spirit', 307.
[4] Siperco, 'The contemporaneity of Coubertin', 105–11.
[5] IOC, *Olympic Movement Anti-Doping Code*.
[6] Oswald, 'Education through Sports', 118–26.
[7] World Anti-Doping Code, 'Article 1–Definition of Doping'.
[8] Papadogiannakis, 'The Legal Aspect of Doping: Crime and Punishment'.
[9] Ren, 'Culturalism and Educational values of Olympism', 250.

[10] Malliori, 'DOPING: Threat for the Sports Community'.
[11] Pound, 'The World Anti-Doping Agency', 110–13.
[12] Heinze, 'The Concept of the IOC on Doping as a Counterpoint to the Olympic Spirit', 65.
[13] Arvaniti, 'Prevention and Education against Doping'.
[14] Ibid.
[15] Nisiotis, 'The Significance of Sport as Play and its effects on Contemporary Olympism', 42.
[16] Nikolaou, Address presented at the International Meeting – Hellenic Olympic Committee, Fight against Doping.
[17] Arvaniti, 'The Olympic Education, in the Learning Society', 96.
[18] Pedagogical Institute, 'Inter-subject Uniform Study Program Framework'.
[19] Arvaniti, and Psarelis, 'A Study on : 1. Beliefs, Attitudes and Knowledge of High – School Students concerning Doping in Sports and 2. Anti – Doping Education: The Beliefs of Physical Education Teachers'
[20] Rontogiannis, 'Undesired Effects of Doping in Athletes', 96.
[21] Ibid., 101.

References

Arvaniti, N. "The Olympic Education, in the Learning Society." In *Olympic Games, Reports – Approaches*. Athens: Ellinika Grammata, 2001.

Arvaniti, N. "Prevention and Education against Doping." Paper presented at the International Meeting – Hellenic Olympic Committee, Fight against Doping, Athens, Greece, 28 June 2003.

Arvaniti, N. and J. Psarelis. "A Study on: 1. Beliefs, Attitudes and Knowledge of High School Students concerning Doping in Sports and 2. Anti-doping Education: The Beliefs of Physical Education Teachers." Paper presented at the World Congress of Sports Management, Sparti, Greece, 3–5 June 2005.

Astrand, P. O. and A. Borgstrom. "Why are Sports Records Improving?" In *Drugs and Performance in Sports*, edited by R. H. Strauss. Philadelphia: N.B. Saunders, 1987.

Butcher, R. B. and A. J. Schneider. "Fair Play as Respect for the Game." In *Ethics in Sport*, edited by William Morgan, Klaus Meier, and Angela Schneider. Champaign, IL: Human Kinetics, 2001.

C.E.O. Council of Europe. *Doping of Athletes. A European Study*. Council of Europe, 1964.

Chantzos, S. *Doping: From School to Death*. Athens: Kaktos, 2004.

Filaretos, N. "The Progress of the Olympic Games the last 35 years." In IOA, *Report of the Thirty-eighth Session 15th July–30th July 1998*. Ancient Olympia and Lausanne: IOC, 1999.

Foundation of Olympic and Sport Education (FOSE). *Be a Champion in Life*. Athens: FOSE, 2000.

Heinze, G. "The Concept of the IOC on Doping as a Counterpoint to the Olympic Spirit." In IOA, *Report of the Twenty-ninth Session 28th June–13th July 1989*, edited by Otto Szymiczek. Ancient Olympia: IOC and HOC, 1989.

International Olympic Committee. *Olympic Charter, International Olympic Committee*. Lausanne: IOC, 1996.

International Olympic Committee. *Olympic Movement Anti-Doping Code*. Lausanne: IOC, 1999.

Ljungqvist, A. "Doping and Medical Control." In IOA, *Report of the Thirty-eighth Session 15th July–30th July 1998*. Ancient Olympia and Lausanne: IOC, 1999.

McNamee, M. J. and S. J. Parry. *Ethics and Sport*. London and New York: E & FN Spon, 1998.

Malliori, M. "DOPING: Threat for the Sports Community." Paper presented at the International Meeting – Hellenic Olympic Committee, Fight against Doping, Athens, Greece, 28 June 2003.

Matthia, A. "The Olympic Movement, Youth and Doping." In *Report on the 29th International Session for Young Participants*, edited by Otto Szymiczek. Lausanne: IOC, 1990.

Muller, N. "Olympism and Olympic Education." in *Report on the IOA's Special Sessions and Seminars Ancient Olympia, Athens 2000.* Lausanne: IOC, 1998.

Nikolaou, L. "Address presented at the International Meeting – Hellenic Olympic Committee." Fight against Doping, Athens, Greece, 28 June 2003.

Nisiotis, N. "The Significance of Sport as Play and its Effects on Contemporary Olympism." in *International Olympic Academy Report of the Twenty-second Session 11th–25th July 1982.* Ancient Olympia: IOC and HOC, 1982.

Oseid, S. and T. Remejorde. "Detection and Control of Doping in Sport." In *Sport Health and Nutrition,* edited by F. I. Katch. Champaign, IL: Human Kinetics, 1986.

Oswald, D. "Education through Sports." In IOA, *Report on the IOA's Forty-third Session for young participants.* Ancient Olympia: IOC and HOC, 2003.

Paloukas, P. "Sports and Olympic Games (Historical and Ethical-Social Conception)." In *Society (Koinonia)* newsletter of the Panhellenic Association of Greek Theologists, 3 (July–Sept. 2004), 235–50.

Panousis, G. "Alteration Forms of the Olympic Spirit." In *Olympic Games, Reports – Approaches.* Athens: Ellinika Grammata, 2001.

Papadogiannakis, I. "The Legal Aspect of Doping: Crime and Punishment." Paper presented at the International Meeting – Hellenic Olympic Committee, Fight against Doping, Athens, Greece, 28 June 2003.

Pedagogical Institute. "Inter-subject Uniform Study Program Framework." Greece: Greek Ministry of Education, 2002 [cited 01 Aug. 2005]. Available from www.ypepth.gr.

Pound, R. "The World Anti-Doping Agency." In *Report on the 41st International Session for Young Participants, Ancient Olympia.* Lausanne: IOC, 2002.

Ren, H. "Culturalism and Educational values of Olympism." In *Report on the IOA's Special Sessions and Seminars 1997.* Athens: IOC, 1998.

Reville, P. *Sport for all, Physical Activity and the Prevention of Disease.* Strasbourg: Council of Europe, 1970.

Rogge, J. "Ethics in sport." In IOA, *2nd International Session for Educationists and Staff of Higher Institutions of Physical Education, Ancient Olympia 1995,* IOC and HOC.

Rontogiannis, G. "Undesired Effects of Doping in Athletes." In *Report of the twenty-ninth Session 28th June–13th July 1989,* edited by Otto Szymiczek. Ancient Olympia: IOC and HOC, 1989.

Schneider, A. "Doping: The Moral Aspect of the Problem." Paper presented at the International Meeting – Hellenic Olympic Committee, Fight against Doping, Athens, Greece, 28 June 2003.

Schneider, A. J. "Ethics and the Challenges of the Potential Use of Genetic Technology in Sport." Paper presented at the WADA Banbury Workshop on Genetic Enhancement of Athletic Performance. Cold Spring Harbor, NY, 17–20 March 2002.

Schneider, A. J. and R. B. Butcher. "For the Love of the Game: A Philosophical Defense of Amateurism." *Quest* 45, 4 (1993): 460–9.

Siperco, A. "The Contemporaneity of Coubertin." In *Report of the twenty-eighth Session 29th June–14th July 1988,* edited by Otto Szymiczek. Ancient Olympia: IOA, 1988.

Theodorakopoulos, I. "Doping and the role of Mass Media." Paper presented at the International Meeting – Hellenic Olympic Committee, Fight against Doping, Athens, Greece, 28 June 2003.

"World Anti-Doping Agency." *World-Anti Doping Code.* Montreal: WADA, 2005.

INDEX

Page numbers in *Italics* represent Tables